Work Organisation
Labour & Globalisation

Volume 2, Number 1, Spring, 2008

Published by Analytica Publications Ltd.
46 Ferntower Road, London N5 2JH, UK
www.analyticapublications.co.uk
phone: +44 (0)20 7226 8411
fax: +44 (0) 7226 0813
email orders@analyticapublications.co.uk
(for subscriptions and editorial queries)

in association with Merlin Press Ltd.
96 Monnow Street,Monmouth NP25 3EQ, UK
www.merlinpress.co.uk
phone: +44 (0)1600 775663
fax: +44 (0)1600 775663
email: orders@merlinpress.co.uk

Printed and bound in the UK by Lightning Source UK Ltd.
6 Precedent Drive
Rooksley
Milton Keynes
MK13 8PR, UK

Edited by Ursula Huws
Designed by Andrew Haig Associates

ISBN: 1-4196-7774-8
ISSN: 1745-641X

Break or weld?

trade union responses to global value chain restructuring

edited by Ursula Huws

About this journal

The globalisation of world trade in combination with the use of information and communications technologies is bringing into being a new international division of labour, not just in manufacturing industry, as in the past, but also in work involving the processing of information.

Organisational restructuring shatters the unity of the traditional workplace, both contractually and spatially, dispersing work across the globe in ever-more attenuated value chains.

A new 'cybertariat' is in the making, sharing common labour processes, but working in remote offices and call centres which may be continents apart and occupying very different cultural and economic places in local economies.

The implications of this are far-reaching, both for policy and for scholarship. The dynamics of this new global division of labour cannot be captured adequately within the framework of any single academic discipline. On the contrary they can only be understood in the light of a combination of insights from fields including political economy, the sociology of work, organisational theory, economic geography, development studies, industrial relations, comparative social policy, communications studies, technology policy and gender studies.

Work Organisation, Labour and Globalisation aims to:

- bring together insights from all these fields to create a single authoritative source of information on the new global division of labour, combining theoretical analysis with the results of empirical research in a way that is accessible both to the research community and to policy makers.
- Provide a single home for articles which specifically address issues relating to the changing international division of labour and the restructuring of work in a global knowledge-based economy.
- Bring together the results of empirical research, both qualitative and quantitative, with theoretical analyses in order to inform the development of new interdisciplinary approaches to the study of the restructuring of work, organisation and labour in a global context.
- Be global in scope, with a particular emphasis on attracting contributions from developing countries as well as from Europe, North America and other developed regions.
- Encourage a dialogue between university-based researchers and their counterparts in international and national government agencies, independent research institutes, trade unions and civil society as well as policy makers. Subject to the requirements of scholarly peer review, it is open to submissions from contributors working outside the academic sphere and encourages an accessible style of writing in order to facilitate this goal.
- Complement, rather than compete with existing discipline-based journals.
- Bring to the attention of English-speaking readers relevant articles originally published in other languages.

Each issue addresses a specific theme and is also published independently as a book. The editor welcomes comments, criticisms, contributions and suggestions for future themes. For further information, visit the website: http://www.analyticapublications.co.uk

Editorial board

Contents

Break or weld?

trade union responses to global value chain restructuring

Ursula Huws

Ursula Huws *is director of Analytica Social and Economic Research and Professor of International Labour Studies at London Metropolitan University in London in the UK.*

ABSTRACT

This paper provides a short introduction to this volume, sketching out some of the main dilemmas confronting trade unions in the context of global value chain restructuring, discussing some of the alternative strategies currently being adopted around the world and summarising the contributions to this volume.

Introduction

International trade union solidarity is certainly not a new phenomenon. The phrase 'workers of the world unite' was coined by Flora Tristan (1803-1844) before Marx and Engels made it famous in their 1848 Communist Manifesto, and throughout the 19th century there were instances of European workers taking action in solidarity with their counterparts in other countries. In 1850, for instance, London brewery workers mounted an attack on the Austrian Field Marshall von Haynau in solidarity with workers in Italy and Hungary whose uprisings he had put down. Whilst they claimed that this was for altruistic reasons saying that 'the infliction of tyranny and cruelty in one country is an outrage to all nations' (Press, 1989:26), many actions had an element of self-interest. For instance in the 1859-61 London building workers' strike, the unions engaged in international solidarity action in order to avoid strike-breaking by foreign workers, and this was also a strong motivation behind the setting up of the International Working Men's Association, or First International, in 1864 (Press, 1989:28).

This uneasy balance between self-interest and altruism still characterises many aspects of trade union internationalism today, but it is by no means the only balancing act trade unions have to carry out in the 21st century. Another challenge is how to balance the defence of existing workers, including the gains they have made in any particular location, with the recruitment and organisation of new groups of workers. And in recruitment drives, what should the priorities be: to try to win over those workers who occupy strategic positions in the value chain and who can thus can help to win disputes? Or to respond to the needs of the most vulnerable workers who may be crying out for an organisation to represent their interests? Then there is the challenge of how to respond to employers' globalisation initiatives: is it better to resist them altogether, running the risk of being accused of protectionism? Or to go 'with the grain' of globalisation and try to win the best deal possible for the workforce, running the risk of being accused of selling out the interests of those who lose by this process?

Given that the multinational companies increasingly span the traditional divisions between sectors and between national economies, how should trade unions restructure themselves to reflect these new configurations: by sector? by occupational identities? by company? by regional or national groupings? or by their political affiliations?

Other questions relate to the broader political roles of trade unions. How, and to what extent, should they get involved in national and international bodies (exposing themselves to the risk of being accused of co-managing neo-liberal capitalism)? And how, and to what extent, should they get involved in broad-based social campaigns, perhaps in partnership with NGOs (exposing themselves to the risk of being accused of abandoning their duty to prioritise the representation of the direct interests of their members)?

These are some of the questions that are addressed in various ways by contributors to this volume. But before introducing them, it is perhaps appropriate to summarise briefly the reasons why such questions have now become so topical. After nearly three decades when, although globalisation has been increasingly discussed, trade unionism has seemed like an old-fashioned issue, or even an anachronistic relic of 1970s culture, the two terms are now suddenly linked together in a range of political agendas as well as in the specialist industrial relations literature. This new interest is evident in a spate of recent publications, including Beiler, Lindberg & Pillay (2008), Pilch (2007), Schmidt (2007), Moody (2007), Kumar & Schenk (2005), Fege (2005) Fairbrother & Yates (2003) and Jose (2002).

Changing attitudes to globalisation

One recent development that seems likely to have contributed to this new-found interest is a change in public attitudes to globalisation. In the early years of the 21st century, it was possible for consultants like the McKinsey Global Institute (2004), as well as government bodies like the Department of Trade and Industry (2004) in the UK, to argue that globalisation was generally beneficial. Citizens of North America, Europe and the rest of the developed world would, they said, benefit partly because of the lower prices of goods manufactured in developing economies and partly because 'their' multinational companies would increase their competitiveness in global markets, which would ultimately lead to the creation of more jobs back home. In the rest of the world, the flow of foreign investment would generate economic growth, new jobs and rising standards of living.

Public belief in such benign win-win forecasts has been somewhat shaken by recent events, including price rises (especially of food and energy) and the effects of the credit crisis of the summer of 2007. In addition, rapid economic growth in China, India, Russia, Brazil and elsewhere has released huge surpluses which, as they have been reinvested elsewhere in the globe, have made it abundantly clear that the multinational companies formerly based on their soil are not the exclusive national property of the citizens of Europe and North America, however much they might identify with iconic national brands. It is, for instance, a Brazilian company[1], that now owns Leffe,

---

[1]   The company in question is Inbev. See http://www.inbev.com for further information

Stella Artois, Becks, Coors, Jupiter, Skol, Boddingtons and many other 'national' and 'regional' brands of beer - often made on the same production lines. IBM's PC business (arguably the product – with its path-breaking link with Microsoft's software – that did more than any other to create the standards that enabled the 'information economy' to spread so rapidly in the early 1980s) now belongs to a Chinese company[2]. Indian companies[3] own most of Europe's steel industry and even Chelsea Football club, in the UK, belongs to a Russian. Meanwhile, as we go to press, it is announced on the news that two of the best-known British auto brands, Jaguar and Landrover, are being bought from Ford by another Indian company, Tata Motors.

In such a context, any idea that national jobs are safe in the hands of national companies is increasingly difficult to sustain. Faith in the long-term stability of global corporations has taken further knocks from other aspects of the financialisation of capital, in the form of a spate of takeovers of well-known companies by private equity trusts, hedge funds, sovereign-wealth funds (owned by governments in the Middle East, Asia. Scandinavia and elsewhere) and state-owned companies from outside the traditional developed triad of North America, Europe and Japan. Private equity firms now own, for instance, such US household names as Dunkin' Donuts, Hospital Corporation of America, Burger King, Toys "R" Us and Chrysler (Economist, 2008) and, in the UK, the pharmacy chain Boots the Chemist[4]. Takeovers by sovereign wealth funds include those of the shipping company and port operator P & O by DP World, owned by the Government of Dubai, and of various telecom companies by Temasek, owned by the Government of Singapore (Economist, 2008b). These funds increasingly own minority shares in other companies too, For instance QIA, owned by the Government of Qatar, which bid (unsuccessfully) in 2007 for the British Sainsbury supermarket chain, owns a significant part of Cadbury Schweppes (Economist, 2007). Such companies are perceived by the general public as seeking only a quick return on their investments, with no long-term commitment even to the future of the brands they have bought, let alone the workers who produce the products sold under these brand names.

In combination with other factors, including the increasingly evident effects of global climate change, public opinion appears to be becoming more mistrustful both of multinational corporations and of the national and international government bodies that seem to be promoting their interests.

The breakdown of national industrial relations models
In a world in which companies are more and more likely to be foreign-owned, whilst workers are more and more likely to be immigrants, and national governments more and more likely to belong to international trading blocs (such as the EU, NAFTA, Mercosur or ASEAN), the idea that industrial relations systems can be adequately regulated and contained within national borders is becoming increasingly anachronistic.

---

2   'IBM sells PC Business to China's Lenovo' (Associated Press, December 8th, 2004)
3   Mittal, the Indian-owned steel company, the largest in the world, purchased Arcelor, itself a merger of steel companies based in Luxembourg, Spain and France with subsidiaries worldwide, in June, 2006. Another Indian company,Tata Steel purchased Corus, Europe's second largest steel company, in April, 2007
4   Alliance Boots was the first UK FTSE 100 (the *Financial Times* list of 100 top UK companies) company to be bought by a private equity fund, Kohlberg Kravis Roberts, in April, 2007

The classic model of an inter-dependent triangular relationship between the state, the trade unions (representing labour) and employers' associations (representing capital) supposed to have characterised what has variously been termed the Fordist period or the 'Golden Age' of capital after the second world war in the West, perhaps never existed in its perfect form but, to the extent that it did, it took distinctively different national forms (Coates, 2000; Hall & Soskice, 2001). In many countries, especially, but not exclusively, in Europe, trade union structures and strategies were shaped by the specific national forms that this relationship took and their own roles in its decision-making processes. Whether or how such structures could or should be dismantled is still an open question in many contexts, although the realisation is growing that they no longer deliver their intended benefits, except, in some cases, to a privileged minority of workers.

Whilst national regulatory regimes continue to make some difference to employment practices between one country and another, there has been considerable convergence over the last three decades, brought about by a combination of factors. These include initiatives from supra-national bodies (such as World Trade Organisation regulations, European Union directives or conditions attached to loans or aid by bodies like the International Monetary Fund or the World Bank). They also include national initiatives, designed to 'modernise' labour markets or attract foreign investment. And of course they include too the actual practices of multinational corporations, either exercised directly, in their capacity as employers, or indirectly, through conditions attached to outsourcing agreements made with their suppliers.

This convergence in employment regimes has not always been matched by convergence on the trade union side. Here, the landscape is marked by considerable diversity both between and within countries. Not only are there varying degrees to which unions are involved in, and committed to, national frameworks of 'social dialogue', and labour market regulation but there is also an enormous variety in the forms of collective bargaining that take place, which may be at national, sectoral or company level, or take the form of inputs into the processes by which national systems of training, qualifications and occupational descriptions are determined. To this must be added another dimension of heteregeneity – the basis on which trade unions have historically been formed and on which they represent their members in any given national context. These may be craft-based, occupation-based, company-based, sector-based or based on allegiances to particular regional and/or ethnic and/or political identitites, ideologies or parties. Whilst some are formally allied to, or closely identified with, particular national political parties, others[5], are closer to social movements, whilst still others remain firmly sectional and non-aligned (Bieler et al, 2008).

It should not be taken for granted that any need for any change will necessarily be recognised when the power positions of existing bureaucrats are well entrenched and the present situation is still producing some positive gains for trade union members. But even if a decision has been taken that a new direction is needed, with such a variety of traditions and models it is by no means obvious what path should be followed. Perhaps more important than any abstract debate about the particular basis on which unions should merge or form alliances with their counterparts in other countries, or with other social or political movements in their own countries, is the reality of who they actually

---

5   for instance the Self-Employed Women's Association (SEWA) in India

represent at present and what negotiating power, if any, these workers have in reality in the actual locations where they based. Without such power, they are unlikely to win anything. As Ellen Woods points out, even though international alliances between workers' organisations are becoming increasingly important, in order to provide mutual support, whether this is in disputes with companies or states, this means that national states remain crucially important arenas of action, (Woods, 1998:15).

As the need for these alliances becomes clearer, it is to be expected that debates will intensify, both nationally and internationally, about the best way to bring them into being. Such debates cannot be separated from broader questions of which workers trade unions can and should represent, in a context in which trade union membership is declining in most countries, as larger and larger proportions of the workforce fall outside their traditional spheres of influence, because of factors including increases in immigration, informalisation, and the decline of traditionally strongly unionised sectors.

Actual changes in employment on the ground

A third factor that has a direct bearing on the new interest in trade union responses to globalisation is perhaps the most important, although it cannot easily be summarised in a few words in an introductory article like this one. This is the actual impact on employment of the global restructuring currently under way and the impacts of these changes on the structure of labour markets on the one hand, and on the daily experiences of workers on the other.

I have already referred to the growth in informalisation of economies. The informal sector is often thought of as a declining relic of pre-capitalist economic relations but it does, in fact, appear to be a defining feature of the most modern form of these relations. As the financialisation of capital progresses, so too does the pressure on employers to produce dividends for shareholders in the short term and, in a context of increasing global competition, such dividends can often only be produced through downward pressure on the wages and conditions of workers (Altvater & Mahnkopf, 2002). A clothing factory in Morocco, for instance, producing goods for global companies, can only compete effectively with alternative factories in China by casualising its workforce, reducing safety standards and paying below the minimum wage (Belghazi, 2005). Multiplied across the world, such effects of globalisation have contributed considerably to the growth in casual and precarious employment which has presented such a challenge for trade union recruitment.

Precariousness outside the formal economy has grown in parallel with precariousness within it. Even if their work is not actually outsourced to another company or relocated to another country (or both) workers in an increasingly large range of companies and industries live with the daily fear that it might be. As work is reorganised on a project basis or on the basis of outsourced contracts, they may, even though nominally in continuous employment, be required to apply for work within the organisation on a project by project or contract by contract basis and, if repeatedly rejected, find their job security little different from how it would be if they were self-employed. Solid occupational identities, based on established skills and recognised qualifications (and that often formed the basis of trade union allegiances) are increasingly giving way to provisional identities made up of changing configurations of increasingly universal 'competences' such as proficiency in particular software packages, knowledge of a particular group of customers, or 'communications skills' 'team skills' or 'mindset flexibility' (Huws, 2006). Instead of being able to see their way forward to a job for life, growing numbers of people now have to negotiate labour markets in the constant fear that they will be seen as only as good as their last job. Like the public sector IT workers whose jobs were outsourced to a global company interviewed in the UK by Simone Dahlmann in 2007, their attitude to their work can be summed up as 'keep your head down, ask for nothing' and just 'hope that you will keep your job for another year' (Huws & Dahlmann, 2007).

Although of course it is possible to point to many cases where jobs have disappeared in large numbers as a direct result of offshore outsourcing, the most important and invidious impact of the global relocation of labour does not lie in the quantitative impact on jobs but the qualitative impact – the disciplinary effect on workers of knowing that their jobs *could* be moved, even if this does not actually happen (Huws, 2006b).

There are, of course, many other ways in which globalisation impacts on employment on the ground, both for those who work directly for multinational companies and those in other sectors of the economy. For the former, they include increasing requirements to speak global languages, adapt to foreign corporate cultures and work to time schedules that are set on the opposite side of the globe. For the latter, they include the many indirect effects of global competition, whether this is on food prices, on natural resources, on the manufacture of the goods, on tourism, or on the environment, and the increasing dominance of local markets by global companies, as well as the effects of new forms of social polarisation, including crime. They also include the effects of migration, both on 'labour exporting' and 'labour importing' regions of the world (Cohen, 2006).

In this volume

This volume aims to add to the literature on trade union responses to globalisation by discussing some of these questions in greater depth.

It begins with an overview by Ronaldo Munck of new forms of labour internationalism in which he argues that trade unions need to 'scale up' their activities beyond the national terrain and that what is needed is a 'transformationalist' alternative that offers labour a multi-layered and flexible response to the new global capitalist order.

This is followed by a paper in which Vincent Mosco examines the actual practices of trade unions in the converging North American communications, culture, and information technology sectors and the extent to which trade union efforts to mirror this convergence by consolidating and merging themselves has been successful. He also looks at worker movements that operate in conjunction with, but outside, the formal trade union structure, including one initiative (Washtech) which is discussed in more detail in a later paper (Rodino-Colocino, this volume). He leaves open the question whether the developments he describes portend a rebirth of North American labour activism or represent its last gasps.

The next paper, by Pamela Meil, demonstrates that, despite the increasingly globalising practices of transnational corporations, specific local institutional contexts still make a difference. She does this using case study evidence from Germany, France and the USA which comparing local trade union responses to the same policy initiatives coming from the same corporate headquarters in two major global companies. She concludes that, in all three countries, the traditional trade union negotiating agendas fail to address the most significant changes that are taking place, omitting important areas that are crucially relevant for bargaining 'unoccupied'. This implies the need for a major revision of these negotiating agendas.

Jürgen Kädtler also draws on case study research on the globalisation strategies of companies, in this case those that dominate the German chemicals, pharmaceuticals, auto and tyre industries, to look at the effects of these strategies on trade union bargaining power. He concludes that the local exercise of power by groups of workers with skills on which the company depends can still bring important gains. However this power may well be held by groups that were traditionally poorly unionised, and depends for its success on a number of other factors, including the national industrial relations system and the success with which trade unions have managed to combine with others internationally in European Works Councils or global union committees. On the analogy of football, he argues that types of work fall into three separate 'leagues'. The first-league workers are those whose skills are absolutely essential to the innovation strategies of companies and who thus have considerable bargaining power. Second-league workers are those who are important to the companies but not indispensible. Their skills are likely to be in somewhat limited supply around the globe so they are likely to be in competition with others of their kind, but only in a few, known, locations and they are likely to remain direct employees of the global companies making it possible for bargaining to take place internationally. Finally, the third-league workers are those whose work has been so standardised that it has become a commodity that can be bought and sold freely on the global market. Theirs are the jobs that are outsourced and subject to the logic of a global race to the bottom and it is dubious whether company-level bargaining can do anything to improve their position.

The next two papers study some of these same developments from a Brazilian perspective. Leonardo Mello e Silva discusses, amongst other issues, the development of international company-based union networks which are now widespread in Brazil and which have been successful in helping build international solidarity in several industries. Marco Aurelio Santana turns a spotlight on the strategies of global auto companies in Brazil, in particular their determination to withdraw from their traditional locations in the so-called ABC region near São Paulo, where workers have developed strong and militant trade union organisation, in favour of green-field sites where they can establish new plants with lower wages and flexibile working conditions on the 'lean production' model. Focusing in particular on the case of Volkswagen, a company also studied by Kädtler, he describes how the local green-field unions quickly learned from their brown-field colleagues on other sites and set up effective forms of communication and a company-based union network on the model described by Silva.

Silva also discusses another way in which Brazilian unions have been working with the state – by participating in the negotiations over the setting up of the Mercosul[6] Latin American free trade area, in particular how union representatives boosted the social agenda within Mercosul and used this experience to develop their general negotiating skills.

This experience can be compared with that of the South African trade unions whose role in national economic policy negotiations is studied by Marlea Clarke and Carolyn Bassett. Their conclusion is that, faced with the challenge of developing a national policy in the context of neo-liberal globalisation, representatives of the South African labour movement abandoned some of their commitment to a 'high road', post-Keynesian restructuring vision and agreed to several policy changes that were more in line with a 'low road', neo-liberal approach, with negative implications for workers in some sectors.

Two further papers, the first by Michelle Rodino-Colocino and the second by Monique Ramioul and Tom de Bruyn, present strongly contrasting – if not antithetical – descriptions of strategies that respond to employers' offshore outsourcing intiatives. The first paper describes, a bottom-up initiative by US workers who developed their own high-tech workers' organisation, WashTech, the Washington Alliance of Technology Workers, to protect their interests in a volatile 'technomadic' labour market. Their actions, which included setting up an 'Offshore Tracker', in a joint project with the Communication Workers of America trade union, are rooted in an explicit opposition to offshoring which is seen as destroying local jobs, and their agenda can be seen as directly counterposed to, or going 'against the grain' of globalisation. The second paper describes a very different, and more top-down, initiative, involving a group of major trade unions, mostly based in high-wage, economies in Northern and Western Europe, together with UNI, the international trade union confederation of white-collar workers in the private sector. This initiative, a project called Make Offshore Outsourcing Sustainable (MOOS), can be seen as going 'with the grain' of globalisation.' Acting within a European tradition of social dialogue, the unions involved in this initiative argue that globalisation is inevitable but that the effects on workers of failed offshore outsourcing experiments are much worse than those of successful ones. It is therefore in workers' interests that their trade unions actively engage in decision-making about global sourcing at the earliest possible stage in order to ensure that the interests of workers are protected and minimum standards are adopted both at the 'source' location, where the jobs are currently based, and at the 'destination', to which some will be relocated. The contrast between these two cases illustrates and concretises a number of important debates currently taking place within the trade union movement internationally, raising issues of protectionism versus internationalism; participation in the co-management of capitalism versus opposition to it; 'corporatist' models versus 'liberal' or 'social-democratic' ones; protection of the sectional interests of well-organised workers versus more generalised demands for protection of the vulnerable; and 'what's right?' versus 'what works?'.

The next two papers step outside formal trade union structures and focus on union relationships with unofficial activities, campaigns and Non-Governmental Organisations (NGOs). Bruce Robinson looks analytically at Internet campaigning, labour activism and the remaking of trade union internationalism, drawing attention to the strengths

6   known in Spanish-speaking countries as 'Mercosur'

and weaknesses of email campaigns and other uses of information and communications technologies in fostering international solidarity. Patrick Develtere and An Huybrechs focus on what they call 'transnational network movements' in which trade unions participate alongside NGOs and other social actors to bring about improvements in working conditions at a global level. Using the example of the campaign for the abolition of child labour, which led to the ILO ratifying a convention more quickly than at any time in its history, they show how such movements can be remarkably effective in bringing about regulatory change. They conclude, however, that while they can complement more traditional forms of trade union action, they cannot substitute for them.

Finally, this issue ends with a review article by Peter Waterman who draws on his own experience, spanning several decades, in international labour studies, both inside and outside the trade union movement, to reflect on its history and, more particularly, the role played in it by activists and scholars from the UK. Through this personal and sometimes idiosyncratic, but always well-informed, lens he reviews some of the recent crop of publications on trade union responses to globalisation as well as commenting critically on web-based resources in the field.

Conclusions

Globalisation is clearly presenting huge new challenges to trade unions. On the one hand it is loosening the authority and leverage they can bring to bear on national governments, at a time when many of those national governments are themselves becoming increasingly incapable of shaping the forms that employment takes within their borders and the mechanisms by which workers can negotiate with their employers. On the other, it is decimating their traditional constituencies and putting obstacles in the way of recruiting new groups of workers and representing their interests.

In the meanwhile, workers themselves are increasingly connected with each other as separate modules in ever-more complex global value chains which link them to each other both spatially and across the boundaries between companies and sectors in sophisticated outsourcing and cross-ownership arrangements. Often with the same employers, the same labour processes and the same relation to capital, but occupying very different social positions across the world, what forms of interaction between these workers are possible or, indeed, desirable, and by whom?

In the past, technological development has brought contradictory developments for workers. Whether it is steam power, electricity, the telephone or the computer, each technology can be seen as having eliminated and deskilled some jobs whilst also creating new ones. And whilst it may have destroyed some aspects of traditional life it has put new resources into the hands of the general population which can be put to new uses. The very technologies that can be said to be degrading some aspects of working life can also, in other words, be seen as liberating. It seems likely that much the same may be said by future historians about the present phase of global value chain restructuring, which has been partially enabled by technological change.

Could the chains that link workers ultimately become a means for the stronger to haul the weaker up towards their level, rather than a means for dragging them down to the depths? In the shorter term, as the papers in this volume show, no consensus has yet emerged on how the workers of the world can unite and it remains an open question whether, in any given circumstances, it is a more successful strategy for trade unions to fight for the workers in their own link in the chain or to extend their solidarity to those along the line, whether, in other words, it is better to seek to break the chain, or to strengthen it. I hope that the papers in this volume will contribute to the debate about such questions.

© *Ursula Huws, 2008*

REFERENCES

Altvater, E. & B. Mahnkopf (2002) *Globalisierung der Unsicherheit – Arbeit im Schatten, schmutziges Geld und informelle Politik,* Münster: Westfälisches Dampfboot

Beiler, A., I. Lindberg & D. Pillay (2008) *Labour and the Challenges if Globalization: What Prospects for Transnational Solidarity?,* London: Pluto Press

Belghazi, S. (2006) in U. Huws, A. Dhudwar & S. Dahlmann, *The Transformation of Work in a Global Knowledge Economy: towards a conceptual framework,* proceedings of conference held in Chania, Greece, 21-22 September, Leuven: Higher Institute of Labour Studies:247-251

Coates D. (2000) *Models of Capitalism: Growth and Stagnation in the Modern Era,* Basingstoke: Polity Press

Cohen, R. (2006) *Migration and its Enemies: Global Capital, Migrant Labour and the Nation State,* Aldershot: Ashgate

Department of Trade and Industry, (2004) *Trade and Investment White Paper: Making Globalisation a Force for Good,* London, DTI, 2004-11-10

Fairbrother, P. & C. Yates (eds) (2003) *Trade Unions in Renewal: A Comparative Study,* London: Routledge

Economist (2007) 'Time to Break off a Chunk', December 13

Economist (2008) 'The Rise and Rise of Private Equity', *World in 2008.* Accessed on March 20, 2008 from http://www.economist.com/theworldin/displaystory.cfm?story_id=10125441

Economist (2008b) 'Asset-backed insecurity', Jan 17

Frege, C.M. & J. Kelly (2005) *Varieties of Unionism: Strategies for Union Revitalization in a Globalizing Economy,* Oxford: Oxford University Press

Hall P.A. & D. Soskice D. (2001) *Varieties of capitalism, the institutional foundations of comparative advantage,* Oxford: Oxford University Press

Huws, U. (2006) 'What will we do? The destruction of occupational identities in the Knowledge-based Economy', *Monthly Review,* Vol 57 No 8 January

Huws, U. (2006b) 'Fixed, Footloose or fractured: work, identity and the spatial division of labour', *Monthly Review,* Vol 57 No 10, March

Huws, U. & S. Dahlmann (2007) 'Global restructuring of Value Chains and Class issues', in proceedings of ISA Conference: *Work and Employment: New Challenges, Montreal,* August 28-30

Jose, A.V. (ed) (2002) *Organized Labour in the 21st Century,* Geneva: International Labour Organisation, 2002

Kumar, P. & C. Schenk (eds) (2005) *Paths to Union Renewal,* Calgary: Broadview Press,

McKinsey Global Institute (2004), 'Offshoring: is it a Win-win Game?'. Accessed in November, 2004 from http://www.McKinsey.com

Moody, K. (2007) US *Labor in Trouble and Transition,* London: Verso

Pilch, T. (ed) (2007)*Trades Unions and Globalisation,* London: Smith Institute

Press, M. (1989)'The People's Movement' in M.Press & U.Huws (eds) *Solidarity for Survival: the Don Thompson Reader,* Nottingham: Spokesman:26-47

Schmidt, V. (ed) (2007) *Trade Union Responses to Globalization: a Review by the Global Union Research Network,* Geneva: International Labour Organisation

Woods. E.M. (1998) 'Labor, Class and State in Global Capitalism', in E.M. Woods, P. Meiksins & M. Yates (eds) *Rising from the Ashes: Labor in the Age of 'Global Capitalism',* New York: Monthly Review Press:3-16

Globalisation and trade unions:
towards a multi-level strategy?

Ronaldo Munck

Ronaldo Munck *is Theme Leader for Internationalisation,*
Interculturalism and Social Development at Dublin City
University in Ireland.

ABSTRACT

International trade unionism is facing a serious challenge from what is commonly called globalisation. Trade unions feel the need to 'scale up' their activities beyond their, once paramount, national terrain and to challenge capital's untrammelled forward march internationalising and commodifying everything in its path. This article examines the new forms of labour internationalism and the way in which trade unions have been creating incipient counter-hegemonic strategies. The only certainty in this globalised and complex situation is that a continuation of national era trade union strategies is not a viable path. A possible 'transformationalist' alternative is posed in this paper, arguing that labour needs a multi-layered and flexible response to the new global capitalist order.

Introduction

'Thoughtful trade unionists have come to recognise that playing safe is the most risky strategy. The present is either the end of the beginning or the beginning of the end' (Hyman, 2004:23). That is, put simply, the dilemma now facing labour activists and critical thinkers. Globalisation has generated a multi-layered and multi-faceted process of social contestation. While the first wave of capitalist globalisation (1875 – 1914) saw the labour movement as the incipient driver of that contestation, the current wave of globalisation (1989 - ?) coincides with what most observers see as the terminal decline of the labour movement, and other social actors are seen as the main agents of contestation. But what if the labour movement is now entering a new cycle of activism and militancy, precisely through the contestation of neo-liberal globalisation? Is it inconceivable that a global contest between labour and capital might now emerge as Marx predicted? Be that as it may, we should certainly now move beyond the verdict of Manuel Castells who argued a decade ago, when globalisation seemed to sweep away all obstacles in its path, that 'the labour movement seems to be historically superseded' (Castells, 1997:360).

This article advances in three distinct moments, in the Gramscian (Gramsci 1971:124) sense, to seek answers to these questions and to advance what I would call a transformationalist labour perspective on globalisation. In the first section, I examine current debates and practical developments around the emergence of global unions. Does global capitalism lead inexorably to global unions or should it? The second section takes up the so-called new internationalism and how labour is joining the new social movements in contesting globalisation. Are we moving towards a global working class taking on global capitalism? Finally, we turn to what a transformationalist or radical reform strategy for labour might mean in the era of globalisation. There are no simple answers, but we have to at least start asking the right questions.

Global capital — global unions?

The year 2007 began auspiciously from an internationalist labour perspective with the announcement by a group of influential US, British and German trade unions that they would join forces to confront the power of transnational corporations (Morgan 2006). The organisations involved were the UK's largest private sector union, Amicus (in the process of amalgamating with the Transport and General Workers Union to form Unite), the influential German engineering union IG Metal and the American United Steel Workers and International Association of Machinists, representing between them nearly six and a half million workers. For traditional. or at least mainstream, trade union leaders to recognise that the days of the national trade union were numbered seemed like a major step forward. While the transnationals were seen to be pitting countries and workforces against one another, trade unionists were now committing to the creation of a transnational union to challenge the power of global capital. Would the 1970s vision of trade unions acting as a 'countervailing power' against the multinational corporations then surging forward across the globe, now belatedly come to fruition?

It is now widely believed amongst labour specialists that the international trade union movement in general, together with its now unified peak organisation, the International Trade Union Confederation (ITUC) which has brought together the International Confederation of Free Trade Unions (ICFTU), the Global Unions (the previous International Trade Secretariats) and the World Confederation of Labour (WCL), is at a crossroads in terms of how to meet the challenge of globalisation. We can but agree with Marcel van der Linden for whom 'it remains very likely that the coming of transnational internationalism will be a difficult process interspersed with failed experiments and moments of deep crisis' (van der Linden 2003). We can probably agree with that statement whether we hold an optimistic or pessimistic view of the likelihood of a new era of labour transnationalism. What is at stake though, in this context, is not our estimation of the capabilities of this or that organisation, but the question of what the main dilemmas facing the global labour movement are. Of course, we cannot discuss this in a few pages but we can try to lay out in a simple way the main scales of activity that labour operates on in the current period, before going on to discuss actual strategies in the next section.

At an international level, the new International Trade Union Confederation (ICFTU/GU/WCL) seeks to articulate labour interests at the level of the international financial institutions and of the TNCs (transnational corporations). Compared to the period of the post-war boom, the era of neo-liberal globalisation has seen very little space for durable class compromises to be negotiated with either of these interlocutors. The main dilemma for international labour organisations is whether they continue to operate as if that class compromise was possible, through the likes of a social partnership and generally 'responsible' modes of engagement and activity. The alternative, I would argue, is a more wholehearted engagement with the global justice movement and activist practices more akin to those of the civil society organisations. What is in question then is whether the existing trade union structures and procedures can adapt to the demands of the new global order.

In terms of the overarching spatial and social divide between workers in the affluent North and those in the dominated South, a major dilemma has been the issue of international labour standards. Should the international labour movement argue, on the basis of fairness and legitimacy, that core labour standards should be incorporated into the remit of the World Trade Organisation? Or are these labour standards a covert form of Northern protectionism vis-à-vis developing countries? As Rebecca Gumbrell-McCormick puts it 'The ICFTU believes that there is a danger of a 'global race to the bottom' and that it must be prevented by binding rules to establish minimum standards for workers in the global economy' (Gumbrell-McCormick 2004:526). The problem is that for workers in the majority world the 'social dialogue' approach and social economy model this is premised on is not available to them. For a global labour movement this is a serious dilemma and not one amenable to cosmetic resolution.

Increasingly, we find the regional moment of labour activity coming to the fore. Whether it is at the level of the EU, North American Free Trade Association (NAFTA), Mercosur (Common Market of the Southern Cone) or the Asian Pacific Economic Co-Operation (APEC), trade unions need to respond to the new regional modalities of capitalist development. As Haworth and Hughes have argued, 'There is a positive aspect to regional labour activity today. A combination of three factors – internationalisation of capital, the Social Clause / Labour Standards debate and regional integration – has provided labour with a need, a platform and a context for action' (Haworth and Hughes 2002:163). While certainly the regional transnationalism of the South does not share the same dynamic as the EU, for example, this domain will clearly gain in importance. The dilemmas it poses for labour are whether it displaces the national terrain and whether it in some way lessens the importance of global labour solidarity.

The regional moment is certainly critical at the European level, not least because of the overwhelming weight of European trade unionists in terms of numbers and even more in terms of resources at a global scale. The ETUC (European Trade Union Congress) currently accounts for more than half of the world's trade unionists (China excluded) and this region's dominance in terms of the International Trade Secretariats (now dubbed Global Unions) is also very clear. However it is less clear whether the European trade unions will be able to achieve the type of renewal necessary to deal with the rigours of neo-liberal globalisation (see Dølvik, 2001). In many ways the performance of the ETUC as a countervailing power within the EU has been disappointing, for all the talk about the European social model. By contrast, regional associations in the South, from the fairly mainstream regional trade union structures within the MERCOSUR (see Munck, 2002 b) to the more radical, but at the same time less influential, SIGTUR (Southern Initiative on Globalization and Trade Union Rights, for which see Lambert, 2002), have been forced to take up the regional level, or moment, of activity as a counter to the regionalizing dynamic of global capitalism.

As to the once dominant, or even exclusive, national level of labour activity, there is now a gradual realisation that the nation state is far from irrelevant as a parameter for much of labour's activity. As Bill Dunn concludes in a recent study of globalisation, labour and the state, 'there appear to be many respects in which it remains both possible and necessary for workers to fight at the national level' (Dunn, 2006:47). Even if labour is mounting a transnational campaign, say on core labour standards, nation states remain key targets insofar as they are the constituent members of the international financial institutions. Upscaling labour struggles because the national terrain is hostile is not always possible or desirable. Because of such dilemmas, however, it is not clear that a national trade union is an adequate vehicle even to defend the national working class from the deleterious effects of neo-liberal globalisation, never mind make substantial gains for the working class.

There is now a growing tendency across social movements to accept that we might 'think globally' but that we also need to 'act locally'. Andrew Herod has argued persuasively that 'workers may think that if they cannot organise globally, there is no point in attempting to organise at other scales' (Herod, 2001:118). This is not only politically paralysing, but ignores the extent to which TNCs can be effectively challenged locally. This is not presented as a 'small is beautiful' or 'local trumps all' argument, but simply recognises that workers need not (indeed often cannot) respond to capital's movement at the same scale. While it is clear that local pressure points may be effective in challenging a TNC, a dilemma is still posed for workers worldwide who might accept that 'another world is possible' in principle but do not see a global vision that is achievable coming from the traditional labour organisations.

Clearly these different scales of labour activity are not like rungs on a ladder, and in practice they overlap, as one would expect, given the uneven and combined development of capitalism itself. Just taking one particular dispute that has received sustained scholarly attention, the Liverpool lock-out of 1995-1998, we can see in practice how complex labour contestation is (see Castree, 2000 for a review of this case). There were sustained arguments that the dockers had to '*go global*' more consistently and that only international labour solidarity could overcome the negative forces prevailing on the national terrain. One could also argue, however, on the evidence, and persuasively, that the dense social networks of the *local* labour and community movements in Liverpool were the only reliable basis for sustaining such a long struggle. Likewise, one could argue that a decisive yet less confrontational approach through the official *national* trade union channels of the transport sector might have produced some more positive results. The point here is not to rake over these debates, but simply to reinforce the point that labour's contestation of capitalism and its effects will more often than not be multiscalar.

At the start of the twenty first century, international trade unionism is confronted by a paradox: there are more wage-earners than ever before (around three billion according to Freeman, 2006) as globalisation has unleashed a new wave of proletarianisation, but the labour movement has been seriously weakened by global neo-liberal policies. There has been a dramatic increase in the effective global labour force over the last two decades with a recent International Monetary Fund study

(IMF, 2007) suggesting it has risen fourfold. A United Nations projection suggests that effective global labour supply could more than double again by 2050 (IMF, 2007:180). While the overwhelming majority of this labour force will remain unskilled it is the increase in the proportion of skilled workers which is its most noticeable feature. The integration of the workers from the 'emerging markets' (ie former state socialist) and 'developing' (ie former Third World) countries has created the conditions for the emergence of a global working class as the ongoing integration of workers into the global marketplace proceeds apace. However the trade union and socialist movements have been emerging from a period when they were seriously weakened, if not decimated, by capitalism's twenty year long neo-liberal offensive.

The new International Trade Union Confederation claims to represent 166 million workers through its 309 affiliated trade union organisations in 156 countries and territories. The ICFTU had already brought the Global Unions under its wing through the Global Unions Council, when the collapsing former state socialist unions were incorporated. The once Christian-oriented WCL was then taken over and eight previously unaffiliated national trade union confederations were brought into its ranks. It was clearly a strategic response to globalisation: 'The international trade union movement is adapting in order to remain a key player in an economic climate that is creating more losers than winners' (ICFTU, 2006). But was this new-found spirit of political collaboration and practical action on the ground too late? Neo-liberal globalisation implied the simultaneous weakening of traditional unionism's century-old national-industrial base, the shift of that base to countries of the South (particularly China), the undermining of traditional job security and union rights, and the decline or disappearance of support from social-democratic parties and reformist governments. Moreover, the traditional Northern unions were being confronted with a fact that they had not had to face previously in the era of national/industrial relations/corporatist type labour relations, namely that in this globalising world of labour, maybe only one worker in 18 was unionised. Finally, with the disappearance of their competitors in communist or national-populist unions, the ICFTU/GU found itself not only in an alien and hostile world but ideologically disoriented now that the old Cold War politics had been superseded.

New internationalisms

Historical parallels with the late 19th century and the emergence of the modern trade union movement teach us is that the necessary shift to a new labour internationalism is unlikely to be a smooth and organic process. It is more likely that alternative social forces (the 'informal sector' for example) and new geographical locations (the South generally and China in particular) will challenge and subvert the current structures and strategies. There are signs that trade unions are looking towards the new social movements in more positive ways than in the past. Even in the USA, as Dan Clawson shows, 'Labour's links with other [social movement] groups are denser and stronger than they have been for half a century' (Clawson, 2003:205) and this interaction has led to new, more progressive policies, for example in relation to undocumented immigrants. Frances O'Grady, deputy general secretary of the British Trade Union

Congress has recognised that 'growing globalisation has demonstrated ever more vividly that going it alone [for the unions] is not an option' (Barber, 2004), and that not only do trade unions need to engage seriously with the global justice movement, but if they wish to change the world they will need to start by changing themselves. Has this begun to happen?

A decade ago, the International Confederation of Free Trade Unions (ICFTU) declared that globalisation posed 'the greatest challenge for unions in the 21st Century' (ICFTU 1997). Since then, there has been a growing mood that labour needs to 'go global' to confront the new, more internationalised capitalist order we live under. An indication of the sea change in official international trade union attitudes can be gauged by considering that while in 1995 the ICFTU was seriously offended when it was offered 'civil society' rather than 'favoured social partner' status at the UN's Social Summit held in Copenhagen, by 2008 it was publicly endorsing the radical counter-movement World Social Forum (WSF) of Porto Alegre and actually called on its members to follow the day of Action called by the WSF (see Waterman, 2008).

If the creation of a global economy is producing a global workforce, then global unions seem a logical development. Global economic power might be seen to inexorably produce a global social counter-power. Or, in Polanyian terms (see Munck, 2002a for a reading of labour and globalisation inspired by Karl Polanyi) the expansion of the market that lies at the heart of what we call globalisation generates a social counter-movement by which society (or social forces therein) protects itself from the ravages of the free or unregulated market. The 'great transformation' of market-led globalisation also creates a broad social movement (with radical and conservative strands) resisting its corrosive effect on social relations. These social relations, however, cannot be conceived without understanding how they are grounded in particular places. Thus the spatial dimensions of transnational labour relations and transnational labour solidarity are crucial to their understanding. Furthermore, contending political projects inevitably contain a particular spatial vision. The forces of capital have their range of spatial fixes, to maintain accumulation and healthy profit rates. Labour also has, or needs to have, its own spatial vision and politics of place. Globalisation has imposed on us a particular vision of space: the 'shrinking globe'; hypermobile investment; and the communications revolution. Its contestation will also generate a new understanding of space: more networked, more interdependent and maybe more sustainable.

If we were to construct a basic social-spatial matrix to set the context for labour's varied and multidimensional responses to globalisation, it would look something like the diagram in Figure 1.

The various points of the diamond might be seen as poles of attraction, setting up force fields affecting the activity of labour in complex and intermingled ways. Thus, workers and unions operate within the parameters of the market (on the left), but they are also always already embedded within social relations (on the right). Trade union strategies might thus be categorised in terms of whether they lean towards market discipline, or the social order. However, they are also pulled in different directions spatially, from the global (at the top) to the local (at the bottom), reflecting the different scales of human activity. Neither the (horizontal) Polanyian tension nor the (vertical) politics of scale can be seen as self-sufficient; rather they act in a manner that is always combined if uneven. The elements detailed in the diamond are illustrative of the type of complex locations of, for example, the European Works Councils as regional and market oriented organisations that we can contrast with the local and social orientation of social movement unionism.

Figure 1. Social and spatial dimensions of labour's responses to globalisation

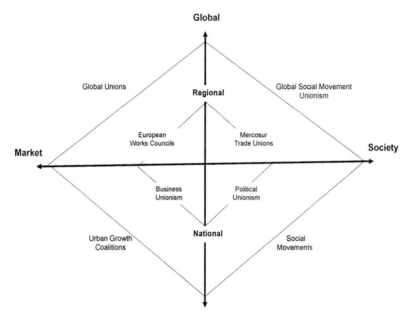

Source: Ronaldo Munck, 2007

The recent, and overdue, spatial turn in international labour studies should not, however, be seen as a panacea because it can, in turn, lead to a neglect of more traditional social, political and, above all, historical forms of analysis and prognosis. There seems to be a tendency, perhaps inevitable, to prioritise or place in a hierarchy the 'scales' of human activity as orthodox Marxists once did with the various 'levels' of capitalist society. Often this leads to binary oppositions and/or hierarchies being established such as 'local is best' or labour 'must go global'. Furthermore, to just add 'space' to the old left trinity of race, gender and class as determinants of human activity as Herod (2001:269) does, does not really subvert that well established, but limited, paradigm. However, overall, an intense focus on the interpenetration of the scales of human activity does contribute considerably to our understanding of the complexity of labour's position and strategies in the era of globalisation, making it possible to open up labour analysis and strategising in ways that acknowledge the complexity and fluidity of the world we live in.

In practice, the new trade union internationalism – as exemplified by the new UK, US and German global super-union referred to above – is largely set within the parameters of traditional industrial relations. The Global Unions had already moved from the voluntary regulation sought by the Codes of Conduct and legal regulation, through the 'social clause' campaign that would have the WTO enforcing labour standards, towards setting up 'International Framework Agreements (IFAs)' with some transnational companies, the main purpose of which was defined as 'establish[ing] a formal ongoing relationship…which can solve problems and work in the interests of both parties' (ICFTU, 2004). These international unions rightly see the TNCs as the major powers in the new global economy. They have thus moved back to 'free collective bargaining' type strategies rather than relying on tripartite relations, including the state, to defend their interests. This is understandable as a syndicalist reaction and it does seem to also lead to a greater emphasis on traditional trade union activities such as recruitment, union building and the defence of basic labour rights. As a transformative strategy, it probably will not work, however, insofar as it moves away from the broader counter-globalisation movements currently organising outside the workplace. But in this context we should be aware of the much more positive reading of Fairbrother and Hammer, for whom 'the pursuit of IFAs represents a singular accomplishment by trade unions at all levels of organization and representation' (Fairbrother and Hammer 2005:421).

Labour internationalism has always taken different forms and these have rarely followed the mythical injunction: 'workers of all countries unite, you have nothing to lose but your chains'. In fact, from the period of the First International until 1968 it was, according to Marcel van der Linden, a 'national internationalism' (van der Linden 2003a) that prevailed. That is to say the prevailing strategy was based on a narrow and Eurocentric conception of the 'international working class' and represented a form of solidarity between national trade unions movements rather than a genuine transnationalism. In the period since 1968 we have seen the rise of new social movements, the collapse of communism and the emergence of globalisation as a dominant societal paradigm. What this means in terms of internationalism is that we have probably entered a transitional phase akin to that associated with the formation of the First International, with new political and organisational forms emerging.

Traditional models of internationalism ignore the complex contingencies at play and the very real contradictions underlying its practice. For example, we might have to recognize that there are often narrow sectional interests lying behind 'internationalism', as when US trade unions promote unionism in the South to dampen competition over wage levels with their own members. Also, we might find that the best way to combat globalization is through a form of national alternativist trade union strategy. Thus one of the new global unions, the ICEM (International Federation of Chemical, Energy, Mine and General Workers Union), in a document arguing for 'global unionism' concludes that 'priority must be given to supporting organising at a local union level' (ICEM 1999:25) in order to build union strength on the ground. There is, in reality, no 'one right way' to practice internationalism and we need to recognise that it is a complex, shifting and transitional phase we are currently experiencing.

That task is tackled more productively, I would argue, by those engaged in bridging the gap between the organised labour movement and the 'new' social movements around environmental, place and gender issues (Clawson, 2004; Waterman, 2005). This is not a politics of nostalgia for an era when the 'class struggle' pitted clearly pre-defined antagonists in battle. It is a call for a politics of articulation between different sectors of the counter-globalisation movement, on the basis of identifying democratic equivalents. Whether it is race/class, blue/green divides or the ever-present gender divisions, unity will not occur through some mystical submerging into a 'multitude'. Taking a broader view, we could say that the move from the hitherto dominant simple, neo-liberal, free market Washington Consensus to a putative post Washington Consensus (see Broad 2004) takes politics out of the equation so that we can all unite around 'globalisation with a human face'. Workers are resisting this on a daily basis and their organisations are beginning to articulate a new labour politics for the era of globalisation.

Transformationalism

Without repeating the Gramscian cliché that what is needed is pessimism of the intellect and optimism of the will (Gramsci 1971:175), we do need to reflect on the good news and the bad news emerging from the above analysis of the contemporary state of transnational labour organising. One recent account of globalisation and labour and its impact on the democratising of global governance manages to make both cases in the same book (Stevis & Boswell, 2008). On the one hand the authors argue that 'we are optimistic that many unions have recognised the necessity of global union collaboration' (Stevis & Boswell, 2008:76) and that 'International Framework Agreements are an accomplishment for global unions' (Stevis & Boswell, 2008:150). But on the other hand they also argue that 'there is no evidence that the authority of the ITUC will grow' (Stevis & Boswell, 2008:72) and that 'so long as national unions persist with business as usual, global union organizations will remain organizations of the protected labor force' (Stevis & Boswell, 2008:74).

I would argue that this dual view of the prospects for and limitations of global unionism realistically mirrors the complexity of the present situation. Thus, for example, the International Chemical, Energy and Mining Workers Federation (ICEM) has been in the vanguard of the new labour internationalism since the mid 1990s, yet its president, John Maitland, resigned in 2006 citing as the cause his disillusionment with the conservative institutional nature of the organisation and the way it had undermined the new local/global organisational forms which had emerged to challenge global corporate power (Webster, Lambert & Bezuindenhout, 2008). While this mixed mode of advance and retreat is normal in any period of transition from one labour organisational form to another, it is understandable why pessimism sets in when transformative change seems to be always set back by conservative inertia. While this pessimistic interpretation dominates in academic analysis (see Myconos, 2005) we can also point to a real process of union renewal based on complex local/regional/global levels of activity and repertoires of action. This complex set of activities is beginning to address and challenge the dominant international political economy and, as Fairbrother and Hammer put it after a close analysis of the trends, 'as part of this process, a genuine international and renewed trade unionism becomes a possibility' (Fairbrother & Hammer, 2005:405).

As to what the future may hold, it is now increasingly common to refer to the 'collapse of globalism' (Saul, 2005) insofar as global peace has clearly not broken out and the nation state (and nationalism) is very much alive and well. Indeed, for many authors, globalisation was always a necessary myth created by the architects of the post-Cold War neo-liberal revolution, at least insofar as this applies to labour (Hirst and Thompson, 2000; Wood, 1997). In terms of economic internationalisation and financial openness, the classic Gold Standard period (1875 – 1914) was seen to more correctly merit the label 'globalisation'. Today, this sceptical case seems more plausible than that of the few remaining true believer globalists. However, it might be more cautious to consider the middle road of David Held's 'transformationalist' perspective which sees globalisation driving rapid economic, political, social and cultural transformations across the globe, but the result of those changes is a contingent historical process replete with contradictions (Held et al, 1999:7). In political terms terms, of course, transformation politics may take on different hues, from the very western social democratic cosmopolitanism of Held et al to the more radical strands emerging from social movement theorising in the global South. Thus Brazilian political philosopher, Roberto Mangabeira Unger, suggests that we should not wait for optimum conditions to emerge or tilt at windmills but, instead, to promote radical reforms where possible, along a transformative path (Unger 1998:18). Society is being transformed by globalisation and politics is changing apace. We need to rediscover our transformative vocations not by fighting yesterday's battles, nor through succumbing to a simple humanising of the existing order. We no longer need to accept neo-liberal globalisation as *la pensée unique* but nor can we, or should we, seek to turn the clock back on the last 20 years, so that we must accept the transformations wrought by globalisation and promote a transformative labour politics on this new social and spatial terrain.

Recently Saskia Sassen (2006) has sought to develop a more mid-range social theory of globalisation that takes us beyond macro-level accounts that tend to simplify the complex social processes underway. In particular, this meso-level narrative would help add 'social thickness' to our analysis of globalisation. By reducing globalisation to the hypermobility of finance capital and the famous time-space compression, dominant accounts strip the global of its social determinants and conditioning factors. This approach also allows us to move beyond impoverished notions of the local and the global in both the pro- and anti-globalisation literatures, that manage to equate the global with placelessness. Sassen's approach also leads us to focus on what she calls the 'countergeographies of globalisation' (Sassen 2006:370) whereby alternative networks develop a multiscalar politics that need not become cosmopolitan in the classical sense, to act as powerful counteracting tendencies to globalisation.

We can argue that there is today a tendency towards the formation of a global working class. For some twenty years now, there has been a tendential process towards the formation of a global labour market. Management consultant William Johnston declared at the start of the 1990s that 'the globalisation of labour is inevitable' (Johnston 1991:126). Of course, in practice no more than one fifth of the world's workers are directly linked to the global political economy in terms of labour relations. Yet the possibility of global unions is not diminished by this fact, when we take into account the much greater impact of what we call globalisation on labour relations worldwide. This leads even cautious labour scholars like Jeffrey Harrod and Robert O' Brien to conclude that 'a global labour force can be discerned, if it is defined as those workers connected to the global economy' (Harrod & O'Brien, 2002:14).

The power of the local to affect the new global capitalism is clear. The local still matters even while globalisation tends to obliterate space. But we need to go beyond the 'local-global paradox' if we are to construct a new internationalism for the era of globalisation. The paradox refers to the fact that 'while economic relationships have become ever more global in scope and nature, political responses to economic globalization are becoming more localized' (Jonas 1999:325). While this might be the case, it is not, I would argue, incompatible with the emergence of a new labour internationalism. Workers are clearly divided by national, regional, gender, ethnic and other fault-lines. The growing internationalisation of capitalist rule may increase competition along national, regional and even city lines. But globalisation is also creating a more numerous global working class and, arguably, a common focus for workers worldwide. Some workers and their organisations have responded with a 'new realism' that simply accepts an irreversible change in the balance of forces against workers. In other cases, national and regional alternatives have developed along traditional political mobilisation lines. Maybe we can develop a 'local transnationalism' based on the notion that workers' internationalism need not mirror the international structures of capitalism of either the multinational corporations or the WTO (World Trade Organisation).

In his final 'search for international union theory' Harvie Ramsay concluded that 'in the end, the success of international unionism remains a contradictory and contingent matter' (Ramsay, 1999:215). There are many contradictions within the global working class, but not least there are the divisions based on social position and geographical location. There is a tension between the transnational labour activity 'from above' and the local contestation of globalisation that may well take particularist and protectionist forms. Then there is a large element of contingency in how labour responds to capitalist strategies and structures that are always changing and show a huge variety of forms across space. We must also, I believe, consider very carefully the Gramscian definition of transitional periods when 'the old is dying but the new has not yet been fully born' (Gramsci 1971:106) and seek to apply it to transnational labour relations. Our conclusion might thus lead us to mirror Harvie Ramsay's, namely, that 'this is not a message of hopelessness, but one which emphasises the complexity and difficulty of the international union project' (Ramsay, 1999:215).

© *Ronaldo Munck, 2008*

REFERENCES

Broad, R. (2004) 'The Washington Consensus Meets the Global Backlash: Shifting Debates and Policies' *Globalizations,* 1(2):129-54

Castells, M. (1997) *The Power of Identity Vol II of The Information Age,* Oxford: Blackwell

Castree, N. (2000) 'Geographic Scales and Grass-Roots Internationalism: The Liverpool Docks Dispute, 1995-1998', *Economic Geography,* 76(3):272-92

Clawson, D. (2003) *The Next Upsurge. Labor and the New Social Movements,* Ithaca and London: ILR Press, Cornell University Press

Clawson, D. et al (2004) Symposium: The Next Upsurge: Labor and the New Social Movements, *Labor History,* Vol 45 No.2:333-382

Dølnik, J. E. (2001) European Trade Unions: Coping with Globalisation? Fafo Paper. Retrieved on December 1, 2007 from http://www.fafo.no/pub/rapp/675/675.htm

Dunn, B (2006) 'Globalisation, Labour and the State' in C. Phelan (ed) *The Future of Organised Labour. Labour Perspectives,* Oxford: Peter Lang

Fairbrother, P & N. Hammer (2005) Global Unions. Past Efforts and Future Prospects', *Relations Industrielles/ Industrial Relations,* 60(3):405-28.

Freeman, R. (2006) 'China, India and the Doubling of the Global Labor Force: Who Pays the Price of Globalization?' Retrieved on December 1, 2007 from http://www.zmag.org/content/showarticle.cfm?ItemID=8617

Gramsci, A. (1971) *Selections from the Prison Notebooks,* London: Lawrence and Wishart

Gumbrell-McCormick, R. (2004) 'Putting the Labor into Labor Standards', *Labor History,* Vol 45 No.4:522-29

Harrod, J. & R. O'Brien, R (2002) 'Organised labour and the global political economy' in J. Harrod and R. O'Brien (eds) *Global Unions? Theory and strategies of organised labour in the global political economy,* London: Routledge

Haworth, N. & S. Hughes (2002) 'International labour and regional integration in the Asia-Pacific', in J. Harrod & R. O' Brien (eds) *Global Unions? Theory and strategies of organised labour in the global political economy,* London: Routledge

Held, D., A. McGrew, D. Goldblatt & J. Perraton (1999) *Global Transformations: Politics, Economics and Culture,* Cambridge: Polity Press

Herod, A (2001) *Labor Geographies, Workers and the Landscapes of Capitalism,* New York & London: The Guildford Press

Hyman, R. (2004) 'Agitation, Organisation, Diplomacy, Bureaucracy: Trends and Dilemmas in International Trade Unionism', *Labor History,* 45(3)

ICEM (1999) *Facing Global Power: Strategies for Global Unionism,* Durban: Second World Congress

ICFTU (1997) *The Global Market: Trade Unionisms Greatest Challenge,* Brussels: ICFTU

ICFTU (2007) 'Strength in unity: a new international trade union confederation is born'. Retrieved on December 1, 2007 from http://www.icftu.org

IMF (2007) *World Economic Outlook. Spillovers and Cycles in the Global Economy.* Retrieved on December 1, 2007 from http://www.imf.org

Johnston, W. (1991) 'Global Work Force 2000: The New World Labor Market', *Harvard Business Review,* March-April:115-127

Jonas, A. (1998) 'Investigating the Local-Global Paradox' in A.Herod (ed) *Organizing the Landscape: Geographical Perspectives on Labor Unionism,* Minneapolis, MN: University of Minnesota Press

Lambert, R. (2002) 'Labour movement renewal in the era of globalization: union responses in the South' in J. Harrod and R. O'Brien (eds) *Global Unions? Theory and strategies of organised labour in the global political economy,* London: Routledge

Mangabeira Unger, R. (1998) *Democracy Realized: The Progressive Alternative,* London: Verso

Moody, K. (1997) *Workers in a Lean World: Unions in the International Economy,* London: Zed Books

Morgan, O. (2006) 'Birth of the first global super-union', *Observer* (December 31st)

Munck, R. (2002a) *Globalisation and Labour: The new 'Great Transformation',* London: Zed Books.

Munck, R. (2002b) ' Globalization, regionalism and Labour: The case of MERCOSUR', *Labour, Capital and Society,* 34 (1):8-25

Myconos, G. (2005) *The Globalization of Organised Labour:1914- 2005,* Basingstoke: Palgrave Macmillan

Ramsay, P. (1999) 'In Search of International Union Theory' in Waddington, J (ed) *Globalisation and Patterns of Labour Resistance* London: Mansell & New York

Sassen, S (2006) *Territory Authority Rights – From Medieval to Global Assemblages,* Princeton & Oxford: Princeton University Press

Saul, J.R. (2006) *The Collapse of Globalism and the Reinvention of the World,* London: Atlantic Books

Stevis, D. (1998) 'International Labor Organizations, 1864-1997', in D. Gallin (ed) *Journal of World-Systems Research,* Vol IV No.1:52-75

Stevis, D. & T. Boswell (2008) *Globalization and Labor: Democratizing Global Governance,* Lanham: Rowland and Littlefield

Urry, J. (2000) *Global Complexity,* Cambridge: Polity Press

van der Linden, M. (2003a) *Transnational Labour History: Explorations,* Aldershot: Ashgate

van der Linden, M. (2003b) 'The ICFTU at the Crossroads: An Historical Interpretation'. Paper delivered to *Labour and New Social Movements in a Globalising World System: The Future of the Past,* conference, Linz: September

Waterman, P., et al (2005) 'Symposium: Labor and the New Social Movements', *Labor History,* Vol 46 No.2:195-244

Waterman, P. (2007) *International Unions Embrace the World Social Forum: Opportunities and…. Limitations?* mimeo

Webster, E., R. Lambert & A. Bezuidenhout (2008) Grounding Globalisation. Labour in the Era of Insecurity, London: Routledge

Wood, E.M. (ed) (1997) *Rising from the Ashes? Labor in the Age of 'Global' Capitalism,* New York: Monthly Review:49

Trade unions and worker movements in the North American communications industries

Vincent Mosco

Vincent Mosco *is Canada Research Chair and Professor of Sociology at Queen's University in Kingston, Ontario, Canada.*

ABSTRACT

This paper reports on a project that examines trends in North American labour movements, and specifically in the workforce, in the converging communications, culture, and information technology sectors. Drawing on documentary evidence and interviews, the paper concentrates on two important developments: efforts to unify workers across the knowledge and communication industries, and the rise of worker movements that operate in conjunction with, but outside, the formal trade union structure. The paper begins by situating these developments within debates about labour in a 'post-industrial', 'information', or 'network' society. It describes the challenges facing workers in the knowledge sector, especially rapid technological change, massive corporate consolidation, the rise of the neo-liberal state and divisions between cultural and technical workers in the knowledge sector. The paper proceeds to describe how North American workers are responding within the traditional trade union system, primarily through forms of consolidation or trade union convergence (such as the Communication Workers of America), and also through worker movements operating outside the traditional trade union system in the information technology and cultural sectors (for example WashTech and the National Writers Union). The paper concludes by addressing the significance of these developments. Do they portend a rebirth of North American labour activism or do they represent its last gasps?

Introduction

Research from a variety of perspectives has demonstrated the importance of information and communication labour in the modern economy (Dyer-Witheford, 1999; Huws, 2003; Terranova, 2004). In an era characterised by declining trade union participation, increasing corporate concentration, and the rise of global conglomerates that feed into - and are fed by - the spread of new communication and information technology, North American knowledge workers have begun to explore new ways to increase the power of labour. This is especially the case in the communications sector, which provides the equipment that makes globalisation possible, and in the production and distribution of the ideas that make it work.

One approach is to pursue trade union mergers, a strategy designed to restructure labour unions along much the same lines as the corporations that employ their members. There is considerable research on the value of mergers or convergence among trade unions, including in the communication and information industries (Batstone, 1984; Katz, 1997; Stone, 2004). Convergent unions like the Communications Workers of America (CWA) or the Communications, Energy and Paperworkers Union of Canada (CEP) bring together workers in what were once independent industries - newspapers, telecommunications, sound recording and broadcasting - but which are now part of cross-media conglomerates. These unions also recognise that it is not just the boundaries between employers that have become blurred; the boundaries between what were once distinct forms of work have also been obscured through the spread of digital technology. Labour convergence, therefore, is seen as an appropriate response to technological and corporate convergence (McKercher, 2002; Swift, 2003; Bahr, 1998).

A second approach is to create non-traditional worker organisations, which draw people into the labour movement who cannot or will not join a traditional trade union. Such groups provide a range of services and support for workers, their families and their communities but do not engage in collective bargaining. In North America, they are particularly prominent in the high-technology area (Stone, 2004; Kline, Dyer-Witheford & de Peuter, 2003; van Jaarsveld, 2004).

Theorising knowledge labour

Call centre employees, university professors, and journalists have very little in common but they do share important roles in the knowledge industries. Analysis and debate about this sector began in earnest shortly after World War II when scholars began to notice growth in the number of jobs outside the manufacturing sector. In the early years, the academic emphasis was on developing measures to track the growth of the information sector as an economic force. Machlup (1962) was among the leaders in charting the expansion of the data and information components of the economy. Porat (1977) later built on this work to document the shift from an economy based on the agriculture (primary) and manufacturing (secondary) sectors to one rooted in services (tertiary) and information (quaternary) occupations. However, neither Machlup nor Porat addressed the political, social, and cultural implications of this transformation with anything approaching the theoretical sophistication of Daniel Bell (1973).

According to Bell, we were not merely experiencing a growth in data and information, nor merely a shift in the major occupational categories, but a transformation in the nature of capitalist society. Capitalism had been governed for two centuries by industrialists and their financiers who comprised the capitalist class. Now, with the rise of a society dependent on technology, and particularly on the production and distribution of information, Bell maintained that a new class of leaders, a genuine knowledge class of well-trained scientific-technical workers was rising to prominence and ultimately to leadership of a post-industrial capitalism. Inherited wealth and power would shrink in significance and a genuine meritocracy would rule. Such a society would not necessarily be more democratic, but it did portend a shift in power from its traditional base in family inheritance to technical and scientific knowledge. The ranks of knowledge workers would literally power and manage this new post-industrial economy, leading to steady economic growth and the decline of historic ideologies. According to Bell, political battles over public policy would diminish as technical algorithms and knowledge-based measures, would govern. No doubt, tensions would exist in such a society, but these would be technical and not ideological. The only potential for serious division lay outside the economic and political spheres and resided in, as Bell (1976) would argue in his next, far darker, book, the cultural sphere. The only significant internal threat to this post-industrial society was a culture sinking deeper into consumer hedonism and irrational beliefs. The conjunction of two apparent opposites, materialism and the counter-culture, threatened the foundations of post-industrialism because they challenged the delayed gratification and support for technical rationality that were required to maintain it.

It did not take long for others to conclude that, cultural issues aside, post-industrialism itself was not inherently progressive. For Herbert Schiller (1973), post-industrialism meant the rise of transnational media and communication businesses that would pump out support for American values, including its military and imperial ambitions, and eliminate alternatives through increasingly concentrated market power. According to Harry Braverman (1973), for the vast majority of workers in the service, retail, and knowledge professions, labour would be as regimented, and ultimately de-skilled, as it had been in assembly-line manufacturing. Indeed, given the immateriality of knowledge work, it would be easier than in the industrial era to separate conception from execution and to concentrate the power of conception (eg design and management) in a dominant class.

There has been widespread debate ever since Bell, Braverman, and Schiller addressed these issues in 1973, but there is some agreement in key areas. For instance, there is consensus that a shift from manufacturing to knowledge work has already occurred in more developed economies and is beginning in some less developed ones. Yes, people agree that there was and still is considerable knowledge required in much of manufacturing as well as in agricultural work. But the difference today is that an increasing amount of work is taken up with the production and distribution of information, communication, and knowledge. Furthermore, there is agreement that a dynamic process of deskilling, upskilling and reskilling is taking place in the occupational hierarchy. At different times and in different sectors one or another of these processes predominates, but the labour process, most concur, cannot be reduced to the singularity of a single process (Barley & Kunda, 2004; Brint, 2001; Powell & Snellman, 2004). Nevertheless, there is also agreement that companies have benefited from reducing the skill component of jobs or eliminating jobs entirely and replacing them with automated systems. This especially applies to jobs traditionally filled by women (Huws, 2003).

Where deskilling or job elimination is not possible, companies have accomplished the same objective by moving jobs to low wage areas within a country or shipping them abroad. Since knowledge work typically does not require movement of material things over long distances (for example, call centres and software engineering contain little or no bulk), the production process requires the use of global telecommunications systems, the costs of which have been declining over years of technological development. This process of outsourcing enables, for example, an American company to use data entry workers in China, call centre employees in Canada, and software programmers in India, while incurring a fraction of the labour costs it would encounter by employing workers in the United States. This process is, by and large, an extension of the general predominance of a business-led neo-liberal agenda that has transformed the business-labour social contract of the 1950s and 1960s (guaranteed jobs at a living wage with a package of benefits) to a business-first agenda that, in the name of productivity, has made jobs, wages, and certainly benefits, far from a guarantee in today's more developed economies. Because outsourcing is part of this wider business agenda, which has also attacked the social policy instruments that protected labour and trade unions, it has been all the more difficult for working people to mount a successful defence (Economic Policy Institute, 2004).

Nevertheless, outsourcing is not without its antimonies. A large share of outsourcing in the knowledge and communication sectors is contained within the developed world where, for example, Canada has become Hollywood North and Ireland continues to benefit from its skilled English-speaking workforce and wage and tax premiums. Moreover, although India is a major source of low wage knowledge labour, its major companies, such as ICICI, Tata, Infosys, and Wipro, are taking a leading role in the outsourcing industry. Their activities in North America suggest that place still matters and that culture still counts. Finally, resistance is growing from labour organisations and that is one reason why the expansion of convergent unions and worker associations in the knowledge and communication sectors is particularly important (Elmer & Gasher, 2005; Mosco, 2006). However, the data on general trade union membership in North America are not encouraging for those who would like to see this resistance expand.

The crisis in North American trade unionism

Trade union membership rates have steadily declined from a high of 20.1 % in 1983, the first year for which comparable union data are available. In 2005, 12.5 % of wage and salary workers in the US were trade union members. According to the US Bureau of Labour Statistics, this was down from 12.9 % in 2003 and 12.7 % in 2004. The figures for private sector members are even lower, about 7.8 %, compared to 36.5 % of government workers. Two occupational groups - education, training, and library occupations, on the one hand, and protective service occupations on the other - had the highest unionisation rates in 2004, at about 38.5 and 37 % respectively. The first of these two groups of workers is centrally located in the knowledge industry and demonstrates the potential for union growth in this rapidly expanding sector (US Bureau of Labour Statistics, 2006). Unionisation is marginally higher in Canada where, in 2005, 30.7 % of workers were union members, an increase from 30.4 % in 2004 (Bédard, 2005). According to a 2004 government report, 72 % of Canadian public sector workers and 18 % of employees in the private sector were union members. However, union density is also down in Canada from the 35 % of workers who were union members in 1990 (Statistics Canada, 2004).

Admittedly, these numbers should be placed in their historical context because while union density rates were at similarly low levels in the 1920s, they bounced to high levels in the 1930s that were maintained through the early 1950s. As late as 1932, an eminent American labour economist speaking to a meeting of the American Economics Association, reflected on the American Federation of Labour's loss of 40 % of its members and pronounced that technological change made it nearly impossible for the union movement to regain its earlier strength (Clawson, 2003). Furthermore, although union density is declining, the absolute number of union members is growing with an overall expansion of the workforce in both the United States and Canada. While it is the case that both countries have more unionised workers than ever before, density rates continue to decline and there is general agreement among scholars and trade unionists themselves that workers in the knowledge economy face serious problems. One strategy that stands out as attempting to rectify this problem is the merger strategy that has been adopted by established trade unions in the United States and Canada to better mobilise and concentrate resources. This has been especially evident in the knowledge and communication sectors. In order to understand this strategy as it applies to the knowledge and media sector, it is useful to consider the concept of convergence.

The concept of convergence

Convergence is one of the central developments taking place across the media, telecommunications and information sectors of the communications industry. Generally speaking, it refers to the integration of technologies, arenas and institutions in these industries and more specifically to the integration of the devices that these industries use and the information they process, distribute and exchange over and through these devices (Babe, 1996; McKercher, 2002; Winseck, 1998). By integrating computers and telecommunications, the internet is now an iconic example of technological convergence.

This form of convergence is also linked to, and partly responsible for, the convergence of once separate industries into a common arena providing electronic information and communication services. Differences in the social relations of technology, including corporate and regulatory arrangements negotiated in the 19th and 20th Centuries that divided up the media into fields of mutually exclusive dominance, once erected thick walls between print media, electronic media, telecommunications, and information services and between labour processes and trade union structures in those industries. Now, owing largely to the power of private communication companies, the weakening enthusiasm of governments to support public service communication, and the decline in social movements committed to public service communication, these walls are breaking down, eliminating many of the distinctive features that divided these separate industries and creating one large electronic information and communication services arena.

Convergence has enabled the interconnection of technologies to create new systems of hardware and new levels of service, such as wireless networking in Wi-Fi and Wi-Max systems. Hardware convergence has been greatly advanced with the development of a common digital language that does not distinguish between audio, video or data transmission; reducing all communication to one language that provides a manifold increase in the quantity and quality of electronic communication. Digitisation has the technological advantage of providing enormous gains in transmission speed and flexibility over earlier forms of electronic communication, which were largely reliant on analogue techniques (Longstaff, 2002). But digitisation takes place in the context of, and greatly expands, the process of commodification, or the transformation of what amounts to a resource into a marketable product or service. On the one hand, the expansion of the commodity form provides the context for who leads the process of digitisation and how it is applied. On the other hand, digitisation is used to expand the commodification of information and entertainment, specifically to enlarge markets for communication products, deepen the commodification of labour involved in the production, distribution and exchange of communication, and expand markets in the audiences that receive and make use of electronic communication (Mosco, 1996).

Companies are taking advantage of technological convergence by creating corporate or institutional convergence. This is embodied in the scope of merger and acquisition activity that is most prominent within the knowledge and media industries, though not limited to these sectors (Mosco, 2004; Nichols & McChesney, 2005; Schiller, 1999). Convergence is bringing together communication firms which want to take advantage of opportunities to integrate products and services, to cross-promote and cross-market products and services in previously separate spheres like entertainment and news, and to cross-produce content for a range of media. Corporate convergence does not, in and of itself, guarantee success. In the short run, it sometimes does not produce the synergies that companies anticipate, such as the integration of the cultures of the print newsroom and the broadcasting station. It also sometimes results in content that cannot attract audiences. These facts help to explain the difficulties experienced by convergent media firms like AT&T, Bell Canada Enterprises and AOL Time Warner. Indeed, according to the *Wall Street Journal*, Time Warner executives no longer talk about 'synergies' but about 'adjacencies' (Karnitschnig, 2006). Moreover, digitisation itself is not a flawless process and technical problems do slow its development.

Another stumbling block in the process of technological and institutional convergence is the state of government regulation. Technological and institutional convergence has raised fundamental problems for regulatory policies that were established for discrete industries based on discrete technologies. But these may be short-term problems, which can result in cyclical declines over the course of a secular trend, rather than as evidence that convergence has failed. Large units enable businesses to better control their environments, limiting competitive pressures even as they benefit by developing internal market competition among divisions.

Convergence is not just a technological, political and organisational process. It is also a myth or a story about how computer communication is revolutionising technology, politics and society. As such, it is part of a sublime vision that, in its strongest form, envisions the technology creating the conditions for the end of history, the end of geography, and the end of politics (Mosco, 2004). Convergence is therefore more than just a term to describe an ostensible change in technology and organisation. It is part of a utopian discourse that aims to lead us from the coarse materiality of, in Nicholas Negroponte's terms, 'the world of atoms', so that we can 'learn to be digital' (Negroponte, 1996). This affirmative vision is used to rationalise deepening social inequalities, tightening surveillance practices, and the growing control of a handful of companies over the production and distribution of communication and information. To say that convergence is a myth is not to imply that it is false. Rather, myths take a basic empirical reality and enlarge it by attributing transformative social and cultural consequences that are not currently justified by empirical evidence. Convergence, as both a political and cultural process, creates considerable pessimism among those who support public service communication, diversity in the form and content of knowledge, information and entertainment, and universal and equitable access to media (Artz & Kamalipour, 2003; Herman & Chomsky, 2002; Winter, 2005). But the growth of trade union convergence is creating some grounds for optimism.

Trade union convergence

In the United States, a range of media unions - the International Typographical Workers Union (ITU), the Newspaper Guild, and the National Association of Broadcast Employees and Technicians (NABET) - have joined the Communications Workers of America (CWA). The model of a convergent union (or, as the CWA likes to call itself, 'a trade union for the information age'), the CWA represents workers employed in telecommunications, broadcasting, cable TV, newspaper and wire service journalism, publishing, electronics and general manufacturing, as well as airline customer service, government service, health care, education and other fields. Among the major employers of CWA members are AT&T, GTE, the Regional Bell telephone companies, Lucent Technologies/Bell Labs, the NBC and ABC television networks, the Canadian Broadcasting Corporation (CBC), and major newspapers such as the *New York Times*, the *Wall Street Journal* and the *Washington Post*.

In Canada, the Communications, Energy and Paperworkers Union (CEP) has pursued a similar pattern. It has merged with many of the Canadian units from the ITU, the Newspaper Guild and Canadian NABET. Its members work in pulp and paper mills, telephone companies, newspapers, radio and television. They are also employed as graphic artists, hotel workers, computer programmers, truck drivers and nurses. Furthermore, the Telecommunications Workers Union (TWU), which historically represented telephone workers in British Columbia, was able to extend its jurisdiction over telecommunications workers in other parts of the country because the Canadian labour regulatory body, the CIRB, determined that technological and industry convergence was best represented by a single converged union.

To a degree, the unions see these actions as defensive, or as ways of protecting their members. But significantly, they also see labour convergence as an attempt to take advantage of synergies brought about by a growing convergence in the nature of their work (Bahr, 1998). Since these unions represent workers who are increasingly involved in producing for a converging electronic information services arena, they see improved opportunities for organising and bargaining. In essence, converging technologies and converging companies have led workers to come together across the knowledge industry (McKercher, 2002).

This strategy has not always been successful. For example, one of the keys to mobilising against the increasingly integrated video and film industries, encompassing mainly television and Hollywood, is to merge unions representing both sectors, just as companies like Disney and Fox have used their merged power to control their respective workers. Without a unified workforce, these companies can dictate the terms of contracts outlining the conditions under which revenues from multiple uses of the same television program or film are to be divided. Specifically, trade union convergence in this sector would mean bringing together the American Federation of Television and Radio Artists (AFTRA) and the Screen Actors Guild (SAG). But attempts to accomplish this have failed, most recently in 1999 and 2003, in very close votes (McKercher & Mosco, 2007).

In Canada, attempts to build closer ties among the major telecommunications unions have also not been particularly successful. Setting up the National Association of Communication Unions created formal federation links between the CEP and the Telecommunications Workers Union (TWU). But perhaps because the latter has a history of radicalism (it once took over the telephone exchanges of Vancouver during a strike action in 1981) and because the TWU has eschewed the convergent union idea, the two unions have not worked closely together (Mosco & McKercher, forthcoming).

Convergence also creates cross-border difficulties, as workers at the CBC experienced when, to facilitate bargaining, the CIRB ordered its unions to merge. Prior to this time, CBC's journalists had been members of the CWA (which won the right of representation when it merged with the Newspaper Guild) and its technicians were part of the CEP. This meant that some employees of Canada's national broadcaster were members of an American union while others were members of a Canadian union. In the ensuing vote, members decided to join the larger CWA, making all employees at Canada's national public broadcaster part of an American union. This form of cross-border convergence has proven to be very useful, contributing significantly to the surprising success of CBC workers against a management that locked them out in August 2005. This case demonstrated the ability of different types of knowledge worker, in this case journalists and technicians, to work together and maintain solidarity with the help of a strong union, even though that union is based in another country (Mosco & McKercher, forthcoming).

In 2005, the merger issue heated up in the United States when, in the wake of the big Republican victory in the 2004 general election and the continued decline in union density rates, one of the major unions in the AFL-CIO threatened to pull out unless the federation permitted significant new mergers and other organisational changes. Specifically, the fastest growing major union in the United States, the Service Employees International Union (SEIU), demanded that the federation consolidate several of its member unions and shift funding from its own research and political activity to grassroots organising. Holding out the threat of withdrawal, the SEIU was backed by the powerful Teamsters Union. The AFL-CIO proposed a compromise but was not successful and several unions left the federation to form their own 'Change to Win Coalition' comprising 5.4 million members committed to stepped-up union organising. Partly in response to this major defection, the AFL-CIO set up an industry coordinating committee made up of ten unions covering the arts, entertainment, media and telecommunications industries. The committee's goal is to build labour power in the industries that have been rocked by corporate concentration and technological change. Convergence, therefore, may also be a response to the failure of an organisation to maintain its membership.

It is uncertain just how far the urge to merge or the convergence movement will take North American trade unions. Will it bring back the idea of One Big Union, once popular a century ago with the Knights of Labour and Industrial Workers of the World? Can it expand democracy and citizen engagement by empowering a segment of society that has declined over the past three decades? Is it a genuine new start for labour or a last gasp? It is too early to answer these questions. But it is useful to consider different perspectives on the significance of this development.

On the one hand, labour union convergence increases the centralisation of power and bureaucracy, thereby making it less likely that union leadership can maintain close contact with the rank-and-file membership. Indeed the evidence from outside North America is not encouraging. For example, in the 1990s the Australian labour movement succeeded in halving the number of its unions, but this did not stop the erosion of union density. Does trade union convergence mean sacrificing union democracy for various forms of cartel unionism?

On the other hand, convergence does give unions greater clout in collective bargaining, thereby diminishing the power that has been concentrated in big companies over the past three decades. To support this view one can point to the CWA's success in organising wireless telecommunication workers and in defending technical and on-air staff at the CBC. Moreover, mergers allow unions to be more involved in social and political activities. For example, Swift (2003) cites the CEP as an example of a converged communication union that has been more deeply involved in major policy issues since it expanded across the converged information industries, including the struggle to limit media concentration in Canada, as well as the fight against lifting restrictions on foreign ownership of Canadian media. The CEP has been in the forefront of lobbying to maintain public telecommunications in the province of Saskatchewan and public electrical power in Ontario.

Moreover, one of the advantages of a converged union is its ability to rise above the narrow interests of some of its members. So, for instance, even though the CEP represents energy workers, it is fully behind the Kyoto Accords to limit the expansion of greenhouse gasses. Furthermore, it was able to stand up for its paper workers against the powerful wood products company Abitibi because convergence permitted the CEP to draw from the strike funds of its energy and communication industry members. The union also has the resources to create a Quebec Solidarity Fund that permitted it to invest in declining Quebec paper mills and keep them from closing. Furthermore, the CEP has been extensively involved in the anti-globalisation movement and in supporting unionisation in Mexico and throughout Latin America with the help of the CEP Humanity Fund. Converged knowledge worker unions also seem to be able to deliver other benefits for their members. For instance, research conducted by Kiss and Mosco (2005) on what unions are doing about surveillance in the workplace demonstrated that knowledge worker unions, especially convergent unions like the CEP, provide the best protection for workers in their collective agreements.

Finally, convergence allows unions to work co-operatively as never before. In the United States the AFL-CIO recently threw its support behind a form of convergent unionism in the cultural sector by setting up an industry coordinating committee made up of ten unions covering the arts, entertainment, media and telecommunications industries. The committee's goal is to build labour power in industries that have been shaken by corporate concentration and technological change.

Nevertheless, it is not entirely clear whether converged unions are genuinely bringing together different kinds of workers in the knowledge, information and communication sectors, such as news workers and telephone operators, or merely becoming federations of what are, in effect, dissimilar employees.

Worker associations

A second response to the crisis in North American organised labour is the formation of worker associations or worker movements that provide benefits to workers without formally negotiating collective agreements. These have been especially prominent in the high-tech sector where union organising has been particularly difficult. They are more evident in the United States than in Canada, though there have been some Canadian initiatives such as the Association des Travailleurs du Multimedia du Quebec, but these have not received substantial support. Worker associations are also more prominent among part-time workers who are difficult to organise by traditional unions because they typically work for an employment agency, not the high-tech company itself. These associations are prominent in California's Silicon Valley where fully 40 % of workers are employed in non-standard ways and in Microsoft's territory in the Pacific Northwest. It was here that the term 'Permatemp' or permanent temporary worker, was coined to describe workers who work full time but on hourly contracts that contain practically no benefits or overtime pay. Among the goals of these associations are the provision of portable benefits for a highly mobile workforce, lifelong training, job placement, assistance to individual workers, dissemination of information to workers and health care plans for workers who are not eligible for employer-paid benefits.

Two types of such associations feature significantly in the knowledge sector, those that represent technology-intensive workers and those that primarily produce content. Perhaps the leading example and model of the former is WashTech, an offshoot of the CWA in the Seattle high-tech industry formed by disgruntled Microsoft permatemps who were successful in a legal action against the company for salary and benefits denied to them because they were placed in the temporary worker category (Brophy, forthcoming; van Jaarsveld, 2004, Rodicino-Colcino, this volume). One of the biggest difficulties workers face in the high tech industry is that many of them do not formally work for the high tech company itself but for companies like Manpower, which provide high tech firms with workers. Nevertheless, what helped forge WashTech was Microsoft's use of its political power to create the 'permatemp' category, thereby denying a large group of otherwise full-time employees the salary and benefits that were available to recognised full-time workers. The lawsuit and the assistance of the CWA helped to galvanise a sufficient number of Microsoft workers to form WashTech.

WashTech includes programmers, editors, web designers, systems analysts, proofers, testers and engineers who aim to win higher pay, health benefits, vacation, access to retirement plans, discounted stock options, and workplace training. In addition to taking legal action against Microsoft, WashTech members used their technical skills to unearth a secret Microsoft database on employee performance and distribute it to members. WashTech also found contract documents dating back to 2001 cementing deals to outsource high-end software architecture to Indian firms that the company hoped to keep secret. WashTech has been successful at Microsoft, helped by its association with research advocacy groups such at the Center for a Changing Workforce and its online site Techsunite.org which provides information and online organising for high tech workers. But it has at best enjoyed mixed success in expanding to other knowledge sector workers. It failed to organise disgruntled workers at the online bookseller Amazon.com, but did succeed in organising workers at Cingular wireless. Today, WashTech is especially involved in fighting the outsourcing of tech jobs to places like India and China and has been successful in convincing some state legislators to stop outsourcing government tech work.

Alliance@IBM was also formed by the CWA and, like WashTech, fought to win benefits that were initially denied to workers based on their status in the loosely defined temporary category by their employer, in this case, IBM. The company has been notoriously associated with concerns about toxic chemicals in the workplace and Alliance has been particularly active in fighting occupational safety and health cases before the courts. Alliance has also been successful in winning some formal representation for workers at both Manpower and IBM.

It is unusual to think of engineers as part of the labour movement but the Society of Professional Engineering Employees in Aerospace (SPEEA) has made it necessary for the management at Boeing to do so because in 2000 the Society led the largest white collar strike in US history against the giant manufacturer. Indeed, what makes the SPEEA particularly interesting to those who believe that knowledge work offers the potential for new forms of organising is that much of their success was achieved by the use of email and the Internet. For example, the union managed to collect home email addresses while building a communications network for their strike against Boeing in 2000. In perhaps the most effective use of its database, SPEEA was able to generate a picket line of 500 people in six hours by email alone, to disrupt an unannounced meeting of the Boeing board of directors in a local hotel. There are other noteworthy high tech worker association organising efforts. Systems Administrators Guilds have been set up in the USA (and in the UK and Australia as well) to organise computer workers and intervene in policy debates.

Worker associations are also increasingly prominent among content producers. Working Today is an advocacy group representing independent workers including freelancers, consultants, temps, and contingent workers based in New York in the area known during the high tech boom as Silicon Alley. The group has been particularly successful in providing basic health insurance to members. The Graphic Artists Guild represents web creators, illustrators, and designers who come together to improve working conditions and intervene in processes concerning copyright, taxation and other important policy issues. The Creators' Federation represents freelance writers and is credited with winning an important case requiring publishers to receive freelancers' approval before putting their work on a database. Additionally, the National Writers' Union in the United States boasts over 5,000 members for whom it provides model contracts, advice on bargaining with publishers and benefits for people without insurance.

One of the primary reasons for the rise of worker associations in the high tech field is that established trade unions have simply not been successful in their organising drives. Nevertheless, some of the old line unions did meet with some success in the heyday of the dotcom boom when unions like the United Food and Commercial Workers successfully organised dotcom workers involved in the online delivery services of supermarkets like Peabodys and Albrittons. Moreover, the AFL-CIO has been successful in building community affiliates like Working America, combining union and non-union members who pledge to co-operate with unions in political and legislative campaigns. Its founding director is Karen Nussbaum who created the first organisation of women office workers in the 1980s with a group called Nine to Five. The Service Employees International Union has also created an online membership organisation called Purpleocean.org in an effort to expand the union's scope and influence beyond the workplace by engaging in social justice activism.

As with trade union convergence, there is uncertainty over the success of worker associations in responding to the crisis facing organised labour. On the one hand, they provide a new form of unionism that makes use of new technology to reach workers who have little experience with unions. They bring into the labour movement people who do not necessarily want to be part of a trade union and they represent a recognition that formal collective agreements do not mean as much in a world of accelerating mobility. But on the other hand one can also make the argument that these new associations are providing little hope for the future. Since they are, by and large, not directly involved in collective bargaining, worker associations offer few, if any, guarantees for wages and working conditions. Arguably they simply provide evidence of the failure to organise unions in the rapidly growing knowledge sector and, since these jobs embody the workplace of the future, they do not offer much hope for genuine trade unionism. Worker associations may provide a new start toward rebuilding the labour movement, perhaps by reinventing the old guild model, but they may also represent little more than organised labour's last gasp.

Conclusion

Drawing on documentary evidence and interviews, this paper has examined the response of North American workers in the converging knowledge and communication industries. On the one hand, traditional unions have reacted with their own form of convergence, bringing together workers across the once separate sectors of journalism, broadcasting, telecommunications, information technology and electronic services. Alternatively, other workers in the knowledge industry, including both technical and creative professionals, are experimenting with new forms of worker association that provide benefits for members without necessarily engaging in formal collective bargaining. Our research has provided evidence that these developments have produced some genuine achievements but have not yet stemmed the tide of labour's decline in North America.

The next step in our project is to examine the process of labour convergence and worker association formation in the international arena. Specifically, we are about to begin a project that will look at organisations like the International Federation of Journalists, the Union Network International, and workers' associations in India like the IT Professional's Forum, the New Trade Union Initiative, and UNITES (the Union for Information Technology & Enabled Services Professionals). Developments in the North American labour movement, especially in the knowledge and communication sectors, are no doubt interesting, and potentially significant. But if labour is to respond successfully to the changing international division of labour then it must respond with new forms of convergence at the global level. Examining the state of global labour federations, new worker associations, and their relationships is therefore essential to determine if labour is able to meet the challenges of a global knowledge economy.
© Vincent Mosco, 2008

REFERENCES

Artz, L. & Y.R. Kamalipour (eds.) (2003) *The globalisation of corporate media hegemony,* Albany: State University of New York Press

Babe, R.E. (1996) 'Convergence and the new technologies', in M. Dorland (ed.), *The cultural industries in Canada,* Toronto: Lorimer:283-307

Bahr, M. (1998) *From the telegraph to the internet,* Washington: National Press Books

Barley, S.R. & G. Kunda (2004) *Gurus, hired guns, and warm bodies: itinerant experts in a knowledge economy,* Princeton: Princeton University Press

Batstone, E. (1984) *Working order: workplace industrial relations over two decades,* Oxford: Basil Blackwell

Bell, D. (1973) *The coming of a post-industrial society,* New York: Basic

Bell, D. (1976) *The cultural contradictions of capitalism,* New York: Basic

Bédard, M. (2005) *Union membership in Canada,* Ottawa: Human Resources and Skills Development Canada, Labour Program

Braverman, H. (1973) *Labour and monopoly capital,* New York: Monthly Review

Brint, S. (2001) 'Professionals and the knowledge economy: rethinking the theory of post-industrial Society', *Current Sociology,* Vol 49, No 4:101-132

Brophy, E. (forthcoming) 'System error: Labour precarity and collective organising at Microsoft', *Canadian Journal of Communication*

Clawson, D. (2003) 'Is Labour on the edge of a new upsurge', *Labour Notes,* September 2

Dyer-Witheford, N. (1999) *Cyber-Marx: cycles and circuits of struggle in high technology capitalism,* Chicago: University of Illinois Press

Economic Policy Institute (2004) *Offshoring* (http://www.epinet.org/content.cfm/issueguide_offshoring)

Elmer, G. & M. Gasher (eds.) (2005) *Contracting out Hollywood: runaway productions and foreign location shooting,* Lanham: Rowman/Littlefield

Herman, E.S. & N. Chomsky (2002) *Manufacturing consent,* New York: Pantheon

Huws, U. (2003) *The making of a cybertariat: virtual work in a real world,* New York: Monthly Review Press

Karnitschnig, M. (2006) 'Time Warner stops pushing synergy', *The Wall Street Journal,* June 2. Reprinted in the Pittsburgh Post-Gazette.com, Accessed, June 3, 2006 from: http://www.post-gazette.com

Katz, H.C. (ed.) (1997) *Telecommunications: restructuring work and employment relations worldwide,* Ithaca: ILR Press

Kiss, S. & V. Mosco (2005) 'Trade union protection of workers' privacy: A content analysis of English and French-language collective agreements in Canada', *Canadian Journal of Communication*, Vol 30, No 4:549-564

Kline, S., N. Dyer-Witheford & G. de Peuter (2003) *Digital play: the interaction of technology, culture and marketing*, Montreal: McGill-Queen's Press

Longstaff, P.F. (2002) *The communication toolkit*, Cambridge: MIT Press

Machlup, F. (1962) *The production and distribution of knowledge in the United States*, Princeton: Princeton University Press

McKercher, C. (2002) *Newsworkers unite: labour, convergence and North American newspapers*, Lanham: Rowman and Littlefield

McKercher, C. & V. Mosco (2007) 'Divided they stand: Hollywood unions in the information age', in Huws, U. (ed) *The Spark in the Engine: Creative Workers in a Global Economy, Work, Organisation, Labour and Globalisation*, Vol I No 1

Mosco, V. (1996) *The political economy of communication*, London: Sage

Mosco, V. (2004) *The digital sublime: myth, power, and cyberspace*, Cambridge: MIT Press

Mosco, V. (forthcoming, November 2006) 'Knowledge workers in the global economy: Antimonies of outsourcing', *Social Identities*, Vol 12, No 6

Mosco, V. & C. McKercher (forthcoming, October 2006) 'Convergence bites back', *Canadian Journal of Communication*

Negroponte, N. (1996) *Being digital*, Cambridge: MIT Press

Nichols, J. & R.W. McChesney (2005) *Tragedy and farce: how the American media sell wars, spin elections, and destroy democracy*, New York: The New Press

Porat, M.U. (1977) *The information economy*, Washington, DC: Office of Telecommunications, Department of Commerce

Powell, W. & K. Snellman (2004) 'The knowledge economy', *Annual Review of Sociology*, Vol 30:199-220

Schiller, D. (1999) *Digital capitalism*, Cambridge, MA: MIT Press

Schiller, H.I. (1973) *The mind managers*, Boston: Beaco .

Statistics Canada (2004) 'Study: the union movement in transition', *The Daily*, August 31.

Stone, K.V.W. (2004) *From widgets to digits: employment regulation for the changing workplace*, Cambridge: Cambridge University Press

Swift, J. (2003) *Walking the union walk*, Ottawa: Communication Energy and Paperworkers Union of Canada

Terranova, T. (2004) *Network culture: politics for the information age*, London: Pluto

US Bureau of Labour Statistics (2006) *Union members in 2005*, Washington, DC: Bureau of Labour Statistics

Van Jaarsveld, D. (2004) 'Collective representation among high-tech workers at Microsoft and beyond: Lessons from WashTech/CWA', *Industrial Relations*, Vol 43, No 2:364-385

Winseck, D. (1998) *Reconvergence: a political economy of telecommunications*, Hampton: Hampton Press

Winter, J. (2005) *Lies the media tell us*, Monteal: Black Rose Press

ACKNOWLEDGEMENTS

This paper was completed with the assistance of a grant from the Social Sciences and Humanities Research Council of Canada to examine Trade Unions and Convergence in the Communications Industry and also with a grant from the Social Sciences and Humanities Research Council which funds The Surveillance Project at Queen's University. I would like to thank the members of numerous unions and worker associations who gave their time for interviews. I would also like to thank my co-investigator on the Trade Unions project, Professor Catherine McKercher, and research assistants Enda Brophy, Laura Glithero, and Simon Kiss.

Multinationals´ Policies and Local Responses:

findings from cross-national case studies in Germany, France and the USA

Pamela Meil

Pamela Meil *is a senior researcher at the Institut für Sozialwissenschaftliche Forschung, eV. (ISF) in Munich, Germany*

ABSTRACT

This paper examines the complex interaction between globalisation practices of multinational corporations and the governing potential of response by local systems of employment regulation in light of rationalisation processes linked to financial market driven strategies. It investigates this issue by looking at optimisation programmes conceived and developed at the central headquarters of two German multinational companies and then traces their implementation at local sites in three different international settings: Germany, the USA and France. A central focus was the role that industrial relations systems play in the transformation process and whether (or how) the response varies according to the strength and coordination of the institutionalised system of industrial relations. The study shows that differences still remain in the form and strength of the industrial relations systems in these three countries. However, in all three cases, a new development in industrial relations is taking place in which areas potentially relevant for bargaining are left 'unoccupied'. That is, they are missed completely in the traditional negotiating agendas of industrial relations actors.

Introduction

This paper examines the complex interaction between the globalisation practices of multinational corporations and the governing potential of local responses in light of rationalisation processes linked to financial market driven strategies. It investigates this issue by looking at optimisation programmes conceived and developed at the central headquarters of two German multinational companies and then traces their implementation at local sites in three different international settings: Germany, the US and France. It first looks at the programme's mission, and then how the programme gets translated into concrete measures that are undertaken in selected sites. In a second step, it considers the potential for local response to the demands coming from central headquarters, either through formal systems of employment regulation or through informal, but concerted efforts (Ram et al.,2001). In this way it offers lessons for two research traditions: one focussing on the dissemination practices of large companies in different national settings (Ferner and Quantanilla,2002), and the other on attempts to understand the modifying potential of different systems of employment regulation (Hall and Soskice,2001; Ebbinghaus and Manow,2001).

Surveying the literature on the role of multinational companies (MNCs) in the process of globalisation can be likened to entering a jungle of entangled causes, effects, levels of analysis and interactions. A variety of findings have pointed to convergence (Berger and Dore,1996; Reich, 1993), regional differentiation or local determination (Storper 1997; Dörre, 1996, Flecker, 2000), corporate isomorphism (Ferner,1997), regime types (Boyer,1992; Hollingsworth,1998, Hall and Soskice 2001), institutional governance (Marginson et al.,1995), institutional decline (Beck,1998; 2002; Schmierl,1998), and host country effects (Kotthof 2001; Ferner 2004) as drivers or explanations of the effects of globalisation.

Initially, as the general streams of convergence vs. local determination in the discussions on the effects of globalisation on workplace practice and relations crystallised, the two different lines of argumentation became more and more polarised. Convergence proponents posited an increasing standardisation of company policy, divorced from considerations of national specificity and traditions (Reich,1993; Berger, Dore,1996). The internationalisation strategies of multinational companies were attributed with an economic logic that washed nationally specific differences away, moving them toward a single world economy and world society (Narr, Schubert,1994). The reasons offered for the ongoing trend toward convergence, as well as the inclination to view it as either a positive or negative trend differed greatly. Some views on convergence saw it as deriving from the dissemination of best practice (Ohmae,1996; Womack et al.,1991). Others were 'negative' scenarios, in which multinationals force their subsidiaries to implement particular work forms or structures without consideration of local specificities or problems.

Local diversity arguments tended to counter the convergence positions by looking at the enterprise level and pointing out how forms of best practice tend to adapt to local conditions or how attempts to force unitary structures simply fail. Thus, in contrast to convergence theses, local diversity perspectives questioned to what extent international companies can pursue their strategies and be unhindered by the need to adapt to local contingencies. Research in this area led to a decisive revision of the approaches that assumed the existence of 'footloose' global enterprises (Dörre,1996; Marginson et al.,1995). For instance, it was shown that the ability of local institutions and actors to exercise influence in global companies is linked to the type of internationalisation strategy the company is pursuing and how that meshes with the factors that the local site offers, including infrastructure, access to markets, qualifications, unemployment rate, wage levels and taxes, etc. (Flecker, 2000). In this type of argumentation, for companies which are pursuing strategies in which the local development of products and the use of differing production conditions are important (i.e. transnational companies), a comparatively strong regional reference and the development of differentiated product and production strategies will lead to high levels of autonomy (Hirsch-Kreinsen,1998). In this scenario, the power that individual sites can wield depends in large part on their resources and attractiveness as production sites. Studies in this genre argue that product type plays a large role in how autonomous local sites can remain. If product complexity is high, use of local conditions is more necessary and therefore divergent strategies are endured by the global company (v. Behr,1999; v. Behr, Hirsch-Kreinsen,1998).

Nevertheless, there are indications that even when so-called autonomy for local sites is permitted, it comes under conditions of high risk to the local site. Goals are set or negotiated and the path to reaching them is left to the discretion of the local site. However, failure to achieve these goals leads to consequences such as a return to centralised controls or, quite possibly, closure. Thus, local autonomy, or even the recognition of necessary variations in product markets and processes by the international company headquarters, does not automatically mean that local companies will remain untouched by strategies of 'coercive comparison' (Flecker, 2000). Goal setting, benchmarking and competition for contracts and investment funds are control mechanisms that can be implemented regardless of the level of standardisation or integration of production. Nonetheless, some researchers take the position that exactly how such control mechanisms get played out at the local level is not necessarily as straightforward or predictable as perhaps intended by the companies. They argue that, behind a surface of standardisation and aggregate information systems very disparate processes and structures actually exist in the majority of multinational companies (Dörrenbacher,1999). Another line of discussion suggests that management and workers at a local site may have similar interests in their response to unpopular directives from the central corporate level. This alliance further facilitates the maintenance of their difference.

Point of Departure

As can be seen in the analyses and studies that have been carried out, there continues to be a persisting diversity in the findings and also growing evidence that a polarisation of positions does not fully capture the picture of what is occurring in global companies at the local level. This paper does not presume to offer a synthesis of the various theoretical and conceptual directions offered up to now. It does, however, recognise the difficulty of presenting a well-balanced and accurate picture of the role of MNCs in the globalisation process and their effects on local sites given that the necessary objects of study are different actors with a variety of interests, diverse institutional settings and national contexts, and changes over time.

More recent studies of the role of MNCs in globalisation have attempted to deal with some of these problems by integrating more than one level of analysis – macro, meso and micro - in the research process to get a more complete explanatory picture. (Meil et al., 2003; Ferner et al., 2004) One outcome is a more contradictory and complex view of multinationals and globalisation in which simultaneous tendencies of centralisation and decentralisation, control and autonomy, convergence and local determination are apparent. These trends are not arbitrary, but also have a certain strategic logic behind them.

This study follows in this path. It first takes a close look at the practices of MNCs and then attempts to link micro level processes with meso level institutional systems. In taking different levels of analysis into account, it tries to explain not a single trajectory of development but a complex and partly contradictory one. We posited that large multinationals will in fact try to impose convergent structures or workplace conditions on their subsidiaries. This is the case for one reason, because the need for central headquarters to control their subsidiaries and engage in benchmarking leads to principles of uniformity and, for another, because central headquarters generally view the methods that they have developed as being the 'best' ones for the strategic orientation of the company. However, we argued that these central convergent strategies will meet with resistance as well as difficulty and will be transformed by local contingencies in their implementation process at the local site. In addition to local effects through varying institutional systems and labour traditions, we also expected host country effects: The thesis was that the content of the programmes and the way the MNCs approach implementation will be affected by the home country in which the programmes were developed. Both the MNCs in this study were of German origin with strong traditions in their home country and a strong German centre. Given that in their home country a strong labour voice and high levels of participation were common operating principles, we expected greater attention to local concerns. Furthermore, German companies, with traditionally less orientation to purely financially driven goals and more long-term perspectives (Jürgens et al. 2000), might be expected to pursue less purely financially motivated policies and should exhibit less centralised and unitary control of local sites than for instance US MNCs (Ferner et al 2004).

The main aim of our study was, however, not to determine whether local conditions matter, but rather to examine exactly how local actors, either formally (through existing institutional structures) or informally, contribute to changes in central company practices when these are implemented at the local level, or when applicable, what forms of resistance arise in response to policies that are centrally mandated from headquarters. Therefore a second aspect of the study was to see and understand how local actors respond to the measures coming from the MNC headquarters. Our assumption was that the institutional framework, for instance in the form of industrial relations systems, would be relevant in the transformation process and that the response would vary according to the strength and co-ordination of the institutionalised system of industrial relations (Albert,1993; Ebbinghaus, Manow, 2001).

Methods
Our empirical research centred on an examination of a comprehensive policy initiative being launched by a multinational electronics company (Company A), which was intended to be implemented at all of its (nearly 200) international sites. Company A seemed a logical choice as a case study. It is a traditional German company with a long history, a strong centre and a reputation for hierarchical organisational structures. However, it also has long term experience with international production sites, which have existed over a long time period at their individual national sites and therefore have established practices and traditions of their own. Another incentive for choosing Company A was that it was in the process of disseminating a comprehensive company-wide optimisation programme at all of its sites. Such 'explicit' (see Marginson et al.,1995) programmes are not

that common. Many companies pursue 'implicit' programmes - best practice, employee involvement, personnel strategies, etc. These programmes are often vague or are not comprehensive – that is, they are geared to one department, one assessment measure, or one procedure. Global programmes with centralised methods, facilitators, training, backing by top management, a special department to carry them out, and lots of publicity are much less common.

For comparative purposes we also decided to examine the implementation of a programme in a company that was not an industrial production enterprise, but rather in the increasingly dominant service sector. We chose an insurance company (Company B) because of its economic importance and its German headquarters: it had sites in all countries relevant to our project and like Company A was in the process of launching a programme to be disseminated to all of its sites. We examined the direct implementation process of the two programmes at the local company level in three different countries and, for the highly diversified Company A, at different business units. In this case, we were able to keep one division constant for all three countries, and another for two of the countries. The national contexts - Germany, France and the USA - were chosen for their variations in institutionalised arrangements of industrial relations.

We conducted intensive interviews based on a pre-formulated list of questions with company managers, works councillors, and when possible, regular employees. We also spoke with union and works council representatives in France and Germany. Altogether 26 in-depth interviews were carried out in the three countries with individuals and groups in the time period between 2000 and 2002. Additionally literature from or about the companies, both from the intra/internet and published documents was analysed, and an extensive review of the secondary literature was carried out.

Description of the cases

This section summarises the study's findings regarding the dissemination of the MNCs' programmes, looking at what kinds of projects or practices were actually implemented at local sites. At the level of strategic programme goals, the attempt to achieve standardisation across the entire company versus the extent to which local specificity was permitted or even systematically encouraged was examined. At the level of practice, for instance in the use of tools and instruments, it was asked to what extent local and nationally specific flexibility is permitted or whether directives from the central headquarters have to be followed and are monitored accordingly. At a third level, the adaptation processes at the local or national levels were described, revealing potential regional differences across the multinational. Also considered were changes in orientation from previous company programmes, the relationship to the centre in the diffusion process, the general attitudes to the programme and implementation strategies by the individual sites, the effects for the site (for instance in terms of organisational changes, pay, job security), the reaction at the local site to the central HQ initiatives, and finally the effects on autonomy and control for the local sites. From these findings more general observations in terms of the interplay between convergence and local diversity were made.

Company A – Traditional manufacturing industry

According to those interviewed in Company A, including the CEO of the US holding, the main and explicit goal of the programme is the clear orientation of all the units toward company success (economic success) and an increase in competitiveness. The programme is geared to change what is seen as the insufficient profit orientation of unit managers and make the company results more transparent (and thus more comparable). At the individual site level, the main goal is the increase in the contribution to value added and 'an orientation to economic results in all areas, down to the smallest unit.' (German works councilor)

The responsibility for the planning and implementation of the programme lies at the German headquarters. There, a programme manager, the head of the programme office, is responsible for all of the sites, world-wide. The service function of the programme office is the development of a toolkit containing instruments that should help the world-wide sites develop programmes to reduce costs and waste and improve quality. These include a range of the current state of the art tools for management and financial methods to optimise, improve, and monitor company processes in a number of different categories (for example, cost reduction, innovation, boosting sales, etc.) In each category there are a number of modules offered to help define and direct projects that are appropriate for a particular unit or problem. So with cost reduction, for example, the emphasis may be on structural change or on lowering purchasing costs or on optimising processes. Within these sub-categories are other sub-categories of more refined modules. The tools are thus a means of information, a form of training and an impetus to get projects off the ground. Since the programme's inception in,1998, the number of individual tools has swelled to about 2000.

The control function of the programme office is reflected in the motto of the programme: 'clear goals, concrete measures, and rigorous consequences' (Company A 2001). 'Clear goals' means reaching EVA (economic value added) targets. 'Concrete measures' means using the catalogue of tools geared toward portfolio optimisation, earnings-oriented sales growth, asset management, cost reduction, quality and innovation as defined by the company headquarters. Finally, 'rigorous consequences' means reviews every three months to monitor results. When there is 'persistent' deviation from targets the Corporate Executive Committee decides between four options: buy, co-operate, sell or close.

This type of programme heralds a clear break with those introduced in the 1980s and early 1990s whose goals were tapping productivity gains through employee participation (Dörre 2001; Applebaum & Batt,1994). The difference is clearly evident in the change in orientation between an earlier programme launched by Company A and the current one. The programme's forerunner at Company A had originally been launched at the beginning of the 1990s at the initiative of the corporation's board of directors. The goals were to identify and improve the company culture and to create a vision for the future development of the enterprise. The central focus of the programme was a re-engineering process, intended to lead to an optimisation of time and process use in response to what was seen as an overly bureaucratic organisation and long development cycles. The goal was to disseminate the programme worldwide, in the 193 countries in which the company was active. The programme was geared toward an increased participation of employees in continuous improvement and more efficient design of work and production processes. In Germany, 105 sites participated in the first programme. The works councils, from the central HQ to each of the sites, were involved in the implementation and strongly supported the programme. The general tenor of the interview responses at the local German sites was a strong emphasis on participation and improvement of company work processes in the first programme. In France, the first programme was apparently also received positively, although it was admitted that a number of existing initiatives were placed under the programme label to fulfill programme requirements; also, the programme was not as widespread in France as in Germany. Interestingly, in the USA, the first programme never really got off the ground. Moreover, for those familiar with it, it had an extremely negative connotation of being completely oriented toward cost-cutting measures, which is exactly opposite to the impression it made in Germany and France.

At some point in the mid 1990s, the first programme began to fizzle out and a new programme generation was re-launched (beginning in 1998). It was linked in name to the first, but with a new orientation geared to designing projects that achieved concrete and measurable economic results, and an overall increase in the transparency of economic performance. Individual practices at the company level in the new programme launched in Europe in late 1998 and worldwide (after some initial problems) in 2001 may still evidence the participatory practices found in the initial programme. However, increasingly the message from the centre being transmitted to the companies, and in particular their management, is that financial results are the ultimate goal; and these must be visible immediately. The consequences of not heeding this message are looming in the form of sell-off or closure. The pressure to meet these demands immediately naturally encourages short-term cost-cutting measures to achieve the desired results without thought for the long term consequences of such measures.

At the German sites that were investigated, there was knowledge of the programmes and tools at the management and works council level, but less actively at the employee level. The introduction of the programme was usually announced through regional presentations in the form of large formal assemblies at which high ranking officials from the central HQ – the chairman of the board in some cases – presented the programme and its goals. In Germany, this meeting was received quite critically, the impression being that the programme was too abstract with no attempt to link the programme to specific problems or the actual situation of the individual site. (In fact, the standardised presentation was a strategy of the centre, which intended to give the same presentation to all of their sites around the world, thereby transmitting a signal of company cohesion. In all three countries, this strategy met with a negative response.) Additional information on the programme was provided on the company's intranet – the main means of dissemination. The relationship with the centre was otherwise very distant. It took the form of reporting of economic results. Intervention from the centre only came about if the economic value-added targets were not met or in cases in which the sites asked for help for programme implementation (which happened rarely).

Although the information for the programme in Company A came from the centre and it was central HQ goals that were being communicated, the implementation process itself proceeded at the local level. Tools and instruments were selected that met the requirements of the projects being launched and were perceived as being appropriate for the particular needs of the site. The programmes tended to be directed toward cost reduction, quality improvement and other internal company processes. The practice of placing already running programmes under the banner of the programme to meet the demands set by the centre was also used.

At the US sites of Company A which were investigated, there was also an emphasis on quality improvement and waste reduction, but there was an additional focus on customer integration and meeting customer needs (to be visible in improved sales figures). As in Germany, the programme was launched by a media presentation at which the US CEO (a German) and members of the German board of directors presenting the programme goals and tools. This assembly was aimed at management, so the knowledge of the programme at the employee level was quite marginal. The programme was officially launched in 1998-99 but was mainly ignored by the US sites, so it got underway very slowly. The actual introduction (under greater pressure to comply) took place in 2001. For most of the sites, the response to the programme was negative; the tools were perceived as being overly complex, thus requiring a large staff to interpret and implement them, which the US sites did not have available. This led to the impression that the German sites, and of course the central HQ in particular, had much more manpower available for such activities, leading to further bad feelings. Other criticisms were that the programme was too geared to internal company processes and incremental change rather than the larger picture, which would in the end, not help the sites to perform well in a difficult economic climate. Most US sites felt that they had already introduced programmes with similar goals and orientations (to improve business performance) before this particular programme was imposed upon them by the Germans. Thus the centralised programme implementation also created negative feelings in that the existing programmes were not valued or recognised unless they were put under the rubric and label of the programme initiated by central HQ.

Other than the kick-off meeting and pressure from their senior management to develop projects and the economic results to go with them, communication with HQ was rare and reduced to a reporting function. Information about the programme was available on the intranet, but it appeared in English rather late, and except in rare cases[1] was not actually used. The practice of using existing programmes and 'selling' them under the programme banner was widespread.

In general, the programme, although centrally launched, did assume that the actual measures would be designed locally with local contingencies in mind. However, the

---

1   In one case, an individual engineer used the information from the Intranet to launch a highly successful project in his company. The group involved described the process as almost accidental. They were looking for information to start a waste reduction project and stumbled across the information which was partly in German. Through individual initiative and getting their local management to agree (at first only haltingly), the group designed one of the most successful projects in the USA.

pressure to report results in terms of economic value added in shorter and shorter intervals has intensified over the last couple of years for the US sites. This has led to concerns at the sites that the orientation to short term financial results will affect their overall ability to grow and innovate. The strict reporting schedules and procedures and the lingering awareness of the consequences of failing to meet economic targets has clearly impinged on the previously very high levels of autonomy enjoyed at the US sites.

In France, the programme in Company A led to practices mainly centred around quality improvement, although there had been a shift away from a focus on the production area toward service departments and customer service oriented projects. As at the other sites, the programme specifics were launched at a large meeting by representatives of the central HQ. Once again this method was criticised as being too abstract and the message as having little relevance since it came from board members with whom the employees were unfamiliar. At one unit that was performing poorly, the presentation was experienced as a type of threat which immediately gave the programme negative connotations. Also, the very financially technical presentation gave the impression that the programme was geared mainly to management and was not relevant for the working situation of individual employees. As in the other international sites, the other information channel was the intranet. Actual implementation in practice was, as in Germany and the US, left up to the individual sites. In the French cases under study, a great deal of emphasis was placed on group development and using employee suggestions to develop measures to achieve the desired economic effects. This worked relatively well and offered a high level of continuity with the forerunner programme. France was in fact one of the few countries in which the personnel from the first programme were often allowed to remain in their positions for the re-launched programme. One problem mentioned, however, was whether funding to develop the projects from the suggestions made by the employees would be sufficient in light of the tight economic framework. Evaluation was also seen as problematic since the financial impact of many of the measures would occur later than the requirements for reporting results. In fact, the French sites stated that a major difference from earlier programmes was the evaluation of the practices undertaken in conjunction with the programme according to their contribution to short-term economic goals. The means of reporting differed between plants: at one, productivity increases of 7-8% were targeted; at another savings of 15 Mio in 1-2 years, the time intervals of reporting were getting shorter everywhere. Best practice sharing between sites of a unit – one of the expressed goals in the programme – occurred through individual initiatives, but not on an organised basis. Help from the centre in the form of training or aiding communication between sites did not exist. Communication was reduced to reporting on economic results.

Company B: Insurance and Investments

Company B headquarters in Germany also initiated a programme that was meant to be disseminated world-wide and was unmistakable in its orientation through it name: EVA (Economic Value Added). Generally, however, the programme was much less structured and also less directed from the centre than the programme in Company A. There was no central department formed solely for the purpose of developing or controlling EVA.

An international task force was formed to design appropriate measures for financial reporting: an interesting difference from Company A in which guidelines and procedures were developed at the central German headquarters. It was expected that the various sites would use the reporting system so that each site's contribution could be monitored. If a site exhibited several poor results in succession and became a problem site, a trouble shooter from the centre might be sent in. Continued poor performance could result in a change of management, a merger, a different arrangement of responsibility areas, or closure. Besides reporting and its possible effects in negative cases, there was little interference from the centre. Exceptions were the co-ordination of projects that it made sense to disseminate and standardise internationally, for example IT systems. In these cases international teams were usually formed. The head of controlling in Germany pointed out that going onto the US stock market demanded a stricter reporting for financial targets and increased disclosure of financial assets, one of the motivations to monitor results more closely in a standardised manner.

At the German site of Company B, the works council supported the EVA programme since it led to transparency in areas that were costly to the company without an accompanying contribution. The background of this support was that at the time of the interviews (2002) there appeared to be little risk of personnel reduction. Moreover, the local sites enjoyed a very high level of autonomy in day to day operations, largely due to the business structure in which knowledge of the local market and local regulations was extremely important to the HQ. The direct effects of the programme for local sites were limited: organisationally there was virtually no effect and the consequences for pay were felt mainly at the middle management level. At the German sites there was an increase in performance-based premiums, but this did not affect base pay which was negotiated with the union. In the USA, performance pay systems and bonus packages which were negotiated directly between the employees and the personnel department did affect employees by creating 'winners'and 'losers.' As a result of profit sharing, the employees at sites with good economic developments earned more at the expense of employees at sites with poor economic performance. Such differences could even occur between different departments on the same site. Referring to the more severe effects of EVA reporting, the US chief of finance remarked that 'company B is slow at giving consequences to under-performers'.

Summary of the Findings

In the programme implementation in both companies, the two aspects of centralisation and decentralisation are clearly recognisable. The programmes and their goals are directed toward convergence to the extent that they are targeted at every company unit and subsidiary worldwide with fixed and centrally-set goals. They also serve to strengthen and especially to systematise company restructuring and optimisation measures. This means that all participation and rationalisation measures that exist at the sites are made more transparent, and those which do not conform to the central programme's goals and orientations are targeted for possible elimination. Thus, the company's control programme does serve to bring all of the sites of the MNC into line. On the other hand, each site has autonomy to decide how to meet the centrally-set goals. In fact, it is more or less accepted that existing rationalisation measures, as long as they are successful, can be defined into the programme, even though they were not specifically designed for, and may even be precursors to it.

There were positive responses to the programmes of the MNCs in terms of using the opportunity in Company A to initiate a change process or to increase transparency in Company B. However, most of the responses tended to be negative, especially in Company A. Expressed were a feeling of increased pressure from the centre without accompanying support, feeling threatened from HQ, and the impression that the programme from Company A might not necessarily hurt them, but it would not necessarily help them to improve performance either. Yet, because of the accountability tied to the programme, which was marketed as a comprehensive company strategy for optimisation, the sites would be held personally responsible for the results of economic downturns over which they might have little control.

There was no evidence of any organised reactions, either through formal institutional mechanisms, or informal means. In Germany, the works council could intervene in the case of personnel reduction with agreements on settlement packages if the reductions were due to benchmarking or best practice activities. However, when there was no direct outsourcing or displacement, it was easy for the company to get around these rules, which were in any case not preventative. By introducing measures for increased flexibility, the company could use temporary or contract workers, thus making permanent jobs obsolete. Collective agreements at the union and employer level protect wage levels. However, personal evaluation systems and performance agreements bypass the regular wage negotiations. For middle level management, pay and career opportunities are increasingly determined by their site's performance.

In France, many of the projects undertaken in conjunction with the programme in Company A were seen as participatory measures that had been generally on the increase in French companies after the implementation of the Auroux laws in the early 1980s. There was no organised response either in company level representation or the union level. Many of the effects on remuneration for individual employees and managers were similar to those in Germany.

In the USA only one site of Company A had union representation which limited its activities to formal issues. Company B had no union in the USA. At the local level the US sites seemed to follow a strategy of ignoring the demands from the centre for as long as possible. In any case, any organised response was bound to be limited because knowledge of the programme at the employee level was limited. Most information remained at management level and was only operationalised in the form of concrete and local optimisation projects. Among regular employees there was little awareness of the central HQ's initiatives, except in very abstract terms.

Shift in orientation towards a market-based regime

As we proceeded with our research, we discovered that some of our initial premises were being called into question. The reason for this was that for the multinationals in our study, in particular Company A, a major shift in orientation for company policy had taken place. The direction of change was not so surprising (DiMaggio 2001; Hall, Soskice 2001). A crucial development with severe consequences for companies listed on the stock exchanges today is that the market is no longer made up of lots of small nameless stockholders. At present, large fund managers in investment, money market or pension funds, with extremely large numbers of shares invested in particular companies have restructured the balance of power between those who run the companies and those who 'own' them. Such 'investor capitalism' (Useem,1996) is characterised by institutional stockholders who are identifiable actors and can exercise power in influencing the activities of multinationals, especially when financial performance is not leading to the desired stock price performance. Investor capitalism creates a situation in which top managers – under pressure themselves – put extreme pressure on their individual site managements to achieve positive financial results on a regular basis (Dörrenbacher, Plehwe 2000; Kühl 2002).

Thus management decisions are now influenced or even controlled by shareholder considerations in a way that did not exist previously. 'Work was organised within corporations in ways that ensured that managers were the key insiders...' (O´Sullivan 2000, p. 71) Having no clearly definable owners to answer to, managers found themselves with a lot of autonomy and power to run multinationals. This did not mean a complete absence of accountability. There was a separation between beneficial owner-ship of corporate stock and strategic control over the allocation of corporate resources. (O`Sullivan 2000). This meant that daily decisions and even long term strategies were much less coupled to instant financial results than seems to be the case today. If managers argued for a certain strategic course in the era of managerial capitalism, they were credited with being most familiar with the needs of the company until proven otherwise. Some authors argue that local management is sometimes pressured into making decisions that are against their own inclinations or will. One example is being induced to raise dividend shares after a good performance (i.e. distributing profits) rather than saving the money for a 'rainy day' fund, which many managers in industrial enterprises will be inclined to do in order to weather the almost certain downturns in business cycles.

That this shift could be so visible even in a traditional German company was unexpected. In Germany, there was a strong historical tradition of managerial control of enterprises even before the war (O`Sullivan 2000). In post-war Germany, the industrial landscape was characterised by a complex system of interlocking shareholding networks including a strong formal presence of bank control in corporations. Labour, represented on the boards of corporations, also has a voice through co-determination. The absence of small shareholders and the role that financial institutions were willing to play in company processes led to a system in which industry was largely insulated from strict market forces. Additionally, the high level managers of industrial enterprises tended to have engineering backgrounds, giving them a different orientation from enterprises run by financial specialists with a background in accountancy. Together, this constellation created a system characterised by the term 'patient capital' – a financial orientation supporting Germany's high quality niche product strategies with a long term perspective (Deutschmann 2002; Jürgens et al 2000). In fact, the German literature expressly argued that contemporary German companies were not characterised by the strong shareholder value strategies found in other industrialised countries, because of specific national bank and financial configurations and goals, as well as low levels of private stock ownership (Jürgens et al. 2000; Vitols 2001).

For the multinational Company A, however, this reorientation was evident, and represents a fundamental shift in ideology: away from an 'engineering' product-driven company to one driven by financial results. Thus the central identity of the company is no longer based on its technological superiority, but rather on its financial performance, the same standard applied to any other multinational in any other industrial branch. The other major change, also deriving from the strong orientation to financial results, represents a shift in philosophy concerning the ties between the various business units, or in other words, the view of what the company as a whole means. Does the corporation as such, which is divided into a number of units by product type, have significance for the individual companies? In the past, the practice of this very solvent company, which had large capital reserves, was to move capital between units to temporarily help out in periods of financial difficulty. This policy has changed so that individual business units are now held responsible for their individual results. Poor performance on the part of a company or business unit is seen as a strain on the corporation as a whole: a kind of malignant tumor that is eating away at the good health of the corporate entity. These shareholder value orientations are apparent in both MNCs in terms of the newly introduced central reporting, transparency and hard consequences for poor performance, but are most obviously visible in the case of Company A.

It also became apparent in the course of our research that the literature on the effects of globalisation in company practice did not adequately recognise the importance of the shifts in company policy for local sites. It became clear, for instance, that the dichotomy between local autonomy and centralisation as clear alternatives for company strategy that is often portrayed in the literature on globalisation is misleading. The programmes at the two multinationals in our study whose implementation we were investigating were the perfect manifestation of this change. Such programmes are geared to utilise two strategies that were previously thought to be in contradiction to one another. The benefits of local autonomy are reaped by utilising the positive attributes of the local setting – skills, costs, expertise, experience, market, resources. Therefore companies are encouraged to make use of the general, often diffuse, tools and methods defined by the company headquarters to custom-make and implement a project or measure at the local company level: autonomy is in this regard welcomed. However, the reporting and benchmarking tools available to measure 'success' are determined using centralised financial monitoring systems and the accountability (or control) linked to this process is very high. This is not merely a formalistic process; it has very concrete effects on work and work practice[2].

---

2 Harrison (1994) called this type of company strategy, 'centralisation without concentration'

As we know, the logic of the market dictates that poor financial performance has to be met with a fairly immediate response. The response is not pre-determined, but 'restructuring' is one of the common answers. Simply cutting personnel won't necessarily have an effect, but rather has to be part of a larger plan which might involve some form of reorganisation (for instance, outsourcing to a supplier, resettlement to a cheaper site, i.e. regime shopping (Streeck,1998; 2001), outplacement, creating a subsidiary, etc.). Although it would be unfair to portray every restructuring measure brought about by financial performance pressure as only being short term and cost motivated, it is true that the extreme orientation to financial outcomes can result in measures that are either cosmetic and not really structural improvements, or are even destructive because of their limited horizon. One example is the use of external contractors for formerly in-house tasks, which takes the costs out of the internal accounts even though the costs still exist. Another is selling off segments that are doing badly temporarily, but have a vital importance for product innovation. It has even been implied that one of the strategies of investor capitalism is to pay extremely high settlements or financial packages to top management as an incentive to side with shareholders rather than internal company interests when a conflict between the two could arise (O'Sullivan 2000).

Obviously the reach of financial orientations embodied in the programmes described here affects the working relationships of employees as well as management. The regular employee possibly feels the direct effects of the programmes only marginally in the form of a variety of measures introduced at the company to improve quality, improve productivity, streamline company processes, and potentially in cost cutting measures and job redundancy. But the ultimate consequence is of course massive job cuts, sell-off or closure. Given companies' new orientation to financial results even at the cost of long term considerations, it is not that surprising that employees at local sites are willing to participate in measures that are designed to achieve economic value added targets to save their jobs.

Conclusion: Market based regimes and local response

Our study revealed that the programmes being implemented by the companies we investigated are geared very much toward principles compatible with the financial orientations of what has been called the 'era of investor (or shareholder) capitalism' in Germany. These programmes place the various sites of the multinational companies under severe pressure to achieve set financial targets within fixed time frames. Especially for the German multinationals in this study, this policy represents a break with past practices in which a product-driven strategy was pursued and in which individual divisions were supported through periods of difficulty. What has changed is a much more pronounced short-term orientation to achieve results and a harder exposure of individual units to the harsh economic consequences of failing to meet targets. A loss of autonomy has taken place to the extent that units at different national sites are more controlled from the central headquarters both with regard to transparency in financial outcomes and with regard to meeting established targets. Autonomy remains, however, to the extent that the means to improve performance is not prescribed, at least up to now.

One stream of literature identifies these financial orientations with a new post-Fordist form of company organisation, characterised by the emergence of new control strategies which consequently transform the previously Fordist mode of control. The new form makes control anonymous, with the use of market-based mechanisms. (Dörre and Röttger 2003). 'Market based control, decentralised firm organisation, flexible work, and management dominated participation are elements of the new production model' (Dörre 2003 p.23). For these authors, it is precisely these aspects of making power and control anonymous that signal a new regulatory regime.

As has been shown here, the subtle connection between the strategies being pursued by global companies in the form of optimisation programmes and the effects on employees makes it difficult for systems of employment regulation to exercise a governance function. Moreover, most of the effects occur within individual companies, so that only internal company interest representatives have direct knowledge of the programmes. However, they do not have the capacity or the means to respond at the level of regulation. In all of our cases, the potential for active response by local industrial relations actors to the programme implementation, or even to the consequences of this implementation, was revealed as being very low. Other studies have also observed that, 'management uses the "diffuse power of the market" (Mann,1993) to keep employees and industrial relations actors in line' (Dörre p.,19-20).

From the point of view of the systems of employment regulation, it is extremely difficult to respond conflictually to a programme that appears so rational and objective. The rules of interaction being laid down by the company central headquarters are to improve your products and processes as you see fit, so that your company makes a profit and contributes to good market results. This sounds very reasonable. The measures of performance seem extremely rational and apply to everyone. Thus every unit and every individual becomes a financial optimiser. The implicit agreement between labour and capital shifts from promises of security and a piece of the pie in return for productivity and labour peace to openness to risk from market fluctuations in return for a piece of a faster growing pie, and possibly greater autonomy, flexibility and participation in the direct work process.

These operating principles of investor capitalism and market-regulated controls weaken the governance potential of existing systems of employment regulation whose negotiating agendas were determined in what regulation theory calls the 'Fordist/Taylorist' production era (Bergmann 2001). Whether or not one subscribes to the theory of production regimes, or agrees that a departure from the Fordist model has occurred, it is clear that the political and regulation forms upon which unions built their negotiation strategies, and which were mostly geared to traditional industries and traditional industrial workers, cannot be transferred to new market based systems. The content of negotiation falls completely outside the range of issues regulated in these systems. The next section looks more closely at the shifts that have taken place in the systems of regulation in the three countries in our study.

Mapping models of employment regulation: from Fordism to 'investor capitalism'

Industrial relations develop in close relationship to the structures in which they are embedded at a national level which shape them as a result of the particular constituents, regulatory supports and historical context in which they were formed. As central instruments in the regulation of work, industrial relations systems are tied to other regulation systems which are, in turn, supported by national labour and welfare laws, education and training systems, and state instruments for labour market policy. The relative immobility of labour and the industrial relations system which represents it has reinforced the national specificity of these systems. However, the specific forms that industrial relations systems take do not only derive from the state regulatory systems in which they are embedded, but also are shaped by the historical form that conflicts between capital and labour have taken and the political ideologies that have inspired them. This becomes especially clear if we look at the history of union development as one of the main pillars of industrial relations systems. In Germany, for instance, unions see themselves as strongly linked to the politics of the German labour movement which was historically social-democratic in orientation - the goal was to achieve a viable democratic state in which labour had co-determination rights. In France, Italy and Spain, by contrast, labour movements were tied to syndicalist, anarchist political movements which led to a splintering of these movements into unions tied to particular political parties. In Great Britain, the shop steward system was based on structures of representation defined along 'craft' or occupational lines of demarcation and tactics of negotiation tailored to the work process. These nationally specific forms of industrial relations determine what the arenas of negotiation between capital and labour will be, the form that conflicts take and the levels and styles of negotiation between collective actors.

In the classic view of industrial relations research the goal of the regulation of work relations is to achieve a balance between the conflicting interests of an autonomous utilisation of capital on the one side, and the protection or improvement of labour's means to reproduce itself on the other. The research carried out from the post-war era to the present shows that a characteristic of industrial relations in Western industrialised economies was the strong link that arose between the orientations of the system of interest representation and the Taylorist/Fordist production model that dominated in the period of economic growth following the second World War. (Bechtle, Lutz,1989) The arenas of conflict and negotiation that emerged in the Taylorist-Fordist production system centre around issues deriving from the work relationship that crystallised in this era, such as wages, working conditions, working time, employment security, etc. This link is particularly strong in German industrial relations which can be clearly seen in the way wage forms are fixed in industry-wide negotiated settlements and in company level negotiated settlements, and also in the concepts underlying the labour process and work organisation that were promoted in this period. (Müller-Jentsch,1991) The wage forms that developed from the 1950s onward were oriented toward an attempt to (objectively) measure and calculate performance, leaving some room for compromise in the form of complaints against standard times (Vorgabezeiten). Because of the central role that the determination of performance levels and the wage setting tied to them has had in German industrial relations, work councils as well as leading union functionaries traditionally concentrated a good deal of their negotiating expertise on wage issues. Conditions of work organisation were thus developed which supported pay based on performance levels - generally in the form of the piece rate wage (Akkordlohn). The control of the system of wage determination by performance levels led to a range of institutionalised forms of regulation such as procedures, work content, routines and norms (REFA[3]) in which the actors in the industrial relations system played a major role. Union representatives received certification in REFA industrial engineering procedures in order to better exercise their codetermination rights in setting performance standards.

Our initial assumption in examining the relationship between global company strategies and industrial relations was that the response at the local level would be affected by the characteristics of the specific systems of industrial relations that are found in the three countries in our study. We expected an effect on the implementation process as well as on the specific character that each programme would take at the different sites. We set out to investigate these assumptions by asking if the particular architecture of the various systems of industrial relations could predict the responses of industrial relations actors to the programmes as they were implemented at the local level. And, if there was no clear institutional response from traditional organisations of interest representation, were there nevertheless identifiable reactions at the company level which could be classified as 'controls' and could be considered as constituting a form of industrial relations, although not in the sense of national level systems of work regulation? Finally, we wanted to determine whether identifiable alterations to the industrial relations practices at the local level resulted from interaction with the programmes implemented by the global companies, which were meant to be instituted universally at all of their sites.

One of the first steps that we had to undertake was to select a way to compare the architecture of the various systems of industrial relations that we would be examining (Germany, France and the USA) in order to identify the reactions and control potential for the globalisation process. Our goal was to steer away from predetermined conceptions of the outcomes based on institutional contexts, such as the German system of industrial relations, that were familiar to us and to avoid abstract functionalist explanations of the demands of globalisation.

We began with the schema developed by Düll and Bechtle (1988) in which systems of industrial relations are classified in a space defined by the four dimensions of negotiation, norm building, conflict, and control (see Figure 1). Between the areas of conflict and control, one finds the poles between which industrial relations have moved historically, while between negotiation and norm building, the forms of institutionalisation are laid out. These latter two make possible a continuous,

3   REFA, the Association for Working Time Studies and Work Organisation, founded in 1924 as the 'Reichausschuss für Arbeitszeitermittlung' or the 'Government association for the determination of working time" carries out studies on work design, industrial organisation and company development. After the war, it became one of the most important instruments of the unions for categorising jobs using complicated time and ergonomic strudies.

albeit limited, balance between conflicting interests, and thus allow the potential explosiveness in the naturally adversarial relationship between labour and capital to be overcome. Norm building represents the concrete form that regulation of the employment relationship takes, for example as rules, procedures, topics and arenas of negotiation.

In the early first attempts at 'mapping' historically formed architectures of industrial relations systems, Germany is typified by a configuration dominated by the link between negotiation and norm building (the normiertes Verhandlungssystem). Open forms of conflict at the company level are rare in such a system and broader forms of conflict are strongly regulated. The 'control' element is anchored in the 'Mitbestimmung' (co-determination) concept of the union. In France, the system of industrial relations originally developed mainly along the poles of conflict negotiation – conflict beyond the individual company level; at the company level the dimension of negotiation was traditionally very weak. Control was reinforced through state agencies (such as the 'inspecteur du travail'). By the mid 1990s, a shift in the system of industrial relations was recognisable toward the poles of conflict and norm building, in which state regulation began to play a more important role (Lallement 2000).

The original model did not include the USA. If one tries to apply the classification system to the traditional US industrial relations system, one could characterise the post-war era's configuration of industrial relations as moving mainly between the fields of conflict and negotiation. Norm building played a role to the extent that the entire system was based on the collective bargaining contract, which often covered the same issues of wages, seniority rules, health and safety, pension funds, and job delineation. The little US legislation that exists supports the regulation process by protecting collective bargaining contracts, prohibiting union busting, penalising discrimination, and protecting the general right to unionise, etc.

The great disadvantage of the classification system presented here is that different levels of interest representation are all missing from it, making it impossible to see the balance between national and local dimensions, the level of institutionalisation and the level at which bargaining takes place. The advantage is that, although it sets the given conditions for action by collective actors in a particular context, it also theoretically allows for some measure of shift if the actors involved in the industrial relations system adopt new strategies. The classification demonstrates links or potential links between dimensions as they have crystallised in specific historical configurations of industrial relations systems in different countries, but existing links can break up, thereby opening up new possibilities for change. Thus it allows a dynamic evaluation of industrial relations response and provides a means to obtain a visual representation of how the response appears with regard to the changes in company strategy and modes of control.

In fact, a reading of the literature on the development of industrial relations in these three countries in the last decade has indeed revealed that a shift has occurred when mapping the system architecture of the German, French and US industrial relations systems using the classification scheme from Düll/Bechtle and this is supported by the empirical research we conducted (see Figure 2). As can be seen, the main dimensions of negotiation and norm building characterising the German system have not changed. However, two aspects have changed: one is that the internal company arena has gained in importance, which has been graphically represented with a larger area covered by negotiation. The other is that the area regulated by the 'normierten Verhandlungssystem' has been narrowed to represent the fact that a number of issues that affect the employment relationship today are simply not considered or covered by the existing processes of negotiation and norm building. In France, the graphic representation of the system of work regulation has shifted considerably from the original portrayal. In a move away from the poles of conflict and negotiation, the French system is now more and more characterised by the state's regulatory influence in the form of broad-based laws affecting the work relationship (for instance on working time and training). The company-based areas of negotiation have also increased in importance, often in conjunction with implementation of state laws. Conflict is less characteristic in the private sector and the unions seem to have a diminishing role and dwindling awareness of company issues and problems. In the USA, the graphic representation also shows a considerable shift away from the post war system in the current situation. Previously moving along the dimensions of conflict and negotiation, with control in the form of rigidly defined job classifications and wage contracts, the USA was characterised by narrowness in the areas in which formal systems of interest representation could negotiate. Increasing marginalisation has resulted in a situation in which formal systems of interest representation exist only in isolated industrial and public sector pockets. Negotiation on formal issues still occurs in these pockets, but conflict plays less and less of a role. (Tilly and Tilly,1998)

The mapping models reveal that a shift in the configuration of industrial relations has taken place in all three countries, although to different degrees, and also that there are still differences between systems of industrial relations. Although this is the case, the mapping models are not good predictive tools for the governance of systems of employment regulation under conditions of 'investor capitalism' because the content of negotiation falls outside the range of issues covered in the rules of regulation. Figure 3 shows the differences in the response potential of the formal systems of industrial relations in the three countries.

In Germany, the strength of the works councils at the company level provides a potential for an organised response, although in our cases they were mainly bypassed in the implementation process of the new generation of programmes geared toward financial results. The works councils, with their high levels of competence regarding company policy, know that new company strategies and financial priorities disempower them to act with the set of issues at their disposal to negotiate, but do not have the capacity or expertise to demand a participatory role.

In France, the state takes an active role in framing labour policy, but this is in relation to 'old,' traditional topics, such as working time, which are increasingly legislated for. The implementation level is the company, where the comité d´entreprise is becoming more involved in negotiations. Nevertheless, the role of the comité d´entreprise is a reactive one. The unions operate beyond the company level, attempting to exercise influence at the political level, but not on issues that are of immediate relevance at the company level because their relationship to internal company practices has become very diffuse. (Lallement 2001)

Figure 1 Classical model of industrial relations in Taylorist-Fordist production systems in Germany, France and the USA (consolidated negotiation)

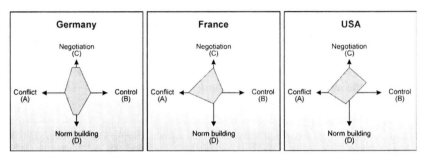

Figure 2 Post-Fordist model of industrial relations in Germany, France and the USA (precarious negotiation)

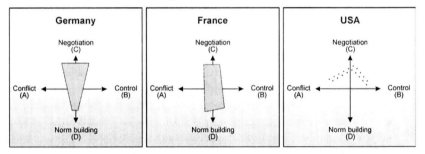

Figure 3 Current forms of 'investor capital' models of industrial relations in Germany, France and the USA (non-occupied negotiation)

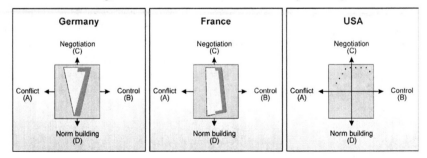

Source: ISF. 2008

In the USA, unions have a marginal presence in industry and their issues for negotiation are very traditional. Some unions in the public sector and in traditionally strong unionised sectors had been involved in the participatory movements of the 1980s (Wheeler,1990). However, in our cases the unions played no role in the implementation and negotiation of programmes aimed at optimising financial performance. In fact, it seems that the most visible level of protest or protection is as citizens and not as employees: issues in which employees lose their jobs as a result of financial practices or regime shopping become voting issues. In this way, protest departs from the realm of the workplace.

In sum, although the systems of employment regulation vary, there was little possibility for local actors to carry out a governance function in response to the pressure imposed on them by the central headquarters in the form of restructuring programmes oriented to financial performance. Informal types of response could be defined as taking control of the restructuring process at a local level to as great an extent as possible, which did indeed occur. However, an organised informal response to counter the pressure from the centre was not recognisable. This does not mean that the sites do not have autonomy, nor does it mean that they do not enact participatory measures which give individual employees a voice in the restructuring process. However, the level of autonomy, the ability to respond actively, not to mention the actual survival of the local unit, depends on an economic situation over which they do not have control.

The current challenge for formal systems of employment regulation, if they do not want to see their co-determination reduced only to the development of social plans for mass dismissals or the protection of seniority, is to reorient their negotiating strategy to deal with issues that do not presume a stable employment relationship in a production-dominated economy. A shift in employment relations has taken place toward a market-mediated work relationship which requires a corresponding shift away from employment regulation based on the Fordist production model. Of course, there are union initiatives at the EU level, in Germany, and the USA as well as workforce initiatives at the company level in new knowledge-intensive sectors which are trying to adapt new strategies to meet company demands for flexibility, and minimise precariousness and market-based controls (Waddington and Hoffman, 2000; Heidling et al, 2004; Hurd et al, 2003; Frege and Kelly, 2003)). At the same time, given the state of the stock market, the present period also has to be seen as a time of flux for the multinationals in terms of defining their strategies for the future. Former strategies of extreme rationality led by financial considerations do not seem to hold up to the arbitrariness of today's financial markets. Although the old social contract based on principles deriving from the Fordist era will most likely continue to disappear, it is still unclear what will replace it.

© *Pamela Meil, 2008*

REFERENCES

Albert, M. (1993) *Capitalism against Capitalism,* London: Whurr Publishers
Applebaum, E. & R.Batt (1994) *The New American Workplace,* Ithaca, New York: ILR Press
Bechtle, G. & B. Lutz (1989) 'Die Unbestimmtheit postTayloristischer Rationalisierungsstrategien und die ungewisse Zukunft industrieller Arbeit', K. Düll, & B.Lutz, B., (eds), *Technikentwicklung*

unnd Arbeitsteilung im internationaler Vergleich. Frankfurt Main: Campus

Beck, U. (2002) *Macht und Gegenmacht im globalen Zeitalter – Neue weltpolitische Ökonomie*, Frankfurt: Suhrkamp

Beck, U. (ed) (1998) *Politik der Globalisierung*, Frankfurt: Suhrkamp

Behr, M. von (1999) 'Power Plant Production: Continuity and Innovation in a Core Business', J. Bélanger, C. Berggren, C. Björkman & C. Köhler (eds) *Being Local Worldwide*, Ithaca: ILR Press:217–232

Behr, M. von; Hirsch-Kreinsen, H. (eds.) (1998) *Globale Produktion und Industriearbeit – Arbeitsorganisation und Kooperation in Produktionsnetzwerken*, Frankfurt, New York

Berger, S.; Dore, R. (1996) *National Diversity and Global Capitalism*, Ithaca and London: New York: Cornell University Press

Bergmann, J. (2001) 'Betriebsräte in Shareholder-Kapitalismus: ratios: Einige Befunde aus einer Befragung von Betriebsräten und Vertrauensleuten', J. Abel & H.J. Sperling (eds), *Umbrüche und Kontinuitäten. Perspektiven nationaler und internationaler Arbeitsbeziehungen*, München: Mering: VS: 101-112

Boyer, R. (1992) 'Neue Richtungen von Management und Arbeitsorganisation – Allgemeine Prinzipien und nationale Entwicklungspfade', A. Demirovic et al. (ed.) *Hegemonie und Staat*.:55–103

Company A (2001) 'Operation 2003 läuft auf vollen Touren' – Pressemitteilung der Company A', 6. December Company A (2001) *'Das "10-Punkte-Programm" der Company A'*, 20. June 2001

Crouch, C. (1993) *Industrial Relations and European State Traditions*, Oxford: Oxford University Press

Deutschmann, Ch. (ed.) (2002) 'Die gesellschaftliche Macht des Geldes', *Leviathan*, Westdeutscher Verlag, Sonderheft (Special issue) 21

Di Maggio, P. (ed.) (2001) *The Twenty-First-Century Firm. Changing Economic Organization in International Perspective*, Princeton, New Jersey: Princeton University Press

Dore, R. (1996) 'Unions between Class and Enterprise', *Industrielle Beziehungen*, Heft 2:154–172

Dörre, K. (1996) 'Globalstrategien von Unternehmen – ein Desintegrationphänomen?' *SOFI-Mitteilungen*, Nr. 24: 15–27

Dörre, K. (2001) 'Das deutsche Produktionsmodell unter dem Druck des Shareholder Value. Beitrag zur Konferenz Shareholder Value und Globalisierung', *Research colloquium of the FIAB*, Recklinghausen, Germany.

Dörre, K. (2003) 'Das flexibel-marktzentrierte Produktionsmodell – Gravitationszentrum eines neuen Kapitalismus?', Dörre, K. & Röttger, B. (eds), *Das neue Marktregime*, Hamburg: VSA Verlag:7-30

Dörre, K.& B. Röttger.(2003) 'Das neue Marktregime – Zwischenbilanz einer Debatte', Dörre, K.& B. Röttger (eds), *Das neue Marktregime*, Hamburg: VSA Verlag:312-321

Dörrenbacher, C. (1999) *Vom Hoflieferanten zum Global Player*, Berlin: Edition Sigma

Dörrenbacher, C. & D. Plehwe (eds) (2000) *Grenzenlose Kontrolle? Organisatorischer Wandel und politische Macht multinationaler Unternehmen*, Berlin: Edition Sigma

Düll, K. & G. Bechtle, G(1988) 'Die Krise des normierten Verhandlungssystems'., K. M. Bolte (ed.) *Mensch, Arbeit und Betrieb*, Weinheim:215–244.

Ebbinghaus, B.& P. Manow (eds.) (2001) *Comparing Welfare Capitalism: Social policy and political economy in Europe, Japan and the USA*, London/New York: Routledge

Ferner A.P. Almond, T. Colling, T. Edwards, L,Holden & M. Muller-Camen (2004) 'The Dynamics of Central Control and Subsidiary Autonomy in the Management of Human Resources: Case Studies Evidence from US MNCs in the UK', *Organizational Studies*, vol. 25, no. 3, March:363-392

Ferner, A. (1997) 'Country of origin effects and HRM in multinational companies', *Human Resource Management Journal*, vol 7., no. 1:19-38

Flecker, J. (2000) 'Transnationale Unternehmen und die Macht des Ortes', C. Dörrenbacher & D. Plehwe (eds) *Grenzenlose Kontrolle?* Berlin: Edition Sigma

Frege, C. & J. Kelly (2003) 'Introduction: Union Revitalization Strategies in Comparative Perspective', *European Journal of Industrial Relations*, vol. 9, no. 1, March:7-24

Ghoshal, S. (1987) 'Global strategy: An organizing framework', *Strategic Management Journal*, Vol. 8:425–440

Hall, P. A. & D. Soskice (eds.) (2001) *Varieties of Capitalism: The Institutional Foundations of Comparative Advantage*, New York: Oxford University Press

Harrison, B. (1994) *Lean and Mean*, New York: Basic Books

Heidling, E., M. Deiss, P. Meil, P& K. Schmierl (2004) 'Restrukturierung der Interessenvertretung', In: U. Beck & C. Lau (eds) *Antiquiertheit der Moderne? Interdisziplinäre Studien zur reflexiven Moderne*, München/New York: Campus

Hirsch-Kreinsen, H. (1998) 'Internationalisierung der Produktion', M. von Behr & H. Hirsch-Kreinsen (eds) *Globale Produktion und Industriearbeit*, Frankfurt/New York: Campus Verlag:37-62

Hirsch-Kreinsen, H. (1999) 'Shareholder Value', *WSI-Mitteilungen* 52:322-330

Hollingsworth, R. J. (1998) 'New perspectives on the spatial dimensions of economic coordination: Tensions between globalization and social systems of production', *Review of International Political Economy* 5:3, Autumn:482-507.

Hurd, R., R. Milkman & L. Turner (2003) 'Reviving the American Labour Movement: Institutions and Mobilization', *European Journal of Industrial Relations*, vol. 9, no.1, March 2003:99-118.

Jacoby, S. M. (1997) *Modern Manors: Welfare Capitalism since the New Deal*, Princeton: Princeton University Press

Jürgens, U., J. Rupp, & K. Vitols (2000) 'Corporate Governance und Shareholder Value in Deutschland', *Discussion Paper FS II 00-202 des WZB*, Berlin: WZB

Kotthoff, H. (2001) 'Pluri-local social spaces in global operating German companies', L. Pries (ed.) *The emergence of transnational social spaces: International migration and transnational companies*, London: Routledge:134-144

Lallement, M. (2000) *Neue Governance Formen in der Beschäftigungspolitik. Industrielle Beziehungen und die Regulierung des Arbeitsmarkts in Frankreich und Deutschland*, Fankfurt/New York: Campus

Lallement, M. (2001) 'The Transformation of Industrial Relations in France: Elements of Analyses at the Time of the Social Refoundation', paper presented at the workshop, *Continuities and Discontinuities in Industrial Relations*, SFB 536, 18./19. January, 2001, Munich

Mann, M. (1993) *The Sources of Social Power, vol. II, The rise of classes and nation-states, 1760-1914*, Cambridge: Cambridge University Press

Marginson, P., P. Armstrong, P. P. K.Edwards & J.Purcell (1995) 'Extending beyond borders: Multinational companies and the international management of labour', *The International Journal of Human Resource Management*, 6:3:702-719

Marginson, P. & K. Sisson (1996) 'Multinational Companies and the Future of Collective Bargaining: A Review of the Research Issues', *European Journal of Industrial Relations*, Vol. 2, No. 2:173-197

Meil, P. (2000) 'The Role of German Labor Organizations in the New Economy'. P. Berg (ed) *Creating Competitive Capacity*, Berlin: Sigma:81-90

Meil, P., E. Heidling,& K.Schmierl (2003) 'Die (un-) sichtbare Hand: Nationale Systeme der Arbeitsregulierung in der Ära des Shareholder Value', *Internationaler Vergleich: Deutschland, USA, Frankreich, München: ISF Forschungsreihe*

Müller-Jentsch, W. (2000) 'Wandel der Unternehmens- und Arbeitsorganisation und seine Auswirkungen auf die Interessenbeziehungen zwischen Arbeitgebern und Arbeitnehmern', H. Funder, Euler & G. Reber (eds) *Entwicklungstrends der Unternehmensreorganisation. Internationalisierung, Dezentralisierung, Flexibilisierung*, Linz, S.:163-177

Müller-Jentsch, W. (ed.) (1991) *Konfliktpartnerschaft. Akteure und Institutionen der industriellen Beziehungen. I. Auflage*, Mering: Hampp Verlag

Narr, W. & A.Schubert (1994) Weltökonomie, *Die Misere der Politik*, Frankfurt am Main: Suhrkamp

O`Sullivan, M. (2000) *Contests for Corporate Control: Corporate Governance and economic performance in the United States and Germany*, Oxford: Oxford University Press

Ohmae, K. (1996) *End of the nation state: The rise of regional economies*, London: Harper Collins

Ram, M., P.Edwards, M. Gilman, & J. Arrowsmith (2001) 'The Dynamics of Informality: Employment Relations in Small Firms and the Effects of Regulatory Change', *Work, Employment and Society*, Vol. 15, No. 4, 19:845-861

Reich, R. (1993) *Die neue Weltwirtschaft – Das Ende der nationalen Ökonomie,* Frankfurt/Berlin: Ullstein Verlag

Roy, W. G. (1997) *Socializing Capital. The Rise of the Large Industrial Corporation in America,* Princeton: Princeton University Press

Schmierl, K. (1998) 'Amorphie im "normierten Verhandlungssystem" – Wandel industrieller Beziehungen im internationalen Unternehmensverbund', M. von Behr; H. Hirsch-Kreinsen (eds) *Globale Produktion und Industriearbeit,* Frankfurt/New York: Campus Verlag:163–207

Storper, M. (1997) *The Regional World. Territorial Development in a Global Economy,* New York: Guilford Press

Streeck, W. (1998) 'Industrielle Beziehungen in einer internationalisierten Wirtschaft', U. Beck (ed) *Politik der Globalisierung,* Frankfurt: Suhrkamp:169–202

Streeck, W. (2001) *The Transformation of Corporate Organization in Europe: An Overview,* MPIfG Working Paper 01/8

Tilly, C. (1998) *Work under Capitalism,* Boulder:Westview Press

Useem, M. (1996) *Investor Capitalism. How Money Managers Are Changing the Face of Corporate America,* New York: Basic Books

Vitols, S. (2001) *Unternehmensführung und Arbeitsbeziehungen in deutschen Tochtergesellschaften großer ausländischer Unternehmen.* Paper prepared for the forum of co-determination and companies, the Bertelsmann and Hans Böckler Foundations, März, 2001.

Waddington, J., Hoffman, E. (2000) *Trade Unions in Europe, Facing Challenges and searching for solutions,* Brussels: ETUI

Wheeler, H. (1990) 'Management-Labor Relations in the USA', G. Bamber & R. Landsbury (eds.), *Comparative Industrial Relations:*57-78.

Womack, J.P., et al. (1991) *The machine that changed the world: The story of lean production,* Cambridge, Maaschusetts: MIT Press

Risking relegation or staying in the first league?

industrial relations and enterprise restructuring in Germany under the impact of globalisation and financialisation

Jürgen Kädtler

Jürgen Kädtler *is the director of the Sociological Research Institute (SOFI) in Göttingen in Germany.*

ABSTRACT

The 'dual system' of industrial relations has formed a crucial component of the 'German Model' of post war capitalism. However it has come under severe pressure since the ending of the 'Golden Age' of Fordism and both nations and companies have been forced to engage with the new demands of globalisation. The focus of this article is on one important aspect of this development: the impact of organisational globalisation in large companies on industrial relations and on employees' bargaining power, drawing on research in the German chemical, pharmaceutical and automotive industries. It is argued that whether employees' primary power will erode, persist, or even increase depends critically on companies' product strategies. The article draws attention to ways in which employees' bargaining positions may be eroded either because the traditional strategies of unions and works councils make it difficult to draw on primary power at a local level or because primary power is shifting to new groups of employees who were traditionally not well organised. However it also points to some ways in which bargaining has been successful under these new circumstances.

Introduction

Germany's unique industrial relations system has indisputably played a crucial part in sustaining the model of post war capitalism that many scholars have characterised as the 'German Model' (Schlupp, 1979; Schroeder, 2000; Schroeder & Esser, 1999), 'Rhineland Capitalism' (Albert, 1991) or a variant of 'Mesocorporatism' (Amable, Barré & Boyer, 1997). Germany's 'dual system', combines a legal system of cooperative 'codetermination' ('*Mitbestimmung*'), whereby works councils, elected by all employees, are responsible for employee representation at the workplace level (Schmidt & Trinczek, 1991; 1999), with a collective bargaining system, known in German as '*Tarifautonomie*', whereby trade unions and employers' organisations have exclusive jurisdiction over the negotiation of general labour standards, such as wages, working hours and the conditions laid down in employment contracts across whole sectors of the economy. This exclusivity of jurisdiction also implies the exclusive right to enter into open conflict to bargain for these standards – but only for these standards (Kädtler, 2003). This dual system proved in the past to be highly efficient in several ways. It significantly improved the living conditions of employees in general; it contributed to bringing about major structural change in the economy whilst avoiding major social conflict; and it provided a high level of social integration and stability at company level, sectoral level and across society as a whole. In large companies, the representation of employees and trade unions on supervisory boards supplied an additional mechanism for achieving social integration by looking for collaborative solutions in cases where there were clashing interests, but always with the alternative back-up option of more conflictual bargaining if this did not bring results (Streeck & Kluge, 1999; Müller-Jentsch, 2003).

This system is regarded as a core element in the German version of 'coordinated capitalism' by Hall and Soskice (2001). It has also been widely regarded internationally as a particularly efficient and stable combination of employees' representation with the regulation of political and societal functions (Markovits, 1986; Silvia, 1993; Silvia & Markovits, 1995; Silvia, 1999; Katz & Darbishire, 2000). Indeed, the economic strength and stability of the welfare system and of democratic relations in post-war West Germany have been largely attributed to the industrial relations system, institutionalised as the 'Social Partnership' (Kädtler & Hertle, 1997). This system can be seen as a specific balance between conflict and cooperation, which Walther Müller-Jentsch has summed up in the term 'conflict partnership' (Müller-Jentsch, 1993).

However it is equally indisputable that both the German industrial relations system in particular and the 'German model' in general have come under pressure in the wake of the decline of the 'Golden Age' (Marglin & Schor, 1990) of Fordist regulation (Streeck, 1995; 1998a; 1998b; Dörre, 1997; 1999; 2001). Both trade unions and employers' organisations have seen sharp falls in membership (Schnabel & Wagner, 1996; Schnabel, 2003; Schroeder & Ruppert, 1996; Ebbinghaus, 2003; Visser, 2006), which has led to a decline in the coverage of sectoral collective agreements (Kohaut & Schnabel, 2003). A further symptom of this development has been a relativisation of those general standards that still exist by a proliferation of loopholes created through the casualisation of regulation, site agreements etc. (Rehder, 2003a; 2003b; Bispinck, 2007). The overall outcome has been a major shift in the distribution of social income from labour to capital[1]. One of the central tenets of Regulation Theory holds that that perfect match between societal subsystems should be understood as the outcome of a highly contingent historical instance (*'trouvaille historique'*) (Coriat, 1994) that is limited in time. Taking this seriously, we argue that the question of whether and how a constellation of comparable coherence and stability can be recaptured, should not be taken as the leading question for an analysis of current developments in industrial relations. Rather, we should be asking how actors and organisations can maintain their room for manoeuvre and capacity to act under conditions of continuing contradictions and uncertainty, and on what resources they can draw whilst doing so. For this reason, in this paper, I do not consider all those aspects of the crisis of industrial relations in Germany that have resulted from the disintegration of the Fordist regulation regime, especially the impact of general mass unemployment on union strategies that are strongly linked to full

---

1   As an important point contributing to this result, reforms in social and labour markets policies have also to be taken into account, because they indicate a significant loss of unions' formerly very strong position in these policy arenas.

employment as their precondition (Kädtler, 1986). Instead, I focus on specific bargaining situations in order to find out what resources might enable trade unions and employee representatives to gain power and use it under these conditions.

I will focus in particular on works councils in large companies, especially companies that are reorientating themselves transnationally, looking especially at the significance of locally-embedded positions and the power resources that are available in these local bargaining situations. As companies become more transnational in their organisational layout, both national units and individual production sites lose their weight and autonomy, at least at the level of formal organisational structures. Large companies have always played a decisive role in shaping industrial relations in Germany and, we submit, will continue to do so. This means that studying the distribution of power within large transnational companies can provide useful insights into several important aspects of possible future developments in industrial relations. It should be emphasised, though, that this focus does not give the whole picture. It leaves out many other important aspects of the ongoing transformation of companies, industry structures, and industrial relations. One important omission here is the question, whether the loosening of sectoral collective agreements by means of site agreements and other exceptions to what were previously universal rules, should be understood as always constituting an erosion of collective regulation or whether – as I would argue – these site agreements also open up at least the potential for a strategic restructuring of collective bargaining that could improve the position of labour where these developments occur (Wendl, 2002; Schroeder, 2003; Rehder, 2003; Bispinck, 2007).

The first section of this paper briefly outlines the connection between institutional arrangements and locally based power positions in the context of German industrial relations. The second section discusses the possible repercussions of 'organisational globalisation', a term which is used here to refer to developments within internationalised corporations, whereby business processes, business units and reporting lines are organised transnationally, and where, as a result, management and decision making is, at least in principle, equidistant from any one of the company's sites, regardless of location[2]. The third and fourth sections present some evidence on restructuring in the chemicals and pharmaceuticals industry and in the automobile industry. The final section presents some tentative conclusions about future developments in industrial relations in the context of the tension that is currently emerging between the production side of the economy and the increasing weight of financial markets.

Industrial relations between local embeddedness and organisational globalisation

In a framework of 'social partnership' the weight of employees' collective representation rests finally on the ability to exercise pressure by means of selectively refusing to co-operate with the employers. Where it can be based on 'primary power' (Jürgens, 1984), that is where companies are dependent on particular groups of employees and where works councils or trade unions are in a position to use this dependence as a tool of power[3], it thus has a

---

2   This makes it possible to take up aspects of what Bartlett & Ghoshal (1989) and Dunning (1992, 1993, 2000) refer to as 'transnational', without having to enter in a more detailed discussion of their concepts for our purpose.

3   Our theoretical point of reference is the concept of strategic organisational analysis developed by Michel Crozier and Erhard Friedberg (Crozier & Friedberg, 1993; Friedberg, 1993; Chazel & Favereau, et al. (1994).

solid basis. Provided it is a credible threat, the severity of this threat of refusing to co-operate is determined by the degree to which companies are forced to rely on this co-operation, and the extent to which they rely on it in practice. The double role of collective employee representation in being able both to guarantee cooperation in normal circumstances and simultaneously to threaten to withdraw it in exceptional circumstances was a basic precondition for the relatively high power of regulation in the conflict-partnership model of German industrial relations in the past.

The regulatory effects of the German system of industrial relations are therefore essentially a function of their deep-seated basis in local bargaining, even though national statutory and organisational structures and the organisational capacities of employers' associations provide the context and preconditions for this local power. This can be seen clearly in negotiations over collective agreements, where unions' bargaining power would not be effective without the ability to mobilise support by employees for strike action if necessary. But it is also the case in the collaborative forms of employee representation covered by the term 'codetermination'. The extent to which employee representatives can use their statutory rights of participation in company decisions or their powers of veto when they are participating in works council business depends crucially on the support that they can muster from employees. Because the vast majority of works council representatives are union members, the reputation that they build when using their statutory codetermination rights at the works council becomes a key factor in the success of union attempts to recruit and mobilise members.

Proximity to relevant decision-makers plays an important role in these processes in the local context. The local power of trade union representatives depends strongly on the room for manoeuvre and scope for decision of their management counterparts. Continuous personal contact between employee representatives and company management representatives also provides an additional channel of influence, which may play a more important role than all the statutory regulation of participation rights. The presence of employee representatives, usually works councillors and union members, on the supervisory boards of large companies is equally important. The way in which these different arenas are related and interlinked to one another (often through personal contacts) determines both the type and the extent of the influence that can be brought effectively to bear on companies by unions, as well as the overall balance of power between them.

Within this nexus of statutory codetermination rights, internal company power positions, and informal relationships of communication and trust, a range of different configurations can be observed. In some companies, employee representatives hold strong primary power positions on the shop floor, but only marginal positions on supervisory boards, while in others the two levels complement and strengthen each other. Others are characterised by intense and highly informal contacts with the board of directors, and the results that are achieved by this means play a crucial role in legitimising works councils members in the eyes of a rather passive work force. The next section of this paper will demonstrate that these established configurations of power and influence strongly affect the way that bargaining develops when companies start becoming active on a global scale.

I refer to the globalisation of companies, rather than the globalisation of markets or even globalisation without further specification, in order to take into account the fact that company strategies are more than direct reflections of market conditions. Several factors, including the elimination of trade barriers, the falling costs of transportation and the dynamic development of information and communication technologies, have placed new options on the bargaining table that cannot simply be ignored in a competitive environment. These options remain the background for behaviour under the conditions of bounded rationality (Simon, 1949; 1995; 1982). This means that they simultaneously define the limits and provide the backdrop for decision-makers' assumptions about the certainties they face when devising their corporate strategies. The implications of this changing environment for the companies thus becomes a component of their choice of strategy (Child, 1972; 1997). Prevailing product and market conditions, existing skills and opportunities, the influence of different actors and maybe even their guiding ideas are all important factors that influence these choices. In the best cases, this results in business strategies that are feasible, but these are by no means inevitable or irreplaceable. Quite different alternative strategies would, in principle, have been possible. To the extent that there is pressure to adopt 'best practice' business models and corporate strategies, this does not come from the inevitable imperatives of the production economy, but from the guiding principles and fads of the financial markets.

Financial markets in this context should not be seen as anonymous markets, but as an institutionalised public realm (Kädtler, 2005)[4]. Since the 1990s, large publicly traded companies in Germany have not been financing their businesses by issuing new shares, but have been heavily buying back their own shares instead. The power exerted by financial markets on business strategies is thus not the outcome of financial dependence but derives from the financial community's ability to define the norms, visions, and even fashions, that then become decisive for business strategies (Kädtler & Sperling, 2002; Orléan, 1999). These come into effect when top management refers to them in order to develop and/or legitimise its business strategies. There is no simple answer to the question to what extent top managers should be seen as driven by, as opposed to actively promoting those requirements of the financial markets (Froud, Haslam et al., 2000; O'Sullivan, 2000; Erturk, Froud et al., 2005). On the one hand it can be argued that the more these ideas become generally adopted, the more difficult it is for individual managers not to follow them. On the other hand, because increases in managers' income are strongly linked to shareholder value management, there is no really strong motivation for managers to dissent from them either (Froud, Sukhdev et al., 2006). In any case, financial markets do not provide unambiguous and binding guidelines that can be implemented in only one way in business strategies.

One important general trend can be singled out in the current development of large German industrial companies in this new business environment. This is a decline in the importance of business strategies solely relating to the national context, i.e. to the export of domestically made products (Beyer, 2001). This is accompanied by a

---

4   Against the background of the theoretical debate on the social constitution or embeddedness of markets (Swedberg, 2003; Callon & Muniesa, 2005; Knorr-Cetina & Preda, 2005; Sassen, 2005) this is of course a very simplistic opposition. However we think it is sufficient for the argument presented here.

trend for (multi)national organisations and governance structures to be replaced by transnational ones. In the formal organisation of companies, particular locations in national contexts are increasingly becoming little more than intersections, or local suppliers within business areas that operate internationally, optimise costs and revenues autonomously on this global scale, and make investment decisions solely on the basis of this kind of optimisation, rather than taking into account particular national or local interests. The term 'organisational globalisation' is used here to describe this trend.

This challenge for the significance of specific locales, already evident in the formal organisational structures of companies, in fact implies a declining role for locally based bargaining. However the magnitude of this effect depends on how important particular locally specific resources and skills still are – or should be – for the firm, and whether such resources can be used to the advantage of the company's employees. Five possible scenarios can be identified. The first of these is that local bargaining power is being eroding, because the resources on which it relies are losing their importance or can be obtained more inexpensively elsewhere within the firm. The second is that local negotiators are losing their influence, despite the fact that the resources on which their power is based remain very important, because global organisational structures and decision making prerogatives are restricting the scope of local influence. A third possibility is that local negotiators are losing their significance, even though the location remains very important, because other resources of that location are becoming more and more important, and these new resources, unlike the ones that used to be crucial, offer no basis for the collective representation of employees' interests. A fourth scenario sees local power positions maintaining and even extending their importance because the complexity of global production networks makes the company increasingly vulnerable to disruptions in the flow of production, and the smooth operation of every single production location is thus becoming ever more important for the overarching scheme (Veltz, 1996). Finally it is possible that local bargaining strength remains intact, because employee representatives play an important role in the 'dominant coalition' (Child, 1972) that makes the decisions about business strategies, or, conversely, that this strength is lost, because the influence of employee representatives was based solely on their membership in that dominant coalition and, because of a failure to mobilise their resources, they were unable either to prevent a loss of this membership or to compensate for that loss.

This is not an exhaustive list. It is possible to imagine still more scenarios, or combinations of those summarised here. The next section presents an analysis of the development of employee representation in a few large companies whose importance extends beyond their own individual cases, because of their position as core companies of the two largest industrial sectors in Germany, which also stand for alternative German industrial relations models. The metal-based manufacturing industries can be taken as the archetype of the 'conflictual partnership' model which is often thought to apply to German industrial relations in general. The chemicals and pharmaceuticals industries, by contrast, represent a more co-operative model, described by the trade union and employers organisations themselves as a 'chemical partnership'. The aim is to identify the factors that governed and may still govern the evolution of the local bargaining positions of employee representatives in these two sectors. All the companies studied have been operating on a global scale for a long time.

Organisational globalisation – erosion or realignment of partnerships in the chemicals industry

For decades the three large chemicals companies Hoechst, Bayer, and BASF stood out among German companies as some of the furthest advanced in their global operations. However the German chemicals and pharmaceuticals industry is also noteworthy for its long-established relationships of cooperation and bargaining which have profoundly shaped industrial relations in the sector. The co-option of the works council leadership into the dominant coalitions, as well as substantial margins for intra-company redistribution, have traditionally curbed any militant ambitions amongst works council representatives and, as a result, have also set limits on the mobilising capacity of the trade union as a whole. At the same time, the breadth of the fields in which the large companies in the chemicals industry operate, as well as their regional scope, have generated an exceptionally unified and firmly institutionalised industrial relations system in an industry that is extremely heterogeneous in the size of its companies and areas of operation. This so-called *'Chemiepartnerschaft'* ('partnership in the chemicals industry') model is now seriously challenged by the realignment of business strategies at a global scale and the repercussions of these changes on internal company bargaining arrangements.

Over the past decade, Hoechst AG has been completely split up (Menz, Becker et al., 1999; Kädtler, 2006:89-140). Its former main site has been replaced by a 'Höchst Industrial Park' with employees scattered across several dozen independent firms, most of which are small and medium sized companies. The only large firm that has its headquarters there is a service and infrastructure provider, the repository of most of Hoechst's service functions when the company was divided up. When it was formed in 1998, this company had more than 4,000 employees, a number that has now been reduced to 1,900. The chemicals and pharmaceuticals plants in the domestic location are all parts of global companies with their headquarters abroad. The works council of Hoechst's immediate successor firm, Sanofi-Aventis Deutschland GmbH, now represents around 10,000 employees, within a global company with 100,000 employees worldwide. But because all the important enterprise functions are governed on a global scale and the national company is now only responsible for domestic marketing, the works council finds itself negotiating with a 'king without a country' [5].

Until 2001 Bayer's top management maintained the profile of an integrated chemicals-pharmaceuticals firm. The company was organised in largely autonomous global business areas, for which the corporation's board of directors had no direct responsibility. Intervention by the board into their strategies were therefore rare exceptions. However because it was responsible for co-ordination and synergies, the

---

5   However it should be noted that the position of German (and also French) employee representatives seems to have improved somewhat since the emergence of the highly financialised Aventis SA, resulting from the acquisition of the pharma businesses of Hoechst and French Rhone-Poulenc (by means of a hostile takeover in 2004). According to German works council members, the more industrial culture of this new pharmaceuticals group is in some respects more like the 'old Hoechst' (Interview in 02/2006).

board did have the ultimate say on business location and in some cases over-ruled the decisions of top management in these business areas. The traditional pattern of exclusive company-wide agreements negotiated at the top level remained in place for all German production sites, albeit on terms that were steadily deteriorating as far as the employee representatives were concerned. Top management could, and actually did, create synergies across business areas while at the same time emphasising to the employees at a company level the unfavourable bargaining position of any single production unit within its global business area. The first site agreement negotiated for the main site in 1997, the business year with the best result ever, included cutbacks in fringe benefits to the amount of DM 320 million (about 165 million euro), in return for an agreed minimal amount of domestic investment and a promise to avoid forced layoffs for the duration of the agreement. So far it is not clear whether the reorganisation of Bayer as a Strategic Management Holding, begun in 2002, and the splitting off of major parts of its traditional chemicals and business services will – as with Hoechst – be an intermediate step on the way to a complete break-up, or just a further reconfiguration of the chemicals-pharmaceuticals conglomerate structure. In any case, it has led to a further weakening of workers' representation, at least within the traditional bargaining context (Kädtler, 2006:174-197).

In neither of these cases has the deterioration in the influence of workers' representatives resulted from a weakening of the companies' dependence on particular assets caused by intensified globalisation. During the restructuring of Hoechst, employees in research and development (R&D) unit at Frankfurt demonstrated a considerable amount of power when confronted with a rigid schedule of cutbacks, devised by the new management. They not only opposed this, but also encouraged the highly unionised laboratory personnel to do the same. This put the management of both the national unit and the entire company under considerable pressure, particularly as the production staff became involved too and the conflict was widely publicised, as part of a strategy to gain public support. Since the internal institutions of conflict resolution, such as bargaining structures, were already missing in this case, this conflict was widely perceived as a stiff confrontation between top management, important parts of the workforce, and the general public. Without this conflict, as union officials openly admit, it would not have been possible to negotiate the comparatively far-reaching transitional agreements for the whole company that were achieved, or the modifications of the cutback plans in R&D that had initially sparked the conflict. But it is important to recognise that this conflict did not represent a situation in which employee representatives could rely on strongly organised parts of the workforce, but, on the contrary, involved poorly organised, but strategically important, groups of employees[6].

Some generalisation is possible beyond this specific case. There are strong indications, that the locally based bargaining power at large R&D sites of employees and their

---

6   It is not quite clear to us whether this special case can be interpreted as evidence for a more general development by which core groups of employees in strategic positions use their primary power exclusively instead of backing the general representation of employees at company or sector level, recently illustrated in Germany by examples including cd|air traffic controllers, flight attendants and train drivers. However it is interpreted, this tendency undoubtedly exists and how such core groups can be (re)integrated is a crucial question for the further development of industrial relations in Germany.

representatives has not declined but has actually increased by becoming part of globally governed networks, and in a similar way, that employees at strategic production sites also have a considerable amount of power within global production networks. In principle, these networks supply the preconditions for internal competition as a means of global governance, but this does not necessarily set in motion an unstoppable race to the bottom. This local strength is all the more remarkable given that it arises from new developments. Traditionally the local reserves of power held by these groups and the bargaining positions of works councils based on them were insignificant.

The real losers from the restructuring processes in both companies are those areas that are left out of the newly constituted global company. At Hoechst, this meant the majority of former employees, but particularly those who were hived off to new small and medium sized service providers. At Bayer the logistics areas were the first to be affected, a group for whom a company agreement was concluded during the outsourcing process. Large parts of technical services followed when the holding structure was established in 2002. As local service providers, they are still part of the global production networks of the newly formed companies, but as external service providers amongst many others – not as insiders. Instead of being able to negotiate for their share of the (historically quite generous) margins for distribution of the chemicals industry, these employees now form part of the local service sector with its much tighter margins. This development has not just had negative consequences for the outsourced workers. It has also been a negative development from the perspective of workers representation within the global chemicals and pharmaceuticals firms themselves, because these traditionally highly organised parts of the workforce are no longer available as a potential power base. At least in the Hoechst case, we would nevertheless argue that there are indications that new forms of workers representation are emerging, following the standard forms of German industrial relations in general. However these conform to standards in the service sector, which fall significantly below the traditional standards of the German chemicals industries with their special '*Chemiepartnerschaft*'

We can conclude that the dramatic loss of influence of formerly powerful employee representatives in the tide of global restructuring at Bayer and Hoechst represents the impossibility of defending a general level of wages and working standards within the traditional German pattern of industrial relations. However it does not demonstrate a decline in the importance of locally-based power positions within global companies, nor does it presage the end of workers representation in these areas, even though these are the localised losers of global restructuring.

BASF AG is – or used to be – different from Hoechst and Bayer in two crucial respects: a very strong union presence in the company and a clear concentration on industrial chemicals based on the '*Verbundchemie*'[7] principle. Here, the cost efficiency of single products is not the strategic focus, but the aim is to produce an extremely broad range of products with high efficiency. This is a technological option, defined

---

7   *Verbundchemie* (literally: compound chemistry) is a technological paradigm in which by-products and energy resulting from one chemical reaction are taken as inputs for new ones. Under this system, industrial chemical production takes the form of large chains or networks of production facilities, where the focus of economic optimisation is not on the single product but on the efficiency of the overall output of this integrated technology.

by the company as a core competence. At the company headquarters and in the main production units, in particular, the union's strength is based on close ties between the company internal structures of employee representation and the industrial union. In addition, by defining 'Verbundchemie' as its core competency the company has committed itself to large and highly complex industrial systems which need constant improvement and further development. BASF thus depends on the collective competence of a highly qualified workforce of workers and technicians who are needed to operate and continually optimise this complex technology. About three quarters of the workforce is unionised, and unions are present in an all-encompassing system of communication and representation maintained by an army of shop stewards and works council members. This strong presence creates the basis for a power position of the employees that is very potent politically.

Although the practical business of intra-company social partnership at BASF hardly differed from the one at Hoechst and Bayer, there was a stark contrast between BASF and the other two firms in the workers' reaction when the management challenged the traditional modes of interaction (Kädtler, 2006:198-253). At Hoechst and Bayer rather far-reaching changes could be implemented without major disruption. The BASF workforce, by contrast, from the mid 1990s onward, staged massive protest demonstrations and reacted very strongly even to relatively minor infractions. The management took these warnings seriously. The abolition of a seniority benefit, originally planned in 1994, was revoked and has been considered taboo ever since; an attempt to cut back sick pay had to be abandoned quickly in 1996; and when, in 2001, the management attempted to reduce an extra benefit that had previously been linked to dividend growth, even though in that very year dividends were extraordinarily high, this too led to massive protests. Such incidents triggered attempts to readjust the internal relationship of cooperation and exchange that went far beyond the scope of the events that had provoked the original conflicts. In the most recent dispute, this attempt at readjustment has taken the form of major negotiations with the head of the production site about the strategic further development of this main business site in Ludwigshafen. The creation of this position of head of the Ludwigshafen site, and the appointment to this post of a member of the company's board of directors, was something that the employee representatives had been demanding for a long time as were the recently-initiated negotiations over the future of the site. Furthermore, a new global organisational and governance structure has been introduced, in which production and manufacturing sites are not subordinated parts of global or regional business units, but where these business units have to negotiate the realisation of their respective strategies with production and manufacturing sites that are organised separately on a continental basis. This entails a strengthening of production sites within the global organisation of the group and thereby – at least potentially – also a strengthening of the position of trade unions and employee representatives backed by local primary power. Interestingly, this company also has an active European Works Council and similar institutions are in the process of being developed for Latin America and Asia as well, forming part of an active worldwide network of employee representation.

In striking contrast with this case, the German tyre manufacturer Continental demonstrates that even strong trade union bargaining positions can fade where local employee representatives cannot rely on a power base of locally-embedded resources and skills on which the company is dependent (Kädtler, 2006:266-281). With over 90% of all its employees in Germany union members, Continental used to be the stronghold of union representation in the rubber industry. But, unlike chemicals, this industry is the classical type of a repository for semi-skilled workers. In its standardised production processes, training times are now, if anything, even shorter than they used to be, and in the areas of higher quality production there has been no increase in skill requirements. As a result, there is a permanent threat of transnational locational competition which creates the all-pervasive context for governance within the company. The traditional high-wage locations do not compete directly with the low-wage locations, but they do compete with one another over the volume of production that remains in their sector, causing a continuous downward spiral in wages and labour standards.

Global Realignments in the Automobile Industry – Stable Conflictual Partnerships?

German automotive companies are the core companies of the German metalworking industries and also dominate the industrial relations in these industries. They can be seen as textbook cases of 'conflictual partnership' (Müller-Jentsch, 1993), combining continuous cooperation between employee representatives and management with conflictual encounters in the realm of wage bargaining, but also, in exceptional situations, at the company level. This 'conflictual partnership' is based on the one hand on statutory rights of codetermination, including representation on the advisory board, and on the other on the company-specific power resources of a highly unionised workforce and its representative institutions. This has resulted in established and reliable bargaining arenas, as well as implicit, and sometimes explicit, productivity pacts. In these pacts high productivity gains combine with wages and social benefits which are well above average standards in Germany.

This pattern of 'conflictual partnership' developed under specific historical conditions. Until the late 1980s, and to some extent even into the 1990s, the major international activities of auto companies in Germany were largely limited to their export businesses. This applied both to the German manufacturers and European subsidiaries of US manufacturers. It was only in the 1990s that the three large German car-makers started to restructure their operations and their strategic business activities with global perspectives that extended beyond this home based export business. At the same time the two German subsidiaries of US car manufacturers, which had always been parts of global systems of production and development, were kept on a much shorter rein. These organisational realignments brought some new pressures to bear on the employee representatives in the majority of these companies, but they did not really jeopardise the established model of industrial relations. There has been a generalisation and intensification of concession bargaining, but this has taken place with the frame of a reconfiguration of bargaining arenas, with intensified interaction between the local or national level and the European level as an important innovation (Pries, 2000; Pries 2002). This outcome can be summarised by the term 'negotiated globalisation' (Kädtler and Sperling 2000; 2002).

The German subsidiary of General Motors provides the most spectacular example of this. Until the 1980s, Opel, like Vauxhall in Great Britain, could be viewed as a paradigmatic example of a multinational company. From the perspective of the Detroit headquarters of General Motors 'these overseas operations largely functioned as independent, parallel industries, rather than integrated divisions of the US parent' (Flynn, 1998:181). The result was that the European production facilities had 'far-reaching autonomy in technological and organisational respects' (Jürgens, Malsch & Dohse, 1989:75). This was true both for the patterns of labour relations and for the room for manoeuvre in these systems, which were adapted to the regulatory frameworks and conventions that prevailed in the countries where they were located. For all practical purposes, industrial relations included, Opel was one German automotive company among others.

This pattern did not change significantly until the early 1990s, when a famous shareholder revolt brought in a new GM top management strongly committed to meeting the demands of the financial markets. This new management implemented a new global governance structure, with all the individual subsidiaries and sites integrated into a highly centralised global network. Cost-driven restructuring was the main driver of this strategic realignment of the company's global activities. In North America this strategy led to plant shutdowns and redundancies and brought about a dramatic deterioration of labour relations in the company, which escalated in the Flint strikes at the end of the decade.

In Europe, the new strategy resulted in an economic disaster. The low cost strategy introduced serious quality problems *per se* but that was not the only difficulty. The Opel development centre at the company's main site in Germany was given worldwide responsibilities outside the USA without any adequate increase in resources and this meant that specialised skills in engineering and production were not available for the planning of products and processes in their original regional markets and brands. This strategy was particularly disastrous because in both national and European markets standard products were losing ground, and there was a growth in demand for customised products, in which competitors were offering extremely innovative products. Market share declined both because of failure to innovate and because of poor quality, dramatically documented in a series of spectacular recall actions. All this caused heavy conflicts between the local and global management, focused precisely on the role of locally-embedded positions of competence and power within a global company. The definition of these positions and roles was strongly contested at many different levels.

The crucial point with respect to industrial relations is that there were at least three moments when the intervention of employee representatives had lasting effects on the outcome of these struggles and on the strategy of reorganisation.

The first of these was when employee representatives on the advisory board used their position to wield some influence on management positions and strategic planning and to get an agreement on 'Guidelines for the Cooperation between Adam Opel AG and General Motors Europe', which established that the German management had autonomous responsibility for the activities of Opel. The lever that was used to achieve this was the company's desire for unanimity over the election of a new CEO. Employee representatives also played an important role in the early resignation of this new CEO and the appointment of his successor. The nomination and election of a German manager with a distinctive background in production management underscored the strategic emphasis on engineering and production competence.

Another decisive intervention came when GM and Fiat created a joint venture for purchasing parts, engines and transmission systems. On this occasion, a local strike at the German site at Bochum, which was the most strongly affected, led to a campaign at the European level that resulted in a binding contract between European management and the European works council, securing the employment status of the employees who would be subject to outsourcing.

A third decisive success for the employee representatives was in January, 2001, when the local management at Luton in the UK withdrew guarantees given to the employees at Luton in exchange for concessions they had made some months before in a plant-centred restructuring contract. The response to this was a local mobilisation campaign which was taken up by employees at other European sites, leading to a day of strikes and demonstrations all across Europe. An important side effect of this was to halt a competitive downward spiral that had been set off by the first of these plant-centred pacts in Germany in 1998.

This prepared the ground for the next stage of negotiations, so that, when in the summer of 2001 the Opel management announced an ambitious restructuring program with a reduction of 15 % capacity, equivalent to 13,000 jobs, among a lot of other measures to increase productivity and efficiency, top management and employee representatives were able to come to an understanding at a European level about a first framework agreement within a remarkably short period of time, even though just a short time before, rumours about plant shutdowns and mass layoffs had been rife. This framework agreement, which applied to all of GM's sixteen European Opel, Vauxhall, and Saab sites, essentially ruled out plant shutdowns and redundancies in the wake of restructuring, and stipulated that measures, to be specified in detail at company, national or plant level, could not be imposed unilaterally by management, but instead must be drawn up in direct consultation and agreement with the relevant employee representatives. A European-level agreement of this scope, embodying the prerequisite for all national negotiations, was a completely new feature of industrial relations. This upgrading of the European bargaining arena did not, however, by any means reduce the local power of employees and their delegates. On the contrary, it was only made possible by this local power and by the ability and willingness of local actors to use it with a European perspective. Perpetuating this European bargaining area remains a challenge, given that site competition is used as a permanent management tool, and there are ongoing tensions, but it appears that the employee representatives are aware of this and are able to find constructive ways forward (Bartmann & Rott, 2008).

The importance of local bargaining as a resource for the representation of employees in transnational organisations is even more obvious in the case of the indigenous German car manufacturer Volkswagen, an extraordinary 'showcase' of the so-called German 'co-operative conflict solution' model of labour relations. Here, bargaining conditions changed significantly in the late 1980s and early 1990s when the company acquired

Seat and Skoda and established new production capacities all over Europe using a new production concept, that of *Global atmendes Produktionsnetzwerk*, which translates loosely as 'globally breathing production network', with 'breathing' being a euphemism for flexibly increasing or decreasing volume and 'global' meaning that this is organised at a global level. This involved integrating different brands under the roof of a single large holding and creating a unified product platform in which the different brands overlapped, thus enlarging the range of possible production decisions and changing the balance of power between company and labour. Continuous internal competition and routinised benchmarking are now used as permanent tools of governance and provide the basis for establishing cost and performance targets, putting local production sites under permanent pressure and increasing competition between them, mainly within Europe (including increasingly Eastern Europe) (Sperling, 2004), but also to a certain extent with non-European sites. This has also intensified competition between parts and component suppliers inside and outside the Group, both at home and abroad.

However, locational competition within the company is also framed by a complex system of social exchanges, interest arrangements and new bargaining arenas that are becoming increasingly important. As units are more closely integrated and intertwined within production networks, there is an increasing need to react to new problems, and this has resulted in extensions and supplements to the traditional institutions and bargaining procedures. The patterns of negotiated globalisation that are emerging within the Volkswagen Group are rooted in the firmly established power and bargaining positions of the general works council at the company's headquarters, buttressed by a highly unionised workforce, strong statutory codetermination rights and long-standing informal contacts within the dominant coalition. By creating a European Works Council in the early 1990s and a world-wide works council later in that decade, Volkswagen enlarged the scope for negotiations over decision-making processes. These institutions provide at least a relative balance between different interests with regard to issues like investment, new models and volume capacities, and establish general standards for social protection and working conditions.

This kind of interest mediation is supported locally by annual 'production site symposia', which provide forums for information and consultation between the local management and employee representatives and often lead to site-specific alliances relating to investment priorities, volume specifications and cost and productivity measures. These strengthen local influence on central decisions, on the part of the employee representatives as well as local management. In fact, the management's potential to exert pressure through transnational mobility options may be regulated, but has not disappeared. However, so far these plant-level arrangements at different Volkswagen sites have not caused a downward spiral or reduced working and social standards below the general level of the German automotive and metal industries. The well-established and proven channels of information and consultation between the local employee representatives in the European (and increasingly world-wide) works councils has enabled a relatively efficient coordination of interests between different locations, which bring into play their own locally-specific resources and skills as part of an integrated production network that is dependent on these competencies. If these well-established bargaining arrangements are currently at risk, this is not because of globalisation or financialisation *per se* but because of the internal degeneration of works council structures at the German main site, where the union and a new core team still need to re-establish their general legitimacy.

The Future of the local basis of industrial relations in global companies

Two general conclusions can be drawn from the developments of corporate strategies in these cases about the future weight of local bargaining positions in globally active firms.

The first of these is that organisational globalisation does not automatically lead to a decline in the importance of the locally-embedded collective skills and cooperation arrangements that can constitute the power basis of employee representation. Instead, the fate of employees' bargaining positions differs across business areas, depending on several different factors. These include the product strategies that companies follow, the extent to which they are dependent on the employees' skills, the extent to which they need the active engagement of these employees to pursue these strategies, and what factors they will have to take into account (or may be able to avoid) by choosing and following these strategies. The most damaging consequences of increasingly global forms of organisation and activity do not occur in those functions that are subject to structural changes within global companies, but instead in those areas that are selected for outsourcing, because they are no longer perceived as a strategic resource but – if needed at all – as a simple standard commodity.

Secondly, companies' dependence on employees' competencies, skills, and engagement in particular locations (a dependence which is implied in many product strategies) does not by itself constitute collective power for labour at those locations. It can only be made effective as a power resource through organisational consolidation. Whether and to what extent the influence and the leverage of local bargaining positions can be sustained or even strengthened when global corporate restructuring takes place therefore depends crucially on the actors and structures of industrial relations. The German system of industrial relations offers considerable room for manoeuvre in the design and the emphasis of the different kinds of bargaining arenas that exist within it. Beyond the national system, there is further scope, both at the level of European industrial relations and in the way in which these different arenas and levels are connected with each other. How this room for manoeuvre is used will affect the potential for local power positions to be consolidated, the scale at which this can be achieved, and how they can be used in the context of global company structures.

The first of these points requires us to distinguish the different configurations of locally-embedded skills and cooperative relationships, which will in turn shape the importance and bargaining power of particular production sites with their locally-embedded skills. Here, the work of Robert Salais and Michael Storper (Storper, 2000; Storper & Salais, 1997) and their analysis of the role of conventions in economic life becomes relevant. Based on the categories in their analysis three ideal-typical constellations of products and production strategies can be identified that characterise the position of individual plants as well as the position of particular corporate functions and business areas in large companies:

The first of these is the production of customer-specific speciality products, based on highly specific, but at the same time broadly employable, skills and resources, as well as industrial standard production on the basis of complex and capital-intensive machinery and skills which are being developed over long periods of time. In the industries discussed here this constellation can be found in R&D, in the manufacturing of the essential part of automobiles in the car industry, in *'Verbundchemie'* with its complex production systems, in other parts of the production of chemicals, in which technologically advanced aggregates play an important role in the production process, and in the manufacture of high-tech products in the tyre industry.

The second category is the production of industrial standard products for particular customers or for anonymous markets, where the demanding requirements of the first constellation are missing; areas that fall into this category are simple, non-critical products in the automobile supply industry, the production of simple pharmaceuticals goods, standard products and standardised machinery in the chemicals industry and standard products in the tyre industry.

The third and final category includes maintenance, infrastructure, and supplier services that are specific to a given production site; examples of this are large parts of the logistics function, but also traditional centres of competence, such as centralised R&D in the chemicals industry, at least in companies that concentrate on a small number of core business areas.

Classifying industrial locations according to these constellations produces a hierarchy of three locational 'leagues'. In the first of these leagues there is a concentration of high wage locations to the disadvantage of peripheral locations, except where specific regional wage differentials between economic zones can be exploited, as is the case in Mexico or Eastern Europe. The second league of locations is made up of those that involve business areas in which production can be moved around on a global scale. Locational competition is important within each of these leagues, but hardly exists between them. The third league finally emerges where – and to the extent to which – the necessary skills and resources can be defined *per se* as generic and substitutable standard products.

Two points should be made about this distinction between ideal-typical constellations. The constellations do not describe objective features of production sites and market segments, as becomes obvious when comparing the position of maintenance functions at BASF with those at Hoechst & Aventis and Bayer, or examining the decline of the formerly centralised R&D capacities at Hoechst. Instead of objective characterisations, these constellations capture the roles ascribed to certain functions and business areas in the context of corporate strategies. Accordingly, the distinctions between the constellations are not only quite fluid, but shifts in these distinctions are an important part of the evolution of firms. Many current industrial restructuring activities, for instance, are geared toward splitting off parts of the central high-wage segment and transferring them into the other two 'leagues'. To what extent this can in fact be realised and to what extent restructuring strategies can be built around this pattern depends ultimately on whether this kind of product strategy is successful on the market. To take the example of Opel/GM, a low cost strategy for GM's European subsidiaries will only be successful at all if such low cost products can be sold on the European car market. Other such risks seem to loom behind different maintenance and logistics strategies in the chemicals and pharmaceuticals industry.

The second important point about the three constellations is that structures of employee representation continue to play an influential role in the strategy choices of corporate management. The influence of employee representatives hits its ultimate limit where there is a descent from the high-wage league into a lower league, where locational competition is strong, and where there is no possibility of escaping this fate by offering a high technology alternative. Insofar as the statutory participation rights and other power positions in the firm can be used at all in such situations, they can only help alleviate the social consequences. There is, of course, nothing new to this, since it is has been a constant thread in union politics in Germany that unions do not prevent rationalisation, but instead support it whilst ensuring socially acceptable conditions for the employees along the way (Kädtler, 1986).

In restructuring initiatives where core units of the company do not drift into the low-cost area but firms try to consolidate them into centres of excellence in the context of a global scheme – and the vast majority of the cases presented here are of that kind – then it is not the lack of power resources in general that poses new challenges to employee representatives. Rather, the main problem is how to consolidate and employ these power resources effectively within global companies. This question becomes increasingly important as the ability to draw on locally-based power resources grows. Some of our examples have demonstrated how decade-old stable and influential positions of employee representatives at the top of enterprises can quickly become worthless if the informal consensus on which they were based is withdrawn unilaterally by management, and employee representatives then do not have effective ties to local power resources. Other examples have shown that demonstrations of local power can be used to push forward the development of durable structures of employee representation and bargaining even beyond the cope of national negotiations.

Such international developments require very traditional forms of support from the local workforce. Mobilising and including groups of employees who were traditionally only weakly unionised poses particular challenges as the skills of highly qualified white collar workers become more and more crucial. How far this can succeed in companies which have traditionally lacked a strong union presence and a solidly based works council is an open question, but it is also a decisive one. That local interests play a major role in any mobilisation of local power resources is self-evident. At the same time, however, our examples also indicate that practices of representation that reach beyond the individual production site, perhaps in the form of trying to regulate locational competition, are more likely where the influence of works councils is not solely based on privileged access to informal relationships of consultation and negotiation but is also backed up by a workforce that can be mobilised. This is particularly true at the transnational level. Where we find efficient coordination in European Works Councils, this is always based on such localised strength at important sites, especially the main sites of corporations, and on the conviction of these locally-based actors that investing part of their local strength in transnational structures might serve their own well-defined interests.

In conclusion, we should emphasise that it is not companies' global operations *per se*, but the instability of these global operations that poses the central problem for employee representation within the new global enterprise structures. Strategic management of the company challenge the realm of production by defending the rationality of financial markets, or, to use Dahrendorf's words, representatives of a new 'global class' challenges the traditional local actors (Dahrendorf, 1999; 2000).

Shared understandings between employees and their representatives, and thus the basis for company-level bargaining, is becoming more unstable as they increasingly face the members of this new 'global class' who challenge the traditional orientation toward long-term growth and intra-company synergies by consistently basing their decisions on the criteria of portfolio management. This situation, in which the bargaining arena itself is unreliable because the operating routines and the codes of behaviour for internal labour relations in the company have to be constantly renegotiated, puts employee representatives under heavy strain. Where management itself does not know what the company will look like two years from now, and individual managers have no idea what their own position in the company will be in the future, then relationships of trust lose their foundations.

At the same time, such instabilities can also open up new opportunities for exerting influence. The greater the distance between strategic top management and the operative areas, the closer the relationship between operative management and employee representatives often is. And since financial management in principle never provides any specific directives for the operative business, the definition and construction of financial indicators is often a contested issue even among top managers. This situation sometimes creates openings for forging alliances across the usual lines of conflict in industrial relations. The main issue, even in these favorable constellations, is the age-old problem of how such selective and situation-specific power resources can be consolidated.

The question of what the consequences of the developments discussed here are for German industrial relations in general must remain open at this point. What should have become clear is that it is not so much local bargaining within global companies that is currently being put under pressure, but rather that which is outside the large firms. This in turn begs the question of what the future role of the large companies, which have in the past been so decisive for German industrial relations, will be in the national context after their global restructuring.

© *Jürgen Kädtler, 2008*

REFERENCES

Albert, M. (1991) *Capitalisme contre capitalisme*, Paris: Èditions du Seuil
Amable, B., R. Barré & R. Boyer (1997) *Les systèmes d'innovation à l'ère de la globalisation*, Paris: Economica
Bartlett, C. A. & S. Ghoshal (1989) *Managing across borders. The Transnational Solution*, London: Century Business
Bartmann, M. & V. Rott (2008) Cooperation versus Competition. Union and Works Council Strategies in Delta Site-Selection Process at General Motors Europe. European Works Councils as Transnational Organisations, in L. Pries, L. Rampeltshammer & M. Hertwig
Beyer, J. (2001) 'One best way oder Varietät? Strategien und Organisationsstrukturen von Großunternehmen im Prozess der Internationalisierung', *Soziale Welt, 52,* 7-28
Bispinck, R., (Ed) (2007) Wohin treibt das Tarifsystem?, Hamburg: VSA
Callon, M. & F. Muniesa (2005) 'Economic Markets as Calculative Collective Devices', *Organization Studies* 26(8):1229-1250

Chazel, F., O. Favereau & E. Friedberg (1994) 'Symposium sur Le Pouvoir et la Règle', *Sociologie du Travail*, 36(1):85-111

Child, J. (1972) 'Organizational structure, environment and performance: the role of strategic choice', *Sociology - The Journal of the British Sociological Association, 6*, 1-23

Child, J. (1997) 'Strategic choice in the analysis of action, structure, organizations and environment: retrospect and prospect', *Organization Studies, 18*, 43-76

Coriat, B. (1994) 'Ecole de la régulation: origines, spécifités et perspectives' in M. Aglietta, F. Sebai & C. Vercellone (eds), *Ecole de la régulation et critique de la raison économique*, Paris: L'Harmattan:102-152

Crozier, M. & E. Friedberg (1993) *Die Zwänge kollektiven Handelns. Über Macht und Organisation*, Frankfurt/Main: Anton Hain

Dahrendorf, R. (1999) 'The Third Way and Liberty', *Foreign Affairs*, 78(5):13-17

Dahrendorf, R. (2000), Die globale Klasse und die neue Ungleichheit', *Merkur*, 54(11):1057-1068

Dörre, K. (1997) 'Unternehmerische Globalstrategien, neue Managementkonzepte und die Zukunft der industriellen Beziehungen' in U. Kadritzke *Unternehmenskulturen unter Druck: neue Managementkonzepte zwischen Anspruch und Wirklichkeit*, Berlin: Edition Sigma:15-44

Dörre, K. (1999) 'Industrielle Beziehungen im Spannungsverhältnis von Globalisierung und europäischer Mehrebeneregulation', in W. Müller-Jentsch *Konfliktpartnerschaft*, München und Mering: Hampp:297-324

Dörre, K. (2001) 'Globalisierung - Ende der rheinischen Kapitalismus? 'in D. Loch & W. Heitmeyer, *Schattenseiten der Globalisierung*, Frankfurt/Main, Surkamp:63-90

Dunning, J. H. (ed) (1992) *Multinational Enterprises and the Global Economy*, Workingham: Addison-Wesley

Dunning, J. H. (1993) *The Globalization of Business*, New York: Routledge

Dunning, J. H. (2000) 'Regions, Globalization and the Knowledge Economy: The Issues Stated' in J. H. Dunning, *Regions, Globalization, and the Knowledge-Based Economy*, Oxford New York: Oxford University Press:7-41

Ebbinghaus, B. (2003) 'Die Mitgliederentwicklung deutscher Gewerkschaften im deutschen und internationalen Vergleich' in W. Schroeder & B. Weßels, *Die Gewerkschaften in Politik und Gesellschaft der Bundesrepublik Deutschland*, Wiesbaden: Westdeutscher Verlag

Erturk, I., J. Froud, S. Johal & K. Williams (2005) 'Pay for Corporate Performance or Pay as Social Division? Rethinking the Problem of Top Management Pay in Giant Corporations', *Competition and Change*, 9(1):49-74

Flynn, M. (1998) 'The General Motors Trajectory: Strategic Shift or Tactical Drift?' in Freyssenet, M., Mair, A., Shimizu & K.Volpato, G. (eds) *One Best Way?*, Oxford & New York: Oxford University Press:179-210

Friedberg, E. (1993) *Le pouvoir et la règle*, Paris: Èditions du Seuil

Froud, J., C. Haslam, et al. (2000) 'Shareholder Value and Financialization: Consultancy Promises, Management moves', *Economy and Society*,29(1):80-110

Froud, J., S. Johal, A. Leaver & K. Williams (2006) *Financialisation and Strategy: Narrative and Numbers*, London & New York: Routledge

Hall, P. A. & D. Soskice (2001) *Varieties of Capitalism*, Oxford & New York: Oxford University Press

Jürgens, U., T. Malsch & K. Dohse (1989): *Moderne Zeiten in der Automobilfabrik. Strategien der Produktionsmodernisierung im Länder- und Konzernvergleich*. Berlin, Heidelberg & New York: Springer

Kädtler, J. (1986) *Gewerkschaften und Arbeitslosigkeit. Zwischen Vollbeschäftigungsziel und selektiver Besitzstandswahrung*, Göttingen: Sovec

Kädtler, J. (2003) 'Tarifpolitik und tarifpolitisches System in der Bundesrepublik 'in W. Schroeder & B. Weßels, *Die Gewerkschaften in Politik und Gesellschaft der Bundesrepublik Deutschland*, Wiesbaden:Westdeutscher Verlag

Kädtler, J. (2005) 'Finanzmärkte - zur Soziologie einer organisierten Öffentlichkeit', *SOFI-Mitteilungen*, 33:31-37

Kädtler, J. (2006) *Sozialpartnerschaft im Umbruch. Industrielle Beziehungen unter den Bedingungen von Globalisierung und Finanzmarktkapitalismus*, Hamburg: VSA

Kädtler, J. & H.-H. Hertle (1997) *Sozialpartnerschaft und Industriepolitik. Strukturwandel im Organisationsbereich der IG Chemie-Papier-Keramik*, Opladen: Westdeutscher Verlag

Kädtler, J. & H.J. Sperling (2000): 'Bargained Globalisation in the German Aotomobile Industry',: GERPISA,International Network conference, *The World that Changed the Machine: The Future of the Auto Industry for the 21st Century* ?,8th International Colloquium, Paris, Palais du Luxembourg, 8.-10. June 2000. Also available from http://www.sofi-goettingen.de/index. php?id=573&no_cache=1&tx_drblob_pi1[downloadUid]=737

Kädtler, J. & H. J. Sperling (2002a) 'After Globalisation and Financialisation: Logics of Bargaining in the German Automotive Industry', *Competition and Change*, 8:149-168

Kädtler, J. & H. J. Sperling (2002b) 'The Power of Financial Markets and the Resilience of Operations: Arguments and Evidence from the German Car Industry, *Competition and Change, 8*, 81-64

Katz, H. C. & O. Darbishire (2000) *Converging Divergence. Worldwide Changes in Employment Systems*, Ithaca:ILR Press

Knorr-Cetina, K. & A. Preda (eds) (2005) *The Sociology of Financial Markets*, Oxford and New York: Oxford University Press

Kohaut, S. & C. Schnabel (2003) 'Zur Erosion des Flächentarifvertrags: Ausmaß, Einflussfaktoren und Gegenmaßnahmen', *Industrielle Beziehungen*, 10(2):193-219

Marglin, S. A. & J.B. Schor (eds) (1990) *The Golden Age of Capitalism: Reinterpreting the Postwar Experience*, Oxford: Clarendon

Markovits, A. S. (1986) *The Politics of the West German Trade Unions: Strategies of Class and Interest Representation in Growth and Crisis*, Cambridge: Cambridge University Press

Menz, W., S. Becker et al. (1999) *Shareholder-Value gegen Belegschaftsinteressen: Der Weg der Hoechst-AG zum 'Life-Sciences'-Konzern*, Hamburg:VSA

Müller-Jentsch, W. (ed) (1993) *Konfliktpartnerschaft. Akteure und Institutionen der industriellen Beziehungen*. München & Mering: Rainer Hampp

Müller-Jentsch, W. (2003) *Mitbestimmungspolitik. Die Gewerkschaften in Politik und Gesellschaft der Bundesrepublik Deutschland*. W. Schroeder & B. Weßels. Wiesbaden: Westdeutscher Verlag:451-477

Orléan, A. (1999) *Le pouvoir de la finance*, Paris: Éditions Odile Jacob

O'Sullivan, M. (2000) *Contests for Corporate Control - Corporate Governance and Economic Performance in the Unites States and Germany*, Oxford andNew York: Oxford University Press

Pries, L. (2000) 'Globalisierung und Wandel internationaler Unternehmen. Konzeptionalle Überlegungen am Beispiel der deutschen Automobilindustrie', *Kölner Zeitschrift für Soziologie und Sozialpsychologie*, 52:670-695

Pries, L. (2002) '5000x5000: Ende gewerkschaftlicher Tarifpolitik oder innovativer betrieblich-tariflicher Sozialpakt?', *Industrielle Beziehungen*, 9(2):222-235

Rehder, B. (2003) *Betriebliche Bündnisse für Arbeit in Deutschland. Mitbestimmung und Flächentarif im Wandel*, Frankfurt am Main & New York: Campu

Sassen, S. (2005) 'The Embeddedness of Electronic Markets: The Case of Global Capital Markets' in K. Knorr-Cetina & A. Preda, *The Sociology of Financial Markets*, Oxford & New York: Oxford University Press:17-37

Schmidt, R. & R. Trinczek (1991) 'Duales System: Tarifliche und betriebliche Interessenvertretung in K. Knorr-Cetina & A. Preda, *Konfliktpartnerschaft*, München und Mering: Hampp:167-200

Schmidt, R. & R. Trinczek (1999) 'Der Betriebsrat als Akteur der industriellen Beziehungen' in K. Knorr-Cetina & A. Preda, *Konfliktpartnerschaft*, München und Mering: Hampp:103-128

Schlupp, F. (1979) Internationalisierung und Krise - das 'Modell Deutschland' im metropolitanen Kapitalismus, *Prokla, 7*, 12-35

Schnabel, C. (2003) 'Determinants of Trade Union Membership' in J. T. Addison & C. Schnabel, *International Handbook of Trade Unions*, Cheltenham & Northampton: Edward Elgar:13-43

Schnabel, C. & J. Wagner (1996) 'Ausmaß und Bestimmungsgründe der Mitgliedschaft in Arbeitgeberverbänden', *Industrielle Beziehungen*, 3(4):293-306

Schroeder, W. (2000) *Das Modell Deutschland auf dem Prüfstand*, Wiesbaden: Westdeutscher Verlag

Schroeder, W. (2003) 'Die Transformation einer bundesdeutschen Basisinstitution - oder:

warum Bob Dylan Recht hatte. Eine Replik auf Michael Wendls konservative Verteidigung des Flächentarifvertrages in PROKLA 129', *Prokla* 33(1):147-158

Schroeder, W. & Esser, J. (1999) Modell Deutschland: Von der Konzertierten Aktion zum Bündnis für Arbeit, *Aus Politik und Zeitgeschichte, 49*:3-12

Schroeder, W. & B. Ruppert (1996) *Austritte aus Arbeitgeberverbänden: Eine Gefahr für das Modell Deutschland?*, Marburg: Schüren

Silvia, S. J. (1993) *Holding The Shop Together: Old and New Challenges to the German System of Industrial Relations in the Mid 1990s*, Berlin: Zentralinstitut für Sozialwissenschaftliche Forschung

Silvia, S. J. (1999) 'Every Which Way but Loose: German Industrial Relations Since 1980' in A. Martin & G. Ross, *The Brave New World of European Labour*, New York: Berghahn

Silvia, S. J. & A. S. Markovits (1995) 'The New World of German Trade Unions: Still Essential Pillars of "Modell Deutschland"'?, *Business and the Contemporary World*, 7:52-66

Simon, H. A. (1949) *Administrative Behavior: A Study of Decision-Making Process in Administrative Organization*, New York: Macmillan

Simon, H. A. (1995) 'Bounded Rationality and Organizational Learning', in Cohen, M. S., L. S. Sproull (eds) *Organizational Learning*, Thousand Oaks, London & New Delhi: Sage:175-187

Simon, H. A. (ed) (1982) *Models of Bounded Rationality*, Cambridge, Massachussets: MIT Press

Sperling, H. J. (2004) 'Going East - A Volkswagen Version of Globalisation', in M. Faust, U. Voskamp & V. Wittke, *European Industrial Restructuring in a Global Economy: Fragmentation and Relocation of Value Chains*, Göttingen, SOFI:181-200

Storper, M. (2000) 'Globalization and Knowledge Flows: An Industrial Geographer's Perspective', in J.H. Dunning (ed): *Regions, Globalization, and the Knowledge Based Economy*, Oxford & New York: Oxford University Press:42-62

Storper, M. & Salais, R. (1997) *Worlds of production. The action frameworks of the economy*, Cambridge, Massachussets & London: Harvard University Press

Streeck, W. (1995) 'German Capitalism: Does It Exist? Can It Survive?' *MPIfG Discussion Papers*, Köln: Max Planck Institut für Gesellschaftsforschung

Streeck, W. (1998a) 'Industrielle Beziehungen in einer internationalisierten Wirtschaft. Politik der Globalisierung' in U. Beck, *Politik der Globalisierung*, Frankfurt am Main:Suhrkamp:169-202

Streeck, W. (1998b) 'The internalization of industrial relation in Europe: prospects and problems', *MPIfG discussion paper,*98:2, Köln:Max Planck Institut für Gesellschaftsforschung

Streeck, W. & N. Kluge (eds) (1999) *Mitbestimmung in Deutschland. Tradition und Effizienz*, Frankfurt/Main & New York: Campus

Swedberg, R. (2003) 'Economic and Sociological Approaches to Markets. Principles of Economic Sociology', in R. Swedberg, *Principles of Economic Sociology*, Princeton: Princeton University Press:104-130

Veltz, P. (1996) *Mondialisation villes et territoires: L'économie d'archipel*, Paris : Presses universitaires de France

Visser, J. (2006) 'Union membership statistics in 24 countries', *Monthly Labour Review*, 129(1):38-49

Wendl, M. (2002) 'Jenseits des "Tarifgitters": Krise und Erosion des Flächentarifvertrages in Deutschland', *Prokla, 32*(4):537-555

ACKNOWLEDGEMENTS

Most of the empirical research for this paper was carried out as part of a research project on 'Globalisation and Industrial Relations in Germany', funded by the Deutsche Forschungsgemeinschaft (DFG) and realised together with my SOFI colleague Hans-Joachim Sperling, who contributed a great deal to the quality of this paper but could not rectify all of the author's errors, for which he is not responsible. I am also grateful to the anonymous reviewers and especially to editor Ursula Huws, who did more for the paper than any author has the right to expect. They are responsible for significant ameliorations, but not for any shortcomings which are the author's sole responsibility.

Brazilian unions face globalisation:
learning to negotiate in regional blocs and global networks

Leonardo Mello e Silva

Leonardo Mello e Silvais is *a lecturer in the Sociology of Work at the Department of Sociology and is a member of the Center of Studies on Rights of Citizenship at the University of São Paulo in Brazil.*

ABSTRACT

This paper discusses how Brazilians trade unions have been reacting to globalisation by analysing their participation in two different, though interrelated, initiatives. The first of these is the process of implementation of the Mercosul Southern Cone Common Market and the prominent role the unions played within it from its inception. The focus here is on how trade unions boosted the social agenda as a core issue in Mercosul's integration policy. The second initiative is the development of international company-based union networks which are now widespread in Brazil. What will be considered in both cases is the increasing importance of the actual practice of negotiation for the ongoing pattern of labour relations in Brazil, whether this is between state agencies and workers' representatives, or between companies and their own workers. The paper points to the difficulties and opportunities for the union movement in each case.

Introduction

Is it really the case that multinational firms come to the South because of the lower labour costs in these countries? This familiar and well-established explanation for the international division of labour that once seemed self-evident now appears to have been shaken by the recent wave of diffusion of flexible accumulation, both in the North and the South.

Not long ago it was believed that the possibility of prosperity was largely within our grasp, down here in the South as well as up there in the North, so long as companies and countries complied with certain prerequisites and made certain adjustments in terms of labour management, company organisation and institutional support (generally involving the elimination of State 'rigidities'). Whether this version of 'the toppling of Fordism' is accurate is accurate, at least when it comes to less industrialised nations like Brazil is contentious. After ten years of debate (both nationally and internationally) on the so-called 'new production models' and what they actually mean, it appears that the economic and social situation in peripheral countries stems much more from the behaviour of financial capitalism than from the vicissitudes of production models. The dominance of the need to meet the requirements of financial accumulation would seem to have successfully subordinated the scope for strategic choices by firms to such an extent that global decisions on where to invest and set up shop are taken along lines that tend to 'detach' them from direct production, in which the workers at least wield some influence. This has clear effects on union practices, both in central and peripheral nations.

It is against this backdrop that this paper will examine recent initiatives of the Brazilian union movement in relation to the globalisation and internationalisation of companies, a phenomenon that – unlike in the past – is now a two-way street, with the arrival of transnational companies on Brazilian soil as well as the expansion of Brazilian companies beyond national frontiers. There are strong grounds for suggesting that the recent wave of financial globalisation is compounding the existing pattern of international division of labour instead of relaxing it, with the labour factor playing the role of adding a 'competitive edge' to increasingly reduced levels of skill and specialisation, while the innovation factor resides in large economic groups at the top of the pyramid in a hierarchy of firms. In this scenario, the role of the unions in Brazil has lost much of its power to regulate industrial relations. However, paradoxically, union institutionalisation has been gaining ground, with a more robust presence in tripartite forums of negotiation and debate, a trend which was given strong a impetus with the election of President Lula in 2002.

Gloomy outlook: a challenge for the unions

For a long period, Southern nations were very attractive to multinational firms, a fact that went a long way toward propelling the 'economic miracles' many of these peripheral societies experienced, including Brazil. Much of this attraction may have arisen from the authoritarian regimes in power in these nations at the time when the multinationals made their first appearance. However, the boom in the NICs (Newly Industrialised Countries) in the 1970s and 80s seems to have been based on a lot more than just the comparative advantage of low wages, unlike the first group of developing countries, which obtained high growth rates during the 60s and early 70s (some authors speak of a second generation of NICs; see Lipietz, 1988), The paradigms of flexibility and lean production, according to the authors who have followed the development of these production models, emphasise the importance of skill and the ability to establish co-operative bonds both within production units and between clients and suppliers along the production chain (Womack et al., 1990).

In both cases, the role of multinationals in driving the economies of peripheral nations has changed between the years of developmental optimism (1950s and 60s) and the recent period of developmental disillusion (Oliveira, 2003). The multinationals have continued to look for cheap labour in these parts of the globe, but no longer worry about staying around for very long. The new economic order has shown itself to be increasingly volatile. Acquisitions and mergers between companies, as well as the availability of fiscal incentives, allied with – and this would seem to be the crux of the matter – the possibility of an internal division of labour within the Fordist factory itself (keeping research and development at the head office and shunting the labour-intensive sections off to the periphery), are making production plant migration and capital mobility much more possible today than they were in the past. Today, when large automobile producers like Ford or Volkswagen, which have been present in Brazil since the days of developmentalism in the 50s, threaten to pull out of the most industrialised belt in São Paulo state (known as the ABC belt) this causes social commotion and rallies public authorities, unions and civil society, precisely because these factories are icons of the 'heroic' age of the modern implantation of Fordism in the country (Negro, 2004).

And yet, on the other hand, such decisions are difficult and painful, for a number of reasons. Whether because of the numbers of staff they employ, the benefits they offer their workforce or the enormous power wielded by the unions that have sprung up around them, companies like these are regarded as dinosaurs in a much more agile and technologically sophisticated age, one that allows for rapid reconversions to meet changes in the global market. Compared with the new plants in the countryside of Rio de Janeiro (Volkswagen) and the metropolitan region of Salvador in Bahia (Ford), the old automobile plants seemed to carry the weight of a slow local obsolescence, the legacy of their own past success. Few would be surprised if the new Ford and Volkswagen plants in Resende and Bahia decided to pack up and leave tomorrow, because they were born, as it were, 'without character', while the old factories in the ABC industrial belt (Santo Andre, São Bernardo and São Caetano), on the other hand, are rooted in an essentially moral context: they form the industrial heart of these sister cities in terms of employment, income and the circulation of symbolic values and social ties. Their decline is the very mirror of the decline of Fordism in a nation that experienced this mode of production without benefiting from any corresponding distribution of the fruits of progress (Boyer, 1990). This was at the root of the importance of the new unionism of the metalworkers in the ABC region. Their goal was to spread the rights they had fought for and won to the rest of society, and to press for the 'social' regulation (dictatorship-free and with free wage bargaining) of the economic results obtained.

Today, the global economy no longer offers a place for developing countries from which they can, within a projected time-frame, come to share in the more civilised and complete standards of a modern industrial society. The positive spiral of development associated with the increasing purchasing power of the wage earner, competitive democracy and a neo-corporatist social contract negotiated between collective agents in the world of labour, have fallen by the wayside; that is, these goals no longer appear to figure as an achievable reality. It is worth remembering that the development blueprint so influential in Latin America, thanks to the theories of ECLA (the Economic Commission for Latin America), a UN regional commission, predicted the gradual absorption of the informal labour market within the formal sector. This prophecy has by no means been fulfilled. In Brazil, for example, the unregistered workforce (without entitlement to the social rights associated with registration) actually outnumbers those in formal employment, not the contrary (see Oliveira: 2003). So what we are now seeing is a new shift in the order of the international division of labour, but for the worse. Southern nations benefit less from hosting multinational structures precisely because the logic of the latter has changed. The Mercosul region is still a well-spring of cheap labour, only now without the prospect of emulating the full cycle of progress enjoyed by the developed countries, as the import substitution strategies of the 1950s and 60s had supposed they would.

Of course, even in the light of this somewhat disheartening scenario for union struggles in the global periphery, and particularly in Brazil, the less empowered players are reacting and attempting to develop initiatives to mitigate this trend, at least to avoid being cast in a passive supporting role to capital restructuring. Some of these contemporary initiatives will be examined below. However, even this active response on the part of the traditionally more combative sectors of the union ranks is not entirely lacking in ambiguities and paradoxes: beyond the horizons of developmentalism and the incorporation of workers as formal wage-earners, no real political project exists for galvanising popular sectors, the union movement included. What has always been seen as a virtue of Brazilian 'new unionism', namely its ability to extend the notion of 'class' beyond the factory walls (Moody, 1997), is now in danger of becoming its main weakness. The absence of long years of experience with a labour culture in Brazil (except via labourism or 'trabalhismo') creates the risk that labout will buy into the 'new world' of soi-disant post-industrial flexibility far too cheaply, with all the vicarious compensations that it promises, such as flexi-time, a supposed increase in free time, self-employment or entrepreneurship.

The coalition between trade unions and social movements, the trademark of 'new unionism' in Brazil (Seidman, 1994), has always been something that has facilitated transitions between the factory environment itself and the world outside it, unlike the far more restricted patterns of the typical traditional skilled industrial worker. The closer ties between the community, the family and other social affiliations (of religion, race, region or gender) have prevented the solidification of a more rigid identity based primarily on the values of the factory floor. This is one side of the problem – albeit a positive side, because it implies a working class that is theoretically better equipped to withstand the neo-liberal assault on labour and the organised unions: something that could be summed up as a 'benefit of backwardness' (measured against the classic Fordist standards of the developed nations).

However, on the other hand, the industrial restructuring of the 1990s seems to have brought about some regression with regard to these democratic achievements, because the new demands of the flexible economy cause the working class to close in on itself, as it were, splintering the labour market, increasing corporatism and narrowing the sense of the term 'workforce', whose identity has now been diluted to that of a 'partner' of the firm rather than the protagonist of new social movements. While citizen-based unionism persists in the discourse of the nation's main umbrella union (the CUT[1]), it is nevertheless losing its real social grounding insofar as the reform of the labour laws (much celebrated by the liberals) is strengthening private company-level trade union agreements[2] that risk creating aristocracies within the working class in a few well-protected locations, rather than generalising the gains that have been negotiated. In recent years, economic growth has created an advantageous bargaining postion have

---

1   Central Única dos Trabalhadores (Workers' Central Labour Union), the largest central union in the country and indeed in Latin America, has more than seven thousand affiliates and represents some 22 thousand workers (Central Union's own figures).

2   'Profit-Related Pay' (Participação nos Lucros e Resultados), a new mechanism of negotiation between the company and the union, could well generate wage differences within the working class that could end up opening a gap between the employees of large, medium and small companies.

made a reality of advantageous bargaining for some employees, but only in privileged sectors. The only existing legal framework (the Consolidation of the Labour Laws of 1943), admittedly of corporatist making, has nonetheless made it possible to curb corporate attempts to weaken labour rights to some extent. The current attack on it is provoking an unprecedented bringing together of different political persuasions within the unionised left that were hitherto somewhat marginalised in the militant base, including Trotskyites and Communists. On the less radical side of the political spectrum wthere has been a strengthening of those more traditional currents that never proposed rupture with the old system of labour relations for fear of compromising the less well-organised unions, as is the position of FS (Força Sindical - Union Power), the main competitor of the CUT.

At Mercedes Benz in São Bernardo, in the ABC region, the workers succeeded in obtaining annual PRP (profit-related pay) of more than twice the average monthly salary of a middle class professional. Hence the symbolic value of being a 'Mercedes employee' spreads throughout the region, opening doors to everything from access to credit to higher stock on the local matrimonial market. If in the hard old days of the struggle of new unionism against the corporate bosses workers' pride derived from a sense of dignity from having their demands publically recognised (see Abramo, 2000), today this has unconsciously been reduced to a mere distinction of class within an ocean of precariousness. In this new context, dignity acquires a somewhat dubious meaning.

It is within this context that we should understand union reactions to the challenge posed by the increasing insertion of Brazil into the international economy, and the global circulation of the company representatives with whom they have to negotiate.

Counter initiatives: participation in regional blocks and union networks

Brazilian unions have recently begun to acquire an active voice on the international scene. The two main central unions in the country, the CUT and FS, set up their International Relations secretariats as a response to the increasingly global character of production and the demands of union bodies in other countries, which requested the participation of Brazilian central unions and federations in their institutional structures. These international bodies included ORIT (Organização Regional Intera-mericana dos Trabalhadores - the Regional Inter-American Workers Organisation), the recently-created CSI (Confederação Sindical Internacional - International Confedera-tion of Unions), ITUC (International Trade Union Confederation), WSF (World Social Forum), ICFTU (International Confederation of Free Trade Unions), CLAT (Central Latinoamericana de Trabajadores - Latin-American Central Workers Union), CCSCS (Coordenadora de Centrais Sindicais do Cone Sul - Coordinator of Central Unions for the Southern Cone) and the ILO (International Labour Organisation).

Prior to this, the unions had a resolutely national, if not nationalist, structure and discourses that originated in a period of rampant state corporatism spearheaded by Getúlio Vargas and João Goulart, the most important labour leaders of the 1940s and 50s, a political force now clearly in decline. PT (Partido dos Trabalhadores - the Workers' Party) and the CUT, as well as FS, inherited the union structures, but not the agendas of labourism ('trabalhismo'). These organisations are the main fruit of the accelerated modernisation of the years of the 'economic miracle' (1968-1975), representing a working class begotten precisely during that period, when the country was undergoing rapid growth. Lula, the leader of PT and current President of the Republic, is also a product of that context. The thirty years that separate the emergence of the new unionism and the first PT mandate testify to the strong modernising impulse that swept through the Brazilian economy and society during that period. The 1980s and 1990s, fraught with hyper-inflation, the strain of external debt and international financial crises, were also a period of mass strikes and growing membership. Union internationalisation was forced onto the agenda by a combination of the institutionalisation of the new unionism, a need to attract affiliates in the more competitive environment created by the emergence of the new central unions and the increasing professionalisation and specialisation of their officers.

This paper will discuss two forms this internationalisation has taken: trade union participation in regional blocks, such as Mercosul (the South American equivalent of the EU), whose earliest manifestations date back to the 1980s; and the establishment of global union networks, which have only very recently been implemented.

Trade unions in the Mercosul

Through the CCSCS (Coordenadora de Centrais Sindicais do Cone Sul - Coordinator of Central Unions for the Southern Cone), Brazilian unions began to participate in the Mercosul – Mercado Comum do Sul (Common Market of the South) before it became a formal customs agreement[3]. It is worth taking a look at the stages of this participation, because they signpost an important cross-over from the more combative Brazilian unionism, starkly hostile to all forums of tripartite negotiation, to a position the leaders of the day described as 'active/propositional', that is, a posture more akin to the models of social reconciliation typical of European social democracies.

The CCSCS was set up in 1986 (without the participation of Uruguay) in response to a need felt by the region's unions to influence the manner in which their respective governments were tackling the economic problems that were at the time fairly universal among the nations of the Southern Cone (external debt, inflation, widespread poverty, etc.). Later, in 1992, thematic sub-groups were created, such as one devoted to 'production and social rights', which conferred a social rather than exclusively economic character upon the Mercosul from the outset, a dimension that was absent from the formative years of the European Union (Costa, 2004).

In those days, the rupture with the old state-bounded models of industrialisation was not clear to the main collective players on the labour side. The prevailing view at the time was that a regional union could be built upon the protectionist policies of the member nations. The effects of competition between economic branches within the block itself were played down.

One year after the Treaty of Asunción, the CCSCS brought out a document entitled 'Carta Social da Confederação Geral do Trabalho' (Social Letter from the General Labour Confederation) in which it presented a more nuanced vision of regional integration. It was no longer enough to insist on the preservation of rights acquired

---

3   The Mercosul was formally established by the Treaty of Asunción on March 26, 1991.

under the existing legislations of the member nations in order to generalise their better points (retaining the aspects most favourable to the wage-earner). Instead it was necessary to try to understand the meaning and depth of the impacts that nations would suffer under a model of adjustment that remained contradictory from the purely commercial standpoint, since the imbalance between the partners tended to create tensions rather than consensus. The economies of the member states were simply not complementary, and similarities in their areas of productive specialisation often created conflicts of interest, resulting in clashes between them. The Latin American unions, with significant Brazilian participation, placed all their reliance on a negotiation-based approach that steered them, politically, toward a deliberative policy format that also had internal repercussions insofar as it signalled a turn toward what public opinion considered a more 'responsible' unionism. The establishment of sectoral chambers, an experiment in tripartite negotiation involving the government, companies and central unions, convened in 1994 on the eve of the first presidential mandate of Fernando Henrique Cardoso, was a sign that the days of making demands without counter-proposals were over and that a new role had been carved out for unionism, especially in terms of intervention in public policy (Oliveira, 2005).

This new union stance would have a far from negligible effect on the Mercosul. The regional principle was factored into the analysis of ways to restart development, acknowledging the need for co-ordination between internal (local) and regional policies to bolster production and the market. With this new emphasis on recognition of inter-regional differences and heterogeneity (most notably between The Mercosul and NAFTA), the relatively easy discourse that had stressed the resuscitation of internal growth alone gave way to a focus on compensatory measures for regions or sectors that were not privileged by company or even state policies. Even if this stance is interpreted as evidence of the frailty of unionism (as opposed to its power), because, to a certain degree it expressed the admission or acceptance of a 'capitalist administration', it must also be recognised that it coincided with a period in the early 1990s when managerial innovations like lean production reached their peak in the industrial fabric.

The working sub-groups were strongly criticised on the grounds that they were incapable of taking account of social rights within a broader and less restricted framework because they limited themselves to purely actuarial studies of 'labour costs' in order to serve as support for commercial policies. The unions' complaints centred on the institutional format of the instruments of participation then available. Their adversaries countered with accusations of a lack of objectivity on the part of the unions, alleging that they had brought no 'concrete' counter-proposals to the debate. To this, the unions retorted that the point of the exercise was to define a new format which made room for social issues, and that this meant reshaping the bodies planned up to that point. Private sector participation was not frowned upon by the unions; quite the contrary: by showing up and stating their legitimate demands, they could be included within a democratically negotiated conflict of interests, an integral aspect of which was the confrontation of ideas and making of reciprocal concessions.

In 1993, the CCSCS assumed its expanded role and sought to make its presence felt in broad general discussions. In order to do this, it focused on three thematic topics: first. the definition of a common external tariff (CET); second, product origin criteria; and third, sectoral restructuring policies, with a view to supporting collective negotiations, whether at the level of sectors (through sectoral union committees) or companies. The sectoral union committee for the metallurgical sector proposed the creation of a reconversion social fund to foster coordinated development and anticipate training requirements wherever these may be necessary. More concretely, what this entailed was that compensatory mechanisms should be employed whenever a particular area was heavily affected by the removal of customs barriers or by factory relocations, which often implied job losses and crises across entire geographical zones. These compensation programmes would be funded via the creation of a single tax on the import of end-consumer goods within Mercosul and would be managed by the fund.

In relation to the CET, the unions settled on the following criteria: the CET would be based on sector or area references, these being the highest tariffs practiced amongst the four member states as of the date on which the CET came into effect (1995). Periodic monitoring would then be conducted over the course of a ten-year transition period (up to 2005) in order to assess the impact of the application of the quotas on the economic policies of the member states. The list of products and sectors considered exempt would be drawn up by agreement and subjected to at least two reviews during the transition period. The purpose of these reviews would be to establish values which the parties would thenceforth take as consensual, namely: product quality targets; incorporation of technical quality standards; price reduction; and job protection (terms that are regarded as mutually contradictory and incompatible in some economic analyses). At the end of the transition period a permanent tariff would be put in place. As is evident, this was a process that was both gradual and selective.

Another point of agreement that emerged from the negotiation between the parties concerned criteria of origin (also referred to as the 'regionalisation rate'), relating to those products not covered by the CET in inter-block transactions. As with the other criteria, the transition period allotted for ironing out internal conflicts was ten years and the starting platform was set at the highest nationalisation rate among the member countries.

However, notwithstanding the effort to find a 'common language' on the union side and the convergence, in practice, with the criteria proposed by the companies (on such items as the CET and criteria of origin), the general orientation that emerged from the Ouro Preto Protocol (1994) gave precedence, above any sectoral, selective or 'vertical' considerations, to the imperative of macroeconomic harmonisation. In this manner, the bipartite concessions between the unions and business class formed partial consensuses that ran up against the 'horizontal' and indistinct industrial dogma of the day, which viewed the concession of subsidies or fiscal incentives not as a means to build development but as feeders of corporatism.

Such comings and goings between the social partners (the representatives of capital and the workers) and the governmental bureaucracies of the member nations encapsulated the main tensions in the Mercosul negotiations up to the early 2000s, when political change in the bloc's heavyweight governments (Argentina and Brazil) gave fresh impetus to the 'social' vein of regional integration. However, in the mid-1990s, despite the unions' efforts to continue to pursue the route of negotiation and multilateral decision-making, a lack of support, in the form of unilateral decisions on the part of the bureaucrats and lobbying by business interests, quickly devalued this course of action and dissolved much of the support that had maintained the productive tension between the letter of the accords (put simply, 'the law') and the creation of new rights (commitments covering training, health and safety at work, the creation of multinational company committees and the recognition of the right to union organisation and membership, etc.).

In fact, these demands did later result in some concrete initiatives. They provide evidence of a coherent stance by the leadership in pursuit of a broader union influence oriented towards the general public. This orientation is also evident in the next section, where we turn our attention to the international commissions of multinational companies.

Union networks

Company union networks exist in both the industrial and service sectors and may be nationwide (bringing together unions from different regions where a given company has sites) or international (bringing together unions from the different countries in which a given group has operations). The main function of these union networks is to monitor the corporation's observance of social clauses, very often associated with concepts of 'decent work' (such as the prohibition of child labour anywhere in the supply chain). One of the core objectives of the trade union networks is the observance of the ILO's Convention 135. The unions involved in these networks typically demand that corporations co-sign what they call International Framework Agreements (IFAs). What lies behind this strategy is the idea of collective agreements on a global level, which is understood by some CUT unionists as an exercise in 'social dialogue'. The networks are organised around large-sized corporations. In Brazil, they are not formed exclusively around multinationals, but also exist in large national companies. These can sometimes behave like 'multinationals' once they begin to operate outside the country, as is the case with Companhia Vale do Rio Doce (CVRD), one of the biggest metallurgical companies in the world[4], or the Gerdau Group, one of the country's largest private enterprises, with operations in South and North America and in Europe (Spain). Gerdau is famous for its anti-union stance in Brazil and the same complaint can now be heard in the USA, although the labour relations systems differ greatly between the two countries. Another corporation that may become a very interesting case in the near future is Petrobras, the state-run petroleum giant which has an enormous presence in South America, including Bolivia, where recent conflict sparked by President Evo Morales' nationalisation initiative has generated a certain tension between the two countries.

The CUT has a policy of encouraging the development of union networks, which it calls 'union committees', in multinational companies. By the end of 2006, approximately 65 of these committees were in operation. It should be noted that even committees in national companies may in fact be monitoring the majority interests not of national capital investors, but of the foreign groups that control these enterprises. Iberdrola, with headquarters in the Basque Country (Spain), is a case in

---

4   CVRD recently acquired the Canadian company INCO.

point. Iberdrola has a global structure that blurs the boundaries between national and foreign, local and global, public and private. In Brazil, the group has a stake in the energy suppliers to three states of the federation (Bahia, Pernambuco and Rio Grande do Norte). This means that the Iberdrola committees are actually monitoring concessionaries of public services.

By contrast, the Carrefour Group, although it is foreign-owned, has an exclusively local union committee, that is, one with no participation of unions from outside the country. The main demand of the Carrefour committee is for a national agreement on performance-related pay (an extremely company-specific demand). The Wal-Mart and C&A committees run along similarly introverted lines. The banking sector has an identical approach, with no foreign trade union participation in its committees, but this can largely be explained by the predominance in Brazil of public, as opposed to private, retail banks. In the latter category there are only three heavyweights in the Brazilian market: ABN Amro, Santander and HSBC.

It is therefore really only among companies in the industrial sector (manufacturing and raw materials) that the trade union committees truly manage to develop 'bottom-up' strategies for responding to globalisation, with an exchange of experiences among unions, reciprocal visits, seminars, conferences and a push for minimum global standards in the corporation's social agenda. Of the German companies, in which the practice seems to be most developed, Basf, Volkswagen, Bayer, DaimlerChrysler and Bosch have committees in place that are generating visible results. In the chemicals/pharmaceuticals sector, in addition to those already mentioned, committees have been set up, or least attempts have been made in that direction, at DuPont, Novartis and AkzoNobel. In the automotive and metallurgical sectors, the large multinationals with committee implementation projects are ThyssenKrupp (Germany), Dana (USA), MagnetiMarelli (Italy), Tower (USA) and Delphi (USA). New networks are under negotiation at transportation and security service companies including Brinks and Prossegur. In the textiles industry, special mention should be made of a committee at Alpargatas Santista, once a paragon of the traditional national company and today a multinational with operations in Chile and Argentina.

One question immediately springs to mind: are these committees effective? The global pact at Daimler-Chrysler gives a clear indication of just how successful international trade union networks can be at mitigating some of the harmful side-effects of globalisation, especially in terms of job security. In the Third World, outsourcing chains pose a risk of becoming a fertile breeding ground for precarious or sometimes even illegal employment regimes (involving unregistered work, without entitlement to employment rights and benefits). As a result of a union committee initiative, one Daimler supplier with a history of problematic relations with the Metallurgical Workers Union in the ABC region ended up being pinned to the wall by its own client, Mercedes Benz (now part of the Daimler-Chrysler group), which threatened to cancel its orders unless the supplier in question started to comply with the good manufacturing practices stipulated in its Global Pact. The union pressured the client, which pressured the supplier, which had no wish to lose a key client. This is the spirit of the Global Pacts for which the central unions are pressing so hard. The CUT passed a specific resolution on multinationals during its 2005 congress[5].

But a sprinkling of relatively successful cases here and there ought not to hide the enormous differences, in scope and in approach, among the 'first rank' trade unions, like the Metallurgical Workers Union of the ABC. One of the activities of the committees, with central union support, is to prepare bulletins and newsletters specifically to showcase their actions both inside the country and abroad in a bid to make them known to the workers on the factory floor in companies where these pacts are in place.

Such cases are interesting because these multinational company committees can end up acting as a stimulus toward more general union organisation around the workplace, which is generally weak, if not non-existent, in Brazil. Unlike in other countries, and perhaps due to a corporatist legacy, union organisation in Brazil is based on a blend of local belonging (to a particular town or region) and identification with sectors, rather than individual companies, as occurs in South Korea, for example (see Moody, 1997:213-218). Only companies with a strong tradition of union struggle (like the car manufacturers in the Greater ABC region of São Paulo) have factory committees with the backing – in some cases very considerable backing – of the region's metallurgical workers' trade union. According to the committee at the Mercedes Benz plant mentioned above, 70% of the staff are unionised. However, multinational company workers' committees are not formally affiliated to the central union, which means that the participants in their networks, as independent entities, are not obliged to follow the network's directives.

Conclusion

We have examined two types of Brazilian union initiative that respond to the challenge of globalisation: the first of a more regional character (Mercosul) and the second with a truly global reach (union networks in multinational companies). This paper has sought to situate these initiatives within the broader political context of the neo-liberal attack on the hard-won achievements of the labour movement worldwide and of the different ways countries and their unions have responded to that attack. Brazil is undergoing a change in how its industrial relations are conducted and this is occurring in parallel with a change in the way the central capitalist economies regulate themselves, which can be characterised as a shift from Fordism towards flexibility. While the unions in developed countries were abandoning the tripartite approach typical of neo-corporatism in the 1990s, Brazilian unionism was choosing precisely this path as offering its best chance of progress[6], emerging as it was from a past of state control over the unions ('trabalhismo') that still lingered in some aspects of Brazilian labour law (Paoli, 1987). The entire agenda of trade union and labour reform now rests on this paradox. There is a real will for change coming from the bottom up which seems, in some instances, to be converging with a will for

---

5   See the text issued by the CUT National Executive Board for the XIX CONCUT, São Paulo, 06 to 09 of June 2005, 'Ação frente às multinacionais', pp 50-51.
6   A gamble that is evident from its participation in Mercosul, as described above.

change trickling down from the top (flexibility as a corporate goal). This remains a complicated feature of the current landscape.

From their participation in the Mercosul negotiations, trade unions learned the exercise of negotiation in practice and the recognition of a technical expertise that would be incorporated definitively into the life of the central unions from that point on. This fact alone is deserving of attention within the pattern of class relations in Brazil (and in Latin America in general), which many believe is condemned to irremediable oscillation between populism and revolutionism, as well as a strong reliance on the State.

The union networks offer an example of an organisational effort to respond to globalisation, this time at the micro level, in other words, where social regulation clashes directly with the company's assertion of its right to private ownership. The success of this initiative is still an open question, but nonetheless it is a process underway as much in the global North as in the global South.

Faced with the discrepancy between the growing mobility of transnational companies and the constraints this places on workers, together with an increasing loss of union influence, what this paper has attempted to do is simply outline some of the paths of resistance. Whether or not these strategies are efficient is another question entirely, and one that lies beyond the intended scope of this paper.

© *Leonardo Mello e Silva*

REFERENCES

Abramo, L. (2000) *O resgate da dignidade: Greve metalúrgica e subjetividade operária*, Campinas: Editora da Unicamp

Boyer, R. (1990) *The Regulation School: A Critical Introduction*, New York: Columbia University Press

Costa, H. (2004)'A acção sindical na EU e Mercosul: limites e desafios', *Revista Crítica de Ciências Sociais*, Vol 62, June 2002:69-95

Lipietz, A. (1985) *Mirages et Miracles: Problèmes d'industrialisation dans Le Tiers Monde*, Paris: La Découverte

Moody, K. (1997) *Workers in a Lean World*, London: Verso

Negro, A. L. (2004) *Linhas de Montagem: O industrialismo nacional-desenvolvimentista e a sindicalização dos trabalhadores*, São Paulo: Boitempo

Oliveira, F. (2003) 'The Duckbilled Platypus', *New Left Review*, Vol 24, Nov-Dec:40-57

Oliveira, F. (2005) 'Quem canta de novo "l'Internationale"?' in B. S. Santos (ed) *Trabalhar o mundo: Os caminhos do novo internacionalismo operário*, Rio de Janeiro: Civilização Brasileira

Paoli, M. C. (1987) *Labour, Law and the State in Brazil 1930-1950*, PhD Thesis, London: University of London

Seidman, G. W. (1994) *Manufacturing Militance: Workers' Movements in Brazil and South Africa 1970-1985*, Berkeley: University of California Press

Womack, J., D. Jones & D. Roos (1990) *The Machine that Changed the World: the Story of Lean Production*, New York: Rawson Associates

ACKNOWLEDGEMENTS

I am grateful to FAPESP for funding the research that made this paper possible.

New industrial areas, old workers' solidarities:

the browning of the auto industry multinationals' green field sites in Brazil

Marco Aurelio Santana

Marco Aurelio Santana *is an Associate Professor in the Graduate Program in Sociology and Anthropology at the Federal University of Rio de Janeiro in Brazil.*

ABSTRACT

This paper describes the ways in which auto workers in Southern Rio de Janeiro State in Brazil have successfully managed to build solidarity with their colleagues in the traditional locations of the auto industry in Brazil in the so-called ABC region near São Paulo, as well as in other parts of the world. This demonstrates the limitations of companies' strategies of seeking 'green field' sites in order to take advantage of low wages and introduce new working concepts such as 'lean production'. When unions are able to build effective links with workers on 'brown field' sites then these strategies can be subverted.

Introduction

The strategy of searching for new areas which offer financial inducements and low wages while avoiding regulation and union strength is one of the most prominent features of the brave new world of the global corporation. From the 1990s onward a wave of relocation has taken place, changing the geography of production throughout the world. Modern plants and their accompanying labour relations have been introduced into places with weak or non-existent industrial traditions. Green field sites are often chosen with the expectation that they will protect companies from union actions with the goal of breaking workers' solidarity across both time and space. By dealing with workers with no tradition of organisation, this strategy can, it is thought, isolate the new workforces spatially from their counterparts on the brown field sites and prevent them from becoming connected with militant traditions, practices and forms of organisation and from other ongoing struggles. However, as we shall see, such plans are not always that easy to put into practice in reality.

Drawing on ongoing research on the installation of European automobile plants (Volkswagen and PSA-Peugeot/Citroen) in the southern region of Rio de Janeiro state (in the cities of Resende and Porto Real), this paper analyses the green field strategies of these companies and how workers have been responding to then. As we shall see, the companies are making strong efforts to maintain the advantages of this strategy and they have been very effective in several respects. However, this is not to say that the actions of workers and unions have had no impact on the companies. Increasing

contact between local workers and others in traditionally industrialised areas with some experience has brought about an important impetus to union action in the southern Rio de Janeiro area.

Southern Rio de Janeiro and the changing Brazilian auto industry

Major changes took place in the vehicle manufacturing sector in Brazil in the late 1990s. These seem set to continue into the next decade and may have an impact on the world industry. All the major assembly companies have invested significantly in new plants and production facilities. These plants are geared to the expanding domestic market facilitated by Mercosul (the Southern Common Market constituted by Argentina, Brazil, Paraguay and Uruguay), and increasingly to the export of cars and trucks to the USA and the expanding new markets of Eastern Europe, South Africa and China.

In Brazil, the assemblers have taken great care in choosing the locations for these new plants and since 1995 most of these have been sited well away from the industrial region surrounding São Paulo (the so-called 'ABC' region). This area has for decades been the most highly unionised part of Brazil and the militant centre of the metal workers' union and the socialist confederation, CUT. The pattern of investment in these new plants has been to move away from traditional industrialised areas in large urban centres, mainly in the South East, in search of the best 'fiscal incentives' from municipalities not too far away from the most important consumer markets. There have also been some extreme cases, as happened when Ford took advantage of competition between the federal states to relocate a projected new development from the South to the industrialising state of Bahia in the North East.

These spatial shifts have been associated with significant changes in the production system and specifically in the relationship between the assembly firms and the component suppliers. This has involved a radical restructuring of the Brazilian component industry. Gitahy and Bresciani (1997) have stressed the increasingly pronounced shift among auto assemblers towards outsourcing their mainstream activities. Salerno (1997) has documented the trend towards 'industrial condominiums' that cluster suppliers around the main assembly plant, reducing transportation costs, streamlining integration and ensuring a steady flow of just-in-time supplies. Humphrey (1998) has developed this account and, in a detailed analysis of one plant, has argued that the commodity production chains emerging in Brazil are complex and not easily deduced from an abstract notion of 'globalisation'.

Located in South East Brazil, Rio de Janeiro was a leading contender for the new foreign investments that reshaped the automotive sector during the 1990s. These changes were facilitated by multi-sector deregulation that allowed imported products to enter the country, in parallel with a regionalisation strategy implemented by the industry itself worldwide. Along with many other parts of the country, Rio de Janeiro State strove to offer attractive conditions to the auto assemblers and their suppliers in order to attract and consolidate new investments.

The official announcement that the town of Resende had been selected as the site for the new Volkswagen manufacturing complex – particularly as this was an experimental plant – generated high expectations of positive effects on the local economy in general, and especially on the labour market. The new jobs that were expected were widely discussed and exploited by local politicians and these high hopes were seemed justified when it was confirmed that the new PSA Peugeot Citroen plant would be sited in the neighbouring town of Porto Real.

The negotiating process that brought these companies to Rio de Janeiro State was based on the incentives offered by the new 'automotive regime', introduced by the Federal Government in 1995 which triggered a new type of industrial policy for the region (Ramalho & Santana, 2001).

The press portrayed this in an upbeat way, seeing it as presaging the channelling of more investments into Southern Rio de Janeiro State. The arrival of the auto assemblers and their suppliers extended the range of action of existing companies, introducing a new set of concepts to a region previously dominated by the overwhelming presence in nearby Volta Redonda of one of Brazil's leading steel mills – CSN (Companhia Siderúrgica Nacional). As some businessmen noted, the companies that decided to reinvest or launch new businesses in the region seem to have shared a vision of a regional shift from a steel belt to a hub with broader characteristics.

Data on the investments announced and actually implemented over the past ten years in Rio de Janeiro State – particularly in Resende and Porto Real – clearly demonstrate the direct effects of the arrival of these auto assemblers, despite the fact that Volkswagen and PSA Peugeot Citroen have adopted very different strategies. Volkswagen did not draw into the region the companies in its modular consortium because the company felt that its proximity to the São Paulo industrial hub and the existence of a relatively modern highway running between Rio de Janeiro and São Paulo could handle the flow of parts and components required for its production activities. By contrast, PSA Peugeot Citroen built up a belt of suppliers around its plant at Porto Real. A survey of the volumes and types of investments in these towns and neighbouring areas indicates that other companies revised their plans in order to take advantage of the general conditions ushered in by the establishment of this automotive hub.

An aspect that has not yet been analysed to any great extent is the role played by basic infrastructure. Established prior to the tax incentives policy, this may have been a decisive supplementary factor in the selection of this region as the focus for new investment in the automotive sector. Although less important in the negotiating process, other factors favouring the region included its strategic location (between Rio de Janeiro and São Paulo and close to the port of Sepetiba). Successive municipal administrations have introduced other infrastructure initiatives designed to buttress industrial growth, in parallel with their efforts to attract new firms. Attractions of the region include high levels of education, housing, and state-level government policies. Education is stressed as a regional comparative advantage of Resende and its surroundings. Not only do the region's schools rank high, but it also houses a Vocational Training Centre run by the National Industrial Apprenticeship Service (SENAI - *Serviço Nacional de Aprendizagem Industrial*) that plays a dual role: training new workers and recruiting skilled labour. This guaranteed the two main incoming auto companies a well-trained labour-force at lower cost than in other regions, such as São Paulo, backed by an existing vocational training infrastructure.

Company strategies

I focus now on two company strategies that have been adopted in the region: low wages policies; and strategies designed to hinder workers' organisation and reduce union activity. Companies in the automotive sector form part of an international production chain and the development of this new industrial hub necessitated new types of institutional relationships, as these giant multinationals are constantly seeking innovative styles of management in order to keep up with the logistics of a highly competitive global economy. The area was chosen as part of a clear-cut trend towards seeking alternatives outside the industrial ABC region surrounding São Paulo, with its long and strong tradition of labour movement. An analysis of the locations of auto assembly plants in Brazil demonstrates a flight from this traditional region, although the sector still remains concentrated in the South and South East of the country. This 'escape from ABC' can be explained by the desire to avoid the trade union element and find a place where it is possible to apply a low wages strategy.

In its move to Resende, Volkswagen, for example, did not attempt to hide the fact that part of its plan was to establish labour relationships that were very different from those in the ABC region of São Paulo. Volkswagen carried out a survey in Resende in order to scale its wages to those of other companies in the industrial district of the region. Its Industrial Director, Luiz de Luca, presented this strategy as resulting from a desire to avoid pumping up the market. He was particularly concerned to emphasise that, on this green-field site, the company was determined to avoid the bad habits of São Bernardo, where it is not possible to negotiate (with the trade union). Claiming that 'everyone is getting out of the ABC region', he said that there was 'perfect harmony' with the metal-workers trade union in southern Rio de Janeiro State (*Folha de São Paulo*, 9 December 1996).

At that time, one of Resende's perceived attractions was that it was a centre of the *Força Sindical* trade union. This union was seen as very responsible and conservative in contrast with the socialist *Central Única dos Trabalhadores, CUT* (Unified Workers Confederation) that dominated the ABC district. Volkswagen considered *Força Sindical* to be more 'affable', with policies that were more in sympathy with the aims of the company. In this new location it was assumed that the trade unions and the workers would be much less experienced in the issues affecting the industry and more receptive to business initiatives.

The cost of labour has always been considered one of the main reasons for the search for new locations in the Brazilian automotive industry of the 1990s. Volkswagen and PSA took obvious advantage of this in Southern Rio de Janeiro.

According to the Inter-Union Department of Statistics and Social and Economic Studies (DIEESE)[1], the average wage of Brazilian metalworkers hovers around 6.2 times the minimum wage (the Brazilian minimum wage is R$ 300 or US$ 134)[2]. In the auto sector, the average wage goes up to 8.1 times the minimum wage.

A recent DIESSE survey, with support from the ABC Metalworkers Union (São Paulo), provided more specific information about the comparative situation of

---

1   *Departamento Intersindical de Estatísticas e Estudos Sócio-Econômicos*
2   Survey carried out by the sub-section of the National Metalworkers' Confederation (CNM – *Confederação Nacional dos Metalúrgicos*) / Central Workers' Union (CUT – *Central Única dos Trabalhadores*).

workers in different parts of the country. In a comparison of data from 17 localities where vehicle assembly takes place, the researchers collected more than five thousand prices of goods at 470 commercial points. The study concluded that there is a large wage gap between different regions and that high prices are concentrated in the new industrial areas. These results contradict the companies' argument that they 'pay less because the cost of living in those regions is low' (DIEESE et al, 2003:11).

From the DIEESE data it is possible to compare Resende and Porto Real with other municipalities in São Paulo where most of the car industry is based. The metalworkers of Resende are at a clear disadvantage compared with their colleagues in São Paulo. The value of wages in the automotive industry in Southern Rio de Janeiro is less than half of the equivalent in São Paulo. The comparison is even more unfavourable if differences in the cost of living are taken into account. If we only look at the value of wages in relation to the acquisition of a bundle of goods and services the difference is astonishing. The disparity between income and the expenditure in the South of Rio de Janeiro is 90.5%. In other words, workers in Resende and Porto Real workers need twice their wages just to buy basic goods and services.

It is clear that the cost of labour is a decisive factor for companies in the selection of new locations in Brazil. This also explains why they pay so much attention to resisting workers' wage demands. In its attempts to diminish the gulf between the wages in Southern Rio de Janeiro and those from other regions, the union has encountered fierce opposition from the companies.

Workers' responses

The arrival of the Volkswagen and PSA Peugeot Citroen auto assemblers presented the Resende Metalworkers' Trade Union with many challenges. In their wage negotiations over the past few years, Union leaders have had to deal with professionals employed by the multinational companies during the wage negotiation processes over the past few years, who have extensive experience in labour relations and are trained to extract the greatest possible benefit from the low wages in the region. In addition to not being accustomed to negotiating with companies in the auto assembly sector, the trade union had traditionally always relied on political support from elsewhere, through its strong and long-established links with the workers at the CSN (Companhia Siderúrgica Nacional) steel mill, which had been State-run until recently. Despite these initial handicaps, the union has been remarkably quick to catch catch up with the new reality.

The arrival of the new plants at Resende and Porto Real introduced changes in regional trade unionism. But despite the efforts of the companies to isolate their workers from the rest of the world, this external world has entered the local arena and the local unions have acquired access to experience at both national and global levels. In illustration of this overcoming of the initial temporal and spatial isolation, the Volkswagen's workers international organisation played an important role in the creation and support of the workers' factory committee, as did the Metalworkers Union from the ABC region. As a result of this support, in a very short space of time the companies found themselves having to deal with a group of workers who were well organised and mobilised.

The first important step was the creation of the Volkswagen factory committee. Just a few years after starting production, the plant had to deal with a range of complaints from the workers about their work conditions. These tensions were expressed in strike movements supported by the union. In 1999, one of these mobilisations demanded that the company should agree to the setting up of a factory committee on the same model that operated in other Volkswagen sites around the world (including in other plants in Brazil) but which up to that point the company had refused to accept in the region. As a result of the workers' action, Volkswagen was forced to agree to the setting up of such a workers' organisation within the Resende plant.

Once they had achieved this form of organisation, it was possible for these Volkswagen workers to be connected with their counterparts not only in other regions of Brazil but also abroad. The factory committee members became strongly involved in the general activities of Volkswagen workers, attending national and international meetings. The company's strategy of isolation the workers had already started to be eroded. Within these meetings, the Resende workers established close contact with the ABC factory committee representatives, so close that the ABC union newspaper started to be distributed within the Resende plant. So friendly did the relationship become between the more militant and experienced representatives from the brown field site and their newer colleagues from the green field site 150 kilometres away that some tensions were created at the official union level, since the Resende union is affiliated to FS and the ABC union to CUT. In generally, however, the local union has supported the factory committee's actions. It could be said that this contact has fuelled a growing radicalisation of the factory committee which has been supporting the union's recruitment drives and campaigns against low wages and for better working conditions.

The struggle against the low wage strategy has been facing fierce opposition from the companies. Little by little the union is beginning to achieve some closing of the gap with traditional areas. However, because the starting point was a very low wage indeed, this struggle is not a simple and easy one. Given the considerable advantages they have gained from this low wage strategy, it is understandable that the companies are so resistant. Nevertheless, the experience at Volkswagen highlights the importance of workers' solidarity, both material and ideological, in the development of effective strategies for negotiating with companies in green field areas.

It is clear that PSA has been watching the developments in the nearby Volkswagen plant and has been taking active steps to prevent its workers from building up an organisation within the plant along the same lines as at Volkswagen workers as well as placing obstacles in the way of their contact with the union. Despite this, the union is working hard not only to establish a proper workers' organisation in the PSA plant, but also to associate PSA and Volkswagen workers.

Conclusion

The new plants in Resende and Porto Real have clearly benefited from government investment in infrastructure, financial incentives, low wages and an inexperienced metalworker's trade union.

The local workers were plunged immediately into lean production patterns which included features such as multi-tasking, the resolution of problems on the shop floor, and team working. These so-called 'modern' labour relations created a work environment that put great pressure onto the workers, leading to stress and the intensification of work. Simultaneously, however, the presence of the new companies in the area has also resulted in the formation of a new working class, which has strengthened trade union organisation.

The fact that the plants were flexible right from the outset did not make the task of the local trade union easy. In addition to its initial lack of experience in dealing with modern multinational companies, the union also had to face the full impact of lean production strategies. However, this situation also had the effect of making the union more aware of the need to claim better wages and job conditions. But the challenge is still enormous. The workplace seems to remain a place where management exerts strong control, that has to be constantly challenged by union action. This can only be achieved by the active involvement of the workers.

The workers and their union first saw the arrival of automotive plants as an opportunity to create more jobs for local workers, welcoming these 'symbolic enterprises' into the local labour market. Getting a job in the automotive plants means a lot to a local worker, firstly, because it is unusual to find a formal job in a labour market characterised by informal labour relations and secondly because, despite being much lower than those of workers in the traditional automotive regions, the wages in these plants are nevertheless above the regional average.

The union has also benefited from the arrival of the new companies in the region, which has enabled it to enter and increase its strength in the automotive sector workers' movement. But this has not prevented the members from complaining about what they consider to be worse treatment at work and lower wages than those to be found in the ABC region.

The establishment of the Volkswagen factory committee can be considered as a landmark in the local workers' struggles, opening up the opportunity to make contact with other Volkswagen workers in Brazil and around the world. This has in turn opened the field for a new type of workers' action connected with other areas.

Building up this solidarity was not an easy process, however, because the ABC and local unions were members of different and competing workers confederations. Recently, the local union has shifted towards the CUT and left the FS. This means that the local union and the ABC one are now under the same confederation, which augurs well for more co-ordinated action in the future. This will enable them to increase pressure on the companies, which, perhaps, in order to keep their market position, will then have to change their relationship with the workers and the organisations that represent them. The green field is becoming brown.

© *Marco Aurelio Santana*

REFERENCES

Abreu, A., H. Beynon & J. Ramalho (2000) 'The Dream Factory: Volkswagen's Modular System in Resende, Brazil'. *Work, Employment and Society*, Vol.14, Issue 2 . UK: Cambridge University Press

Abreu, A., L. Gitahy, J.R. Ramalho & R. Ruas (1999), 'Industrial Restructuring and Inter-Firm Relations in the Auto-Parts Industry in Brazil', *Occasional Papers 20*,. Institute of Latin American Studies, University of London

Abreu, A. & J.R. Ramalho (2000) 'A indústria automobilística brasileira e a implantação de novos pólos de desenvolvimento regional – o caso do Rio de Janeiro', III Congreso Latinoamericano de Sociologia del Trabajo. Buenos Aires, May 17 20

Abreu, A. & J.R. Ramalho (2003) 'Regional development and new labour strategies: trade unions and the new car plants in Resende, Brazil', in D. B. Cornfield & H. J. McCammon (eds) *Labour Revitalization: global perspectives and new initiatives*, New York: Elsevier

Arbix, G. & A. Rodríguez-Pose (1999) 'Estratégias do Desperdício - A Guerra entre Estados e Municípios por Novos Investimentos e as Incertezas do Desenvolvimento', *Novos Estudos CEBRAP*, No 54, July 1999

Arbix, G. (2000) 'Guerra Fiscal e Competição Intermunicipal por Novos Investimentos no Setor Automotivo Brasileiro', *Dados*, Vol.43, N.1

Beynon, H. (2003) 'O Sindicalismo tem futuro no século XXI?' in M.A. Santana, & J.R. Ramalho (eds) *Além da Fábrica: trabalhadores, sindicatos e a nova questão social* São Paulo: Boitempo Editorial

Beynon, H. & J.R. Ramalho (1999) 'The transformation of the automobile sector in Brazil - a new way of producing cars?' Conference, *Approaches to Varieties of Capitalism*. CRIC, ESRC, University of Manchester

Carvalho, R.Q. (1997) 'Restructuring and globalisation in the Brazilian automobile industry', Gerpisa Conference, *The Trajectories of Internationalisation of Firms in the Automobile Industry*, Paris, June

Castro, N. (ed) (1996) *A Máquina e o Equilibrista - inovações na indústria automobilística brasileira*, São Paulo, Paz e Terra

DIEESE, CUT-CMN, Sindicato dos Metalúrgicos do ABC (2003) *Do Holerite às compras – remuneração, preços e poder aquisitivo do tempo de trabalho em 17 municípios com produção automobilística no Brasil,*. São Paulo, SMABC

Durand, J. & J. Durand-Sebag (2001) 'PSA s'installe au Brésil', *Lettre du Gerpisa* N°150, March 2001

Freyssenet, M. & Y. Lung (1997) 'Between Globalization and Regionalization: What is the Future of the Automobile Industry?', *Actes du GERPISA*, n. 18, France: Université de Evry

Gitahy, L. & L. Bresciani (1997) 'Reestruturação Produtiva e Trabalho na Indústria Automobilística Brasileira', Campinas: Unicamp, Mimeo

Humphrey, J. (1998) 'Globalisation and supply chain networks in the auto industry: Brazil and India', *Conference Paper*, Geneva, 9-10 March

Martin, S. (2001) 'Globalização e imbricamento da flexibilidade do trabalho: perspectivas contemporâneas da indústria automobilística nas Américas (Brasil, México e Estados Unidos)', in N. A.Guimarães & S. Martin (eds), *Competitividade e Desenvolvimento – atores e instituições locais,* São Paulo: Editora Senac

Posthuma, A.C. (1997) 'Autopeças na encruzilhada: modernização desarticulada e desnacionalização', in G. Arbix. & M. Zilbovicius (eds), *De JK a FHC - A Reinvenção dos Carros,* São Paulo: Scritta

Ramalho, J.R. & M.A. Santana (2001a) 'The Volkswagen's modular system: regional development and workers' organisation in Resende, Brazil', 9th GERPISA International Colloquium Reconfiguring the auto industry: merger & acquisition, alliances and exit, Palais du Luxembourg, Paris, June 7-9, 2001

Ramalho, J.R. & M.A. Santana (2001b) 'Promessas e efeitos práticos da implantação da indústria automobilística no Sul Fluminense', XXV Encontro Anual da ANPOCS, Caxambú, October 16-20, 2001

Ramalho, J.R. M.A. & Santana (2001c) 'Um perfil dos Metalúrgicos da Volkswagen de Resende – RJ', Rio de Janeiro: Unitrabalho/UFRJ

Ramalho, J.R. & M.A. Santana (2002) 'The Volkswagen's modular system and workers' organisation in Resende, Brazil', *International Journal of Urban and Regional Research*, Vol. 26, No 4. Oxford: Blackwell

Salerno, M.S. (1997) 'A Indústria Automobilística na virada do século', in G. Arbix & M. Zilbovicius (eds), *De JK a FHC - A Reinvenção dos Carro,,* São Paulo: Scritta

Salerno, M.S., et al (2002) 'A nova configuração da cadeia automotiva brasileira. Relatório de Pesquisa', Pesquisa, EPUSP/PRO/TTO/BNDES, Mimeo

Santana, M. (2006) 'The PSA experience in Porto Real (Rio de Janeiro – Brazil): state commitment, firm strategies and workers' responses', Paper presented at 152th *GERPISA Monthly Seminar*, Paris, April

Stewart, P., et al (2001) 'Control for whom? Work organisation automobile industry in the North America', *Actes du GERPISA*, No 30, Paris, October 2001

Stewart, P., J.R.Ramalho, A. Danford, V. Pulignano & M.A. Santana (2004), 'Novas estratégias gerenciais e a qualidade de vida no trabalho na indústria automobilística (Grã-Bretanha, Brasil e Itália)', *Revista Latinoamericana de Estudios Del Trabajo*, Uruguay, v. 1, n. 17:165-187, 2005

Vallas, S. (2005) 'Theorizing Teamwork under Contemporary Capitalism', Keynote Address at the 9th Annual Meeting of the *International Workshop on Teamwork* (IWOT) in Lisbon, Portugal, September 8-9 2005

ACKNOWLEDGEMENTS

This article benefits from the results of the research projects 'O Global e o Local: os impactos sociais da implantação da indústria automotiva no sul fluminense' and 'Desenvolvimento regional, indústria automobilística e relações de trabalho em uma perspectiva comparada: os casos do Sul fluminense e do ABC paulista', sponsored by FAPERJ (Programa 'Cientistas do Nosso Estado') and by CNP, under the co-ordination of José Ricardo Ramalho (UFRJ). I would like to thank CAPES for its support.

Technomadic Work:
From Promotional Vision to WashTech's Opposition

Michelle Rodino-Colocino

Michelle Rodino-Colocino *is an Assistant Professor of Film/Video Media in the College of Communications at Pennsylvania State University, USA.*

ABSTRACT

The purpose of this paper is to examine 'technomadic', or 'technomediated' mobile work at the levels of labour process and labour market. It investigates the promise of technomadic work at the level of the labour process, analyses the exploitation of technomadic work at the level of the labour market, and presents an instructive case study of the ways in which US workers are collectively struggling against such arrangements through the high-tech workers' union WashTech, the Washington Alliance of Technology Workers. The following analysis remedies gaps in the literature on technology and work by examining two overlooked phenomena: firstly the way in which the production of mobile labour markets contradicts the liberatory promise of technomadic labour processes; and secondly, workers' collective action against exploitation in the mobile, global labour market. By combining methods that interpret meanings within texts about labour processes with an empirical overview of trends regarding the labour market, this essay aims to contribute to the productive conversation between research in political economy and in cultural studies and to an understanding of divergence between the representations and experiences of technomadic work.

Introduction

Movement is pivotal to the development of industrial capitalist production. So are the newest information and communication technologies (ICTs). At the turn of the twentieth century, time and motion studies used photography and later motion picture film to scrutinise workers' movements and expenditures of energy (Braverman, 1974; Brown, 2005; Burns, 1973; Ferguson, 1997). One century later, via technologies like surveillant computer networks that monitor keystrokes, management continues to employ the latest media to move workers more efficiently throughout their workday (Nolan, 2003; Nord, McCubbins & Nord, 2006; Parenti, 2003). Management has long been concerned, more specifically, with using the newest ICTs to reduce labour costs by streamlining the labour process. I use the term 'labour process' to describe how the tasks that comprise a job are organised and carried out at the micro levels by workers. Labour historians from Karl Marx (1977) to Joan Greenbaum (1995) have critiqued the use of the latest technologies in the labour process to extract more surplus labour from workers. Such critics are concerned with studying the way 'people of one class set into motion people of another class' (Braverman, 1974:179)[1]. I use the term 'labour market', in contrast with 'labour process', to describe the organisation of work at the macro level, including the global demand, distribution and division of work[2]. Although sophisticated and robust, critiques of management's use of technology to reorganise work at the level of the labour market have largely ignored two phenomena: firstly, the reality of mobile labour markets which contradict the liberatory promise of technomadic labour processes; and secondly, workers' collective action against exploitation in mobile, global labour markets[3].

To fill these gaps, this paper examines the promise of technomadic work at the level of labour process, analyses the exploitation of technomadic work at the level of labour market, and presents a case study of the ways in which US workers are collectively struggling against such arrangements. The first section discusses the early promise of technomadic labour processes, promoted as liberating, even empowering individual workers. Technomadic labour processes describe work made flexible across space and mediated by technology; ICTs mediate work while moving in or out of the office. Brought to the market as the overwork of US employees gained publicity in the commercial press, cell phones, PDAs, portable computers, LAN networks, and strategies like telecommuting and the portable office promised to 'create more time' (Haynes, 1991:x).

My analysis then turns to the technomadic labour market, where high-tech work has been reorganised. Technomadic labour markets include work that has been outsourced and offshored (made mobile across space). I discuss how workers are challenging such arrangements through WashTech (the Washington Alliance of Technology), a union for US technology workers whose labour is mobile at the level of the labour market. WashTech is also significant for using technomadic strategies in both organising and legislative activities. Finally, I issue a note of caution and a call to action. Labour activists and scholars, I argue, should view offshoring as a galvanising issue but move on to embrace a wider platform that seeks to address the structural causes and effects of an economy that mobilises labour only to squeeze out more in return for less.

Methods borrowed from cultural studies and political economy inform my analysis. The investigation presented here combines critical analysis of key texts from management literature with an examination of the IT labour market and an assessment of union opposition. By combining methods that interpret texts about labour processes with an empirical overview of trends regarding the labour market, this paper aims to contribute to the conversation between research in political economy and cultural studies (Mosco, 1998). My experiences as an active member of WashTech since 1999

---

1   Taylor and Bain (2005) analyse the ways in which labour processes in Indian call centres are circumscribed by globalisation. Other investigations of labour process include Braverman (1974), Fraser (2001), Greenbaum (1995), Huws (2003), and Noble (1984, 2001), whose works examine how management uses technology to augment control over the labour process.
2   Fernandez and Sosa (2005) study the call centre labour market by investigating the mechanisms that segregate such work according to gender. Spitz-Oener's (2006) labour market analysis looks at the relationship between computerisation and rising skill demands through a case study of occupations in West Germany.
3   Scholarship critical of specific forms of telemediated mobile work arrangements, from telecommuting to offshoring, also overlook workers' collective resistance (Frauenheim, 2006 ; Golden, 2006; Harpaz, 2002; McNally, 2003; Kitou & Horvath, 2003; Westfall, 2004). Studies of collective action against exploitative telemediated work include Noble (2001) and against exploitative media work include Wasko (1998).

also informs the analysis. This project, then, also integrates an 'advocacy' approach because I engaged in the movement I am studying (Park & Pellow, 2002). Although this experience has enriched my interpretation of the union's activities, the texts analysed here are available in the public domain, as cited.

A note on the limitations of methods is warranted. I use textual analysis in the first section of the paper to underscore the disconnect between promotional discourse on labour processes that promises liberation and efficiencies for workers and the growing problem of overwork, as evidenced by labour market trends and workers' struggles. This methodological choice practically guarantees there will be a disjuncture between what I find in the texts and wider trends in the labour market and labour movement. Management's promotional discourse on mobile technology, however, merits a corrective grounded in workers' experiences.

Technomadic Labour Process

Since the mid 1990s, management and academic discourses have described how employers have made professional work mobile at the level of labour process. Talk of technologically-linked nomadic workers proliferated in articles like 'Nomadicity in the National Information Infrastructure' (XIWT, 1995). The XIWT (Cross-Industry Working Team) is a consortium of academics and corporations like Intel, IBM, and AT&T, who define 'nomadicity' as the 'ability of people to move easily from place to place, retaining access to a rich set of services while they're moving, at intermediate stops, and at their destination' (XIWT, 1995). The XIWT assert that electronic connection is crucial for making workers mobile during the workday: 'it is the character of the nomad that he needs to do his job irrespective of location'.

In 'Technomadness and the Internet' (Roberts, 1993), freelance journalist and 'technomadic' researcher Steve Roberts offered a more poetic description of digitally mediated work at the level of the labour process. Recounting his 'adventures' working as a freelance journalist traversing the USA aboard a bicycle laden with electronic gadgetry, Roberts portrayed himself as a 'technomad' who is 'physically rootless, but wired into [his] electronic home in the Internet'. He believed his communications technology-laden recumbent bicycle, 'Winnebiko' to be 'a machine that eloquently symbolised the daring notion that people could indeed be free, follow their dreams, and break the chains that had always bound them to their desks'[4]. For Roberts, technomadic work yielded heightened individual freedom while working. Other management texts agree: 'The portable office offers us freedom to work when and where we please, to realise our aspirations to set up and run our own businesses, to pursue business and leisure interests, and to create more time' (Haynes, 1991:x).

Less glamorous than pedalling technomads are telecommuters who do their jobs 'remotely' (Sproull and Kiesler, 1994). Jack Nilles, who coined the term 'telecommuting' in the 1970s, defined the arrangement as 'periodic work out of the principal office, one or more days per week' (Ellison, 1999). Telecommuting affects the labour process by enabling 'place independence' that promises to boost workers' loyalty (Hodel,

---

4   See Roberts (1993) and excerpts from *Computing Across America* (1988), both available at: http://www.microship.com/ bike/ winnebiko/across.html.

Holdregger & Luthi, 1998). Management literature seems to agree that US employees value telecommuting because the workforce is becoming 'more independent' and 'self-sufficient' (Shaw, 1996:33). Telecommuting is promoted elsewhere as an efficient way for working parents to fulfil work and family responsibilities (US Department of Labor, 1999; Nilles in Duxbury, Higgins, & Neufeld, 1998:224).

Management texts have also promoted technomadic work as making workers more mobile *at* the office. *Business Communications Review (BCR)* (Moran, 1999) touted mobile ICTs as a solution to the communication problems of the 'distributed workforce', that 'emerging category of employees who need to be highly mobile, albeit within an enterprise's campus or cluster of buildings'. In *BCR*'s vernacular, these employees are 'hall warriors,' workers who 'typically spend 30 to 40 percent of their working day collaborating with colleagues in conference rooms or working in multiple locations around a corporate campus'. Time spent in conference rooms and moving between offices at the 'campus' constitutes an opportunity to boost productivity. Information and communication technology 'is well-suited for on-premise mobile employees who require updates from their desktop environment as they move about the campus' (Moran, 1999). *BCR* advocates ICTs, in other words, as a means to mediate workers' daily tasks and consequently the labour process in which they engage.

These various forms of technomadic labour processes contribute to the constitution of a notion of the placeless workplace. In the fourth edition of their book on the 'networked organisation', Sproull and Kiesler (1994) argued that new computer-based communication technologies 'overcome temporal and geographical barriers to the exchange of information' in ways that profoundly change the way organisations operate (Sproull & Kiesler,1994:ix). Hodel et al. referenced the new technological and global reorganisation of work when describing work decoupled from specific physical locations. 'Place independence' is the result of 'local and global computer networks [that] make distances irrelevant' (Hodel et al., 1998:1057). Such technologies similarly inspired Castells (1996) to argue that the 'space of flows' had overtaken the 'space of place' and Cairncross (1997) to announce the 'death of distance'.

Has technomadic work borne out the promises of efficiencies and freedoms of its promotional discourse? Although debates around 'the productivity paradox' have not been settled (Lina & Shao, 2006; Willcocks, 1999), one way to answer this question is to look for clues in the labour market. At the very least, statistical descriptions of the labour market point toward a correlation between work hours and technological diffusion. But the statistics certainly do not suggest that new mobile communication technologies are liberating workers from long, intense workdays. Since the 1990s US workers have endured longer, harder hours, 'anytime, anywhere' for less pay and security. In 1997 the average married couple worked 717 hours longer annually than they did in 1969. Between 1979 and 1998, the percentage of men and women who worked over forty hours per week also grew. Nearly twice as many men as women worked long weeks in 1998 (US Department of Labor, 1999).

Marketing discourses for mobile information and communication technologies (MICTs) have constructed 'technomadic' work as a solution for the overworked by promising to mediate work across space and time. Promotional discourses` for mobile information and communication technologies, moreover, promised 'anytime, anywhere' work, while the new economy called for labour to be available whenever and wherever employers desired. As 'the precariat' knows too well, however, post-industrial workers face longer, more intense workdays with fleeting job security (Brophy, 2006). The organisation of technomadic work helps explain this contradiction. The spatial dispersion of labour means overworked technomads are increasingly likely to find themselves liberated from work (i.e., laid off) rather than 'physically rootless' but gainfully employed (Roberts, 1993).

Technomadic Labour Market

New ICTs have helped extend the spatial dispersion of labour markets. During the 1980s, following the movement of manufacturing jobs from the First to the Third World, clerical services used ICTs to move data processing to cheaper labour markets[5]. Over the past decade and a half, high-tech firms have also reorganised work in ways that are producing a global labour market for professional and service work. The same companies that manufactured the ICTs that 'set into motion' workers in various labour processes have also set the labour market into motion via offshore outsourcing.[6] Info-tech employment, however, is technomadic in ways that depart significantly from the romantic images conjured up by the freewheeling, freelancing journalist Steve Roberts or idealised portrayals of 'independent telecommuters' and connected 'hall warriors'. Contrary to such utopian characterisations, technomadic work at the level of the labour market has disempowered workers. Facilitated by ICTs that mediate spatially distributed production, offshoring has enabled the exploitation of workers through the production of a technomadic labour market.

Since the late 1990s, high-tech workers in the USA have increasingly toiled under the threat of seeing their jobs outsourced or offshored to cheaper labour markets beyond their reach. Offshoring promises to cut labour costs by employing workers at a fraction of the US cost. In 2000, Amazon.com announced plans to outsource 150 jobs to India, where it would employ up to 80% of its customer service workers for one-tenth the wage (Layoffs, 2000)[7]. Two years later, one Microsoft executive described plans for offshoring work to India, where the company sought 'quality work at 50-60% of the cost…that's two heads for the price of one' (Microsoft's Indian Outsourcing Documents, 2002). The first decline in median salary in 31 years for US IEEE (Institute of Electrical and Electronics Engineers) members has been at least partly attributed to offshoring (Incomes of Technical Professionals Decline, 2004; Schneiderman, 2005)[8]. Because offshoring has reduced the number of entry level jobs, the UK's Association of Technology Staffing Companies blames offshoring for the 'salary slump' that permanent and contract IT helpdesk workers

---

5   See, for example, Skinner (1998).
6   These workers include those employed in computer hardware, software, and other information services mobile professionals require.
7   Although Amazon.com's customer service workers earned less than unionised customer service employees across the United States, they earned upwards of $11 an hour or $1900 per month if they worked forty-hour workweeks. The same worker in India would cost $150 per month.
8   Between 2002-2003, full-time IEEE workers experienced a 1.49% wage reduction.

have experienced (Hadfield, 2005)[9]. Workers displaced by offshoring report that they are frustrated in finding equivalent pay. Of the 5.3 million full-time US workers displaced by plant closures and relocations between 2001-2003, more than half landed full-time jobs that paid less than their previous positions. A whopping 29% experienced a 20% (or greater) reduction in earnings (US Department of Labor, 2004).

What should we make of arguments that offshoring creates wealth on both sides of the transaction? Agrawal, Farrell and Remes (2003) contend that offshoring lowers labour costs in countries that send work overseas and boosts wages in countries that receive offshored work. This argument, however, hinges on a logical fallacy that universalises corporate interests via the claim that cutting wages 'creates wealth' (Levy, 2005). Instead of creating new sources of revenue, lowering wages in sending countries transfers capital upwards to wealthy elites. Although some workers in countries receiving offshored work will enjoy higher pay, those countries also experience expanded wage gaps. Offshoring, therefore, does not result in a benign labour market marked by 'friction-free capitalism' (Gates, 1995) or a placeless 'space of flows' (Castells, 1996). Place matters, as evidenced by the need to find cheaper labour markets not just anywhere, but in lower waged Third World economies. As the challenge WashTech poses to offshoring suggests, this strategy is not without friction (Brophy, 2006; Rodino-Colocino, 2007; van Jaarsveld, 2004).

As we examine WashTech's mobilisation around technomadic labour markets, a note of caution on the effectiveness of offshoring is in order. As Doug Henwood (2004) points out, we may be making too much of offshoring as the cause of job loss. The USA, particularly its manufacturing sector, is losing many times more jobs than can be attributed to offshoring. Receiving countries like Brazil and China are also experiencing significant job losses. Foreign countries make an easy scapegoat, one that distracts Americans from the need to make fundamental changes and launch wide scale job-creation and welfare programmes (including public healthcare and childcare programmes) that can benefit all workers rather than help only those directly affected by offshoring.

Nevertheless, the mobilisation of today's IT workers is noteworthy for at least four reasons[10]. First, IT workers have been conceived of as 'symbolic analysts' best positioned to exploit the 'riches of the Information Age' (Reich, 1992; US Department of Commerce, 1995). Second, IT workers are leading the resistance against exploitative mobile labour arrangements. Third, both technomadic work and the struggle against it are facilitated by ICTs. Finally, the struggle of professional high-tech workers, difficult to organise since they have not traditionally viewed themselves as workers, is a bellwether for the labour movement that is as transglobal as the twin problems of labour precarity and overwork.

WashTech Challenges the Technomadic Labour Market
Since March 1998, WashTech (the Washington Alliance of Technology) has represented technomadic worker's rights largely at the level of the labour market. After affiliating

---

9   In the UK contract and temporary IT helpdesk workers watched their pay tumble further than that of their permanent counterparts. Pay for contract and temporary help desk workers fell by 25% between 2004 and 2005; pay for permanent workers fell by 3% (Hadfield, 2005).
10   For more on the uneven proletarianisation and feminisation of clerical work, see Strom (1989).

with CWA (Communication Workers of America, the 700,000 member large affiliate of the AFL-CIO) in August 1998, the Seattle-based union for high-tech workers spent five years advocating for long term temporary IT contractors (known as 'permatemps') who worked at Microsoft without the lucrative benefits that were available to permanent staff, like employee stock options (ESOPs). The permatemps ultimately won a \$97 million judgment against Microsoft in 1999.

WashTech's 'new model of unionism' proved a more significant victory (Rodino-Colocino, 2007). The union's free listserv and membership at large have helped WashTech grow into a more general advocacy group for high-tech workers. As of January 2008, the listserv reaches 17,000, over eight times its dues-paying membership of 2,000. WashTech's paid membership structure is unusual in that it boasts approximately 500 members at large and 150 members under contract at AT&T Wireless (previously Cingular; see Nachtigal, 2005). Championing issues relevant to 'precarious' workers beyond permatemps has enabled WashTech to serve as a social movement labour union (Brophy, 2006).

From 2003 to the present, offshoring has been a central organising and legislative issue at WashTech. With 395,600 jobs in high-tech industries lost nationally between 2001 and 2004, 9,600 high-tech jobs lost in Seattle between 2001-2002 and millions of dollars for state contracts going overseas, it is not surprising that offshoring was a major concern for Washington's technical workers (Srivastava and Theodore, 2006; Doussard and Mastracci, 2003). In 2002 and 2003, WashTech conducted protests at Microsoft, gave interviews to print and broadcast media and posted corporate offshoring plans on the web to spur organising efforts and inspire action against offshoring (Dobbs, 2003; Engardio et al., 2003; Microsoft's Indian Outsourcing Documents, 2002). Such publicity across media led to an increase in listserv membership, which jumped from 2,000 in January 2003 to over 15,000 in September 2003. Union President Marcus Courtney attributes this upsurge to the union's exposure of offshoring as a labour issue and its original reporting on the issue via WashTech news, an informative component of the union's website[11]. When workers at Cingular Wireless (now AT&T) won the campaign to represent workers through WashTech, one member partly attributed the victory to concerns over outsourcing (Nachtigal, 2005). As the first of its kind, the successful Cingular campaign constitutes a significant victory for the growing union[12].

WashTech also pursued legislation to boost job security and create safety nets for workers. In the 2004 legislative session WashTech joined with other labour unions to support HB 3187, which aimed to prohibit Washington State contract work from flowing overseas. The bill died at the state level but passed at the federal level as part of the Omnibus Budget Act of 2004. In 2006 and 2007, WashTech supported the expansion of Trade Adjustment Assistance (TAA) to all high-tech and service workers. Established as part of the Trade Act of 1974, TAA provides benefits to workers laid off because of declining sales or production or increased imports. Benefits include job training, job relocation assistance, subsidised healthcare, and cash payments (US

---

11   Courtney, personal communications, August 10, 2006 and August 14, 2006. Also see WashTech News at http://www.washtech.org/news.

12   Nearly one thousand paying members belong to the Cingular Wireless-WashTech.

Department of Labor, 2006). Because the Senate failed to extend TAA past its expiry date of December 31, 2007 its status remains uncertain and it has become a likely focus of legislative advocacy[13].

WashTech has taken some flak for opposing offshoring. The union has been linked with the rhetoric of 'white collar nationalism' that constructs Indian (and Third World) workers as thieves of US jobs and hapless victims of globalisation (Chakravartty, 2006). Portraying WashTech's position as nationalist protectionism, however, is unproductive on several counts. The characterisation homogenises WashTech's and labour activists' perspectives. Some activist IT workers in the USA oppose offshoring and agitate for immigrants' rights (Rodino-Colocino, 2007; 220). In addition, WashTech supports the principle of organisation of workers in outsource-receiving countries like India. CWA, WashTech's union affiliate, is working toward such ends by joining with Indian union coalitions and organisations, including the New Trade Union Initiative, the Young Professionals Collective, the Centre for Education and Communication, and Jobs with Justice-India to explore transnational union alliances (CWA, 2006). Associating WashTech's legislative agenda with white-collar nationalism also plays into the right-wing 'friction-free' economic development rhetoric that regards national regulations as hindrances to unfettered free trade. WashTech President, Marcus Courtney, describes the union's position as neither anti-trade nor protectionist but supportive of a human-centred rather than a profit-centered trade system:

'We need to change our current trade model that is undermining human and environmental rights into one that recognises these [as] fundamental to any global system of trade. We are not opposed to trade, but [we] are opposed to the trading system that encourages the undermining of good paying family wage jobs in the race to the bottom. Trade needs to encompass more than a corporate bottom line agenda.'[14]

The charge of white collar nationalism is not without some justification, however, because it does underscore a real and strategic deficit within the labour movement and more generally, within the lexicon that describes labour's relationship to globalisation. The problem with the offshoring debate is that it deflects critiques of larger job losses in sending and receiving countries and sidetracks any examination of the causes and effects of these declines (Henwood, 2004). Before turning to how WashTech might mobilise its members against wider structural problems that could globally unite workers, let us examine how WashTech uses technomadic labour processes. Doing so suggests that technomadicity is not inherently exploitative and opens up the possibility that its manifestation in arrangements like offshoring need not be either. Offshoring would not be so destructive if our global labour movement won protections for living wages, health, retirement, and family benefits, unemployment benefits, and shorter, less intense workweeks. Perhaps WashTech's nomadic, technological organisation strategies can inform a new wave of activism that seeks to achieve such ends.

---

13   The Department of Labor has given assurances that it will use appropriated funds.
14   Marcus Courtney, personal communication, January 29, 2008.

WashTech's Technomadic Labour Process

Although WashTech focuses on stemming the exploitation of workers in the global labour market, the union uses technomadic labour processes in its daily work of organising (building membership), making legislative appeals, and generating media attention. These tactics help overcome obstacles to organising IT workers. Such obstacles include anti-union sentiment among employers and employees, resistance to supporting the issues that matter most to precarious and contingent workers, and the recently-overturned legal requirement that client firms and temporary agencies should consent to recognise collective bargaining units (van Jaarsveld, 2004)[15].

If we accept the XIWT definition of 'nomadicity' as 'the ability of people to move easily from place to place, retaining access to a rich set of services while they're moving, at intermediate stops, and at their destination', then the WashTech members are nomadic. Members enjoy the ability to retain membership of the union while moving from job to job, across the country, and out of the country. Most dues-paying WashTech members are 'members-at-large' rather than traditional chapter members. I joined WashTech as a graduate student in 1999 to participate in the movement I was researching for my dissertation in communication studies at the University of Pittsburgh[16]. As a WashTech member, one may be a temporary worker, a student, self-employed, unemployed, working at home, or working for a large corporation like Microsoft.

WashTech also practices *tech*nomadicity to inform and recruit members. Since its foundation in 1998, the organisation has used email to communicate with current and prospective members and has featured 'WashTech News' prominently on its homepage[17]. Founding organisers wrote most of the articles until 2001, when members with journalism backgrounds began contributing articles. In 2001, WashTech launched TechsUnite.org to serve national list members[18]. TechsUnite is home to the 'Offshore Tracker', a joint project of WashTech and CWA[19]. Launched in 2004, the tracker reports offshoring events covered by the news media and accepts submissions detailing such events on its website. According to the tracker, 528,478 jobs were offshored between January 1, 2000 and January 29, 2007 and 263,069 jobs were lost as a result. Union staff verify all posts, but these estimated figures are conservative because of corporate secrecy around offshoring plans (Beckman, 2004).

The union also employs digital media to encourage paying and listserv members to lobby legislators about timely policy issues. Since 2003, WashTech has used email appeals produced by GetActive, a company that designs 'relationship management products' to help non-profit bodies 'recruit, engage, and retain' members[20]. GetActive software mediates online petitions, appeals for donations, and solicitations for membership recruitment. CWA has praised WashTech for its adept use of technomadic labour and as a leading source of IT industry news (Hartman, 2006).

---

15   This legal requirement was overturned by the National Labor Relations Board's (NLRB) decision in M.B. Sturgis, Inc. (331 NLRB No 171, August 25, 2000); see van Jaarsveld (2004).
16   Living in Seattle, WA, as I wrote my dissertation, I worked as a nomadic student.
17   See http://www.washtech.org.
18   See http://www.techunite.org.
19   See http://www.techsunite.org/ offshore/index.cfm
20   See http://www.getactive.com.

Conclusion

The concept of technomadic work captures the promise and perils of techno-mediated mobile labour. Proponents of technomadic labour processes envision a placeless workplace in a 'space of flows' marked by the 'death of distance'. Glamorous accounts imagine mobile workers who roam, 'physically rootless', while scholarly descriptions assert the 'place independence' that ICTs afford. The mobility that workers are promised at the level of labour process, however, is experienced quite differently in the labour market. Offshoring, which relies on ICTs to facilitate work between disparate parties, creates a technomadic labour market that erodes job security and wages in sending countries and aggravates inequality in receiving countries. Paradoxically, ICTs enable the death of distance at the level of labour processes but reassert the significance of geographical place in the labour market. ICTs enable companies like Microsoft, Amazon, and IBM to tap into cheaper labour markets beyond US borders. Place matters to corporate owners and executives, as illustrated by the senior vice president who urged colleagues to 'Think India' (Microsoft's Indian Outsourcing Documents, 2002). Touting the death of geographical place discounts how offshoring affects the labour market in IT and other sectors. Technology, furthermore, cannot overcome the importance of geographical place as long as wages diverge so greatly across the globe.

Wage divergence points to the political and structural aspects of the technomadic labour market in general and offshoring in particular. 'Offshoring strategies,' Levy (2005) argues, 'are more about shifting relations of power than gaining efficiency' (Levy, 2005:690). Labour, management, and technology scholars, then, should view offshoring as a political strategy, because executives use the arrangement to expand the labour pool. By expanding the labour pool, offshoring reduces First World workers' leverage for demanding secure, living wage jobs. Enlarging the labour pool is a familiar tactic for controlling workers and busting unions. What is novel about offshoring in the twenty-first century, however, is the extent to which electronic networks facilitate the creation of globally dispersed labour and the separation of value creation and wealth distribution. The latest version of techno-mediated offshoring is structural in nature; it does not affect one sector exclusively but rather, affects entire skill sets that can be reduced to communication tasks (Levy, 2005).

Labour scholars and activists, however, should approach offshoring as a management strategy that serves a familiar end: squeezing more out of workers for less in return. Offshoring is a means, like outsourcing, automation, and downsizing, to reduce labour costs but also displaces labour within a workplace. All too often surviving workers pick up the slack for the 'pink slipped'[21] (Henwood, 2004). Workers face obsolescence or overwork because they are still required to produce a surplus. As Karl Marx put it over one hundred years ago, 'Capital has one sole driving force, the drive to valorise itself, to create surplus value, to make its constant part, the means of production, absorb the greatest possible amount of surplus labour' (Marx, 1977). Managers' preoccupation with motion and mobility throughout industrial capitalist development can be explained by their search for more output from workers at less cost. This point is important for unions like WashTech's CWA to remember when

---

21   Pink is the colour of the employee's copy of an official redundancy notice in the USA.

seeking to create a broad-based labour movement, inclusive of all workers in the First and Third Worlds (CWA, 2006). When this is acknowledged, offshoring can be given its due as a galvanising issue that has sparked a movement of professional workers who understand labour markets as global formations. To build on such success, a broad-based, inclusive labour movement must move forwards and toward global solidarity. Workers facing job loss in offshoring countries and their counterparts in offshored countries have similar needs: affordable healthcare, family care, unemployment, retirement, housing, clean air, adequate food, water, energy supplies, transportation, education, living wages, and secure jobs. Attaining these basic necessities for the working class demands that we make room for the struggle over offshoring to recede as the smaller, less productive battle.

© *Michelle Rodino-Colocino, 2008*

REFERENCES

Agrawal, V., D. Farrell, & J.K. Remes (2004) 'Offshoring and beyond', *McKinsey Quarterly*, Vol. 4:24-35

Beckman, D. (2004) 'Washington Alliance of Technology Workers launches web-based Offshore Tracker for jobs going overseas', *WashTech News*, 16 April 2004. Accessed on January 28, 2008 from http://www.washtech.org/news/ industry/display.php?ID_Content=4661

Braverman, H. (1974) *Labor and Monopoly Capital: the Degradation of Work in the Twentieth Century*, New York: Monthly Review Press

Brophy, E. (2006) 'System error: Labour precarity and collective action at Microsoft'. *Canadian Journal of Communication* 31: 619-638

Brown, E. (2005) *The Corporate Eye: Photography and the Rationalization of American Commercial Culture, 1884-1929*, Johns Hopkins University Press, Baltimore

Burns, J.E. (1973) 'Allan H. Mogensen, the man who started it all', *Industrial Management*, Vol. 15, No. 6:7-11

Cairncross, F. (1997) *The Death of Distance: How the Communications Revolution Will Change the World*, Harvard Business School Press, Boston

Castells, M. (1996) *The Rise of the Network Society*, London: Blackwell

Chittum, R. (2004) 'Rise in offshore jobs expected', *Wall Street Journal* (Eastern edition), 5 May 2004:B.6

'CWA, Indian unions join forces on call center work', *CWA News*, 11 August 2006. Accessed on January 28, 2008 from http://www.cwa-union.org/news/ page.jsp?itemID=27826809

Dobbs, L. (2003) 'The exporting of America', 21 May 2003, CNN

Doussard, M. & S. Mastracci (2003) *Uncertain Futures: The Real Impact of the High Tech Boom and Bust on Seattle's IT Workers*, Center for Urban Economic Development, Chicago: University of Illinois

Duxbury, L., C. Higgins & D. Neufeld (1998) 'Telework and the balance between work and family: Is telework part of the problem or part of the solution?', M. Igbaria & M. Tan (eds), *The Virtual Workplace*, Hershey: Idea Group Publishing:218-255

Engardio, P., A. Bernstein, M, Kripalani, F.Balfour, B.Grow & J.Greene (2003) 'The new global job shift', *BusinessWeek*, 3 February 2003. Accessed January 28, 2008 from http://www.businessweek.com/magazine/content/03_05/b3818001.htm

Edwards, C. (2005) 'Wherever you go, you're on the job', *BusinessWeek*, 20 June 2005 Accessed January 28, 2008 from http://www.businessweek.com/magazine/content/05_25/b3938612.htm

Ellison, N. (1999) 'Social impacts: New perspectives on telework', *Social Science Computer Review*, Vol. 17, No. 3:338-356

Ferguson, D. S. (1997) 'Don't call it "time and motion study"', *IIE Solutions*, Vol. 29 No. 5:22-23

Fernandez, R. M. & L. Sosa (2005) 'Gendering the job: networks and recruitment at a call center', *The American Journal of Sociology*, Vol. 111, No. 3:859- 907

Fraser, J. A. (2001) *White-collar sweatshop: The deterioration of work and its rewards in Corporate America*, New York: W.W. Norton & Company

Frauenheim, E. (2006) 'Telecommuting cutbacks at HP represent shift', *Workforce Management*, Vol. 85 No. 12:4-5

Gates, B. Myhrvold, N. & P. Rinearson (1995) *The Road Ahead*, New York: Viking

Manufacturing Engineering (2005) 'Going offshore cuts technology jobs', *Manufacturing Engineering*, Vol. 134 No. 5:40

Golden, T. (2006) 'The role of relationships in understanding telecommuter satisfaction', *Journal of Organizational Behavior*, 27:319-340

Greenbaum, J. (1995) *Windows on the Workplace: Computers, Jobs, and the Organization: Office Work in the Late Twentieth Century*, New York: Monthly Review

Hadfield, W. (2005) 'Offshoring blamed for salary slump', *Computer Weekly*, 18 October 2005. Available at: http://www.computerweekly.com/Articles/2005/ 10/19/212531/ Offshoringblamedforsalaryslump.htm. Accessed on 22 August 2006

Harpaz, I. (2002) 'Advantages and disadvantages of telecommuting for the individual, organization, and society', *Work Study*, Vol. 51 No. 2:74-80

Hartman, J. (2006) 'From Ink to I-Pods: Communicating with Members: Key to Building, Strengthening CWA', *CWA News*. Accessed on January 28, 2008 from http://www.cwa-union. org/news/cwa-news/page.jsp?itemID=27400331

Harvard Business Review (2006) 'Conversation: William MacGowan on continuity and communication' *Harvard Business Review*, 1 May:38

Haynes, C. (1991) *Portable Computing: Work on the Go*, New York: Amacom

Henwood, D. (2004, March 22) 'Toward a progressive view on outsourcing', *The Nation*. Accessed on January 28, 2008 from http://www.thenation.com/doc/20040322/cavanagh/5

Hodel, T., A. Holdregger & A.Luthi (1998) 'Ethical guidelines for a networked world under construction', *Journal of Business Ethics*, Vol. 17:1057-1071

Huws, U. (2003) *The Making of a Cybertariat: Virtual Work in a Real World*, New York: Monthly Review 'Incomes of technical professionals decline' (2004) *IEEE-USA, Communications*, 22 December 2004. Accessed on January 28, 2008 from http://www.ieeeusa.org/communications/releases/2004/ 122204pr.asp

Kitou, E. & A. Horvath (2003) 'Energy-related emissions from telework', *Environmental Science and Technology*, Vol. 37, No. 16:3467-3475

'Layoffs: One click away' (2000) *Washington Free Press*, November/December 2000. Previously available at http://www.washingtonfreepress.org/48/layoffs.html; contact author for text on mlr31@psu.edu

Levy, D. (2005) 'Offshoring in the new global political economy', *Journal of Management Studies*, Vol. 42, No. 3:685-693

Marx, K. (1977) *Capital*, Volume I. (B. Fowkes, Trans.), New York: Vintage Books

McNally, R. (2003) 'High tech hopes', *Alternatives Journal*, Vol. 29, No. 3:30

'Microsoft's Indian Outsourcing Documents' (2002). Accessed on January 28, 2008 from http:// www.washtech.org/news/industry/display.php?ID_Content=441

Moran, R. (1999) 'Supporting a distributed workforce: What's available now', *Business Communications Review*, October 1999:15-19

Lina, W. & B. Shao (2006) 'The business value of information technology and inputs substitution: The productivity paradox revisited', *Decision Support Systems*, Vol. 42, No. 2:493

Mosco, V. (1998) 'Political economy, communication, and labour', in G. Sussman, G. & J. A.Lent (eds), *Global Productions: Labor Making in the 'Information Society'*, Cresskill: Hampton Press Inc.:13-38

Nachtigal, J. (2005) 'Cingular organizing drive a success'. *WashTech News*, 21 November 2005. Available at: http://www.washtech.org/news/inthenews/ display.php?ID_Content=5025. Accessed on August 22, 2006

Noble, D. (1984) *Forces of Production: A Social History of Industrial Automation,* New York: Oxford University Press

Noble, D. (2001) *Digital Diploma Mills: The Automation of Higher Education,* New York: Monthly Review

Nolan, D. R. (2003) 'Privacy and profitability in the technological workplace', *Journal of Labor Research,* Vol. 24, No. 2:207-232

Nord, G. D., McGubbins, F., and Nord, J.H. (2006) 'E-monitoring in the workplace: Privacy, Legislation, and surveillance software', *Communications of the ACM,* Vol. 49 No. 8:73-77

Parenti, C. (2003) *The Soft Cage: Surveillance in America from Slavery to the War on Terror,* New York: Basic Books

Pellow, D. N.& L. S. H. Park (2002) *The Silicon Valley of Dreams: Environmental Injustice, Immigrant Workers, and the High-Tech Global Economy,* New York: New York University Press

Reich, R. (1992) *The Work of Nations,* New York: Vintage Books

Roberts, S. (1993) 'Technomadness and the Internet rev 2.0', 29 September 1993. Accessed January 28, 2007 from http://www.microship.com/ technomads/article.html

Rodino-Colocino, M. (2007) 'High-tech workers of the world, unionize! A case study of WashTech's "new model of unionism"', in C. McKercher & V. Mosco (eds) *Knowledge workers in the information society,* Lanham: Lexington:209-227

Shaw, L. (1996) *Telecommute! Go to Work Without Leaving Home,* New York: John Wiley

Schneiderman, R. (2005) 'IEEE cites outsourcing as wages drop and US loses 221,000 jobs', *Electronic Design,* 14 April 2005:25

Skinner, E. C. (1998) 'The Caribbean data processors', in Sussman, G. and Lent, J.A. (eds), *Global Productions: Labor in the Making of the 'Information Society',* Cresskill: Hampton Press:57-90

Spitz-Oener, A. (2006) 'Technical Change, Job Tasks, and Rising Educational Demands: Looking outside the Wage Structure', *Journal of Labor Economics,* Vol. 24, No. 2:235-272

Sproull, L. & S. Kiesler (1994) *Connections: New Ways of Working in the Networked Organization,* Cambridge, Massachussets: MIT Press

Srivastava, S. & N. Theodore (2006) *Information Technology Labor Markets: Rebounding, but Slowly,* June 2006,Chicago: Center for Urban Economic Development, University of Illinois

Strom, S.H. (1989) '"Light Manufacturing": The feminization of American office work 1900-1930',*Industrial and Labor Relations Review,* Vol. 43, No. 1:53-71

Taylor, P. & P. Bain (2005) 'India calling to the far away towns: the call centre labour process and globalization', *Work, Employment and Society,* Vol. 19, No. 2:261-282

US Department of Commerce, National Telecommunication and Information Administration, (1995) *Falling Through the Net: A Survey of the 'Have-Nots' in Rural and Urban America.* Available at: http://www.ntia.doc.gov/ ntiahome/fallingthru.html

US Department of Labor, (1999) *Report on the American Workforce,* Washington, D.C.: Bureau of Labor Statistics. Accessed on August 14, 2006

US Department of Labor, Bureau of Labor Statistics (2004) *Displaced workers summary,* 29 September, 2004. Available at: http://www.bls.gov/news. release/disp.nr0.htm. Accessed on August 14, 2006

US Department of Labor (2006) *Employment and training administration fact sheet'.* Available at: http://www.doleta.gov/programs/factsht/taa.htm. Accessed on August 15, 2006

Van Jaarsveld, D. (2004) 'Collective representation among high-tech workers at Microsoft and beyond: Lessons from WashTech/CWA', *Industrial Relations,* Vol. 43, No. 2:364-385

Wasko, J. (1998) 'Challenges to Hollywood's labour force in the 1990s', G. Sussman, & J.A. Lent, (eds), *Global Productions: Labor Making in the 'Information Society',* Cresskill: Hampton Press Inc.:173-189

Westfall, R. D. (2004) 'Does telecommuting really increase productivity?' *Communications of the ACM,* Vol. 47, No. 8:93-96

Willcocks, L. & S. Lester (1999) *Beyond the IT productivity paradox,* New York: John Wiley & Sons

XIWT (Cross Industry Working Team) (1995) *Nomadicity in the National Information Infrastructure.* Accessed on January 28, 2007 from http://www.xiwt.org/ documents/documents.html

Towards strategies for making offshore outsourcing economically and socially sustainable

Monique Ramioul and Tom De Bruyn

Monique Ramioul *is a research manager at the Higher Institute for Labour Studies at the Catholic University of Leuven in Belgium.*
Tom de Bruyn *is a senior research associate at the Higher Institute for Labour Studies at the Catholic University of Leuven in Belgium.*

ABSTRACT

This paper looks at the role trade unions and employee representatives can play in workplaces where offshoring and outsourcing projects are introduced. Starting with an overview of the literature on the employment impacts of offshore outsourcing, it highlights a strong contrast between the generally optimistic macro-economic studies focusing on the net effects, and the realities of offshore projects revealed through case studies, in which failure and mismanagement are common. It describes a situation in which increasing numbers of European trade unions, acknowledging that offshore outsourcing is 'here to stay', have reacted to this situation by developing a more pro-active approach to the introduction of outsourcing and offshoring which seeks to avoid the negative impacts on employees of failed or badly managed offshore outsourcing projects. Finally, the paper discusses the MOOS (Making Offshore Outsourcing Sustainable) project which exemplified this approach, aiming at contributing to a better informed and more effective role for employee representatives, to enable them to assess and influence the offshore outsourcing practices of their employers.

Fears and facts about offshore outsourcing

The fear of globalisation

In 2003 the European Commission published a Flash Eurobarometer on Globalisation (Sofres, 2003). More than 7,500 residents of the EU 15 countries were interviewed by telephone and asked about their opinions about the impact of globalisation in relation to several different social questions. Half of the respondents (52%) thought that globalisation ' has a rather negative effect on employment' in their own country, while 40% assessed the effects as positive. A breakdown by country shows that in France, Germany, Greece and Belgium a large majority (over 60%) does not expect much good from globalisation as far as employment is concerned. In most of the fifteen countries a majority of respondents had negative rather than positive expectations, and in countries where this expectation was positive it did not exceed 51% except in one case. This was in Ireland where 63% of respondents though that globalisation was beneficial. This is probably a reflection of the fact that the Irish economy, the so-called 'Celtic Tiger', has famously been a favoured destination for activities offshored from the United States.

The Spring 2005 Eurobarometer concludes that the dominant perception among EU citizens of the consequences of globalisation is that it leads to company relocation to countries where labour is cheaper. The fear of relocation is at its strongest in France (59%), Belgium (56%) and Germany (51%) but is lower in the Netherlands (13%), Lithuania (14%) and Latvia (14%). In so-called 'candidate states' which are currently outside the EU public opinion focuses more opportunities that globalisation might bring in terms of inward foreign investment, in particular in Romania (32%) and Turkey (30%) (TNS Opinion and Social, 2005:59-60). There are no straightforward explanations for these country differences but they might indicate a difference in the perceived employment effects of globalisation between typical 'source' countries from which work is more likely to migrate (in 'old' EU countries in Western and Northern Europe) and countries that can be identified as 'destinations', such as Ireland and the new EU Member States.

These results illustrate the fear of the employment impacts of globalisation that is widespread in Europe. The dominant sentiment among employees, trade unions and politicians is that increased globalisation will result in an acceleration of job moves and losses, downward pressure on wages and working conditions, and – more broadly – a loss of control in the economic sphere.

The facts about offshore outsourcing

In the meanwhile, intensified political interest in the increase in job relocations, especially in the IT and business service sectors, has prompted policymakers in several EU countries and at the international level to instigate a number of studies aimed at developing a better understanding of the scale, scope and impact of offshore outsourcing on their economies and labour markets.

National studies are sometimes based on (one-off) company surveys, asking companies about their practices and intentions with regard to offshore outsourcing, and sometimes on national statistics, depending on the quality of available national statistical indicators (which is highly variable within the EU). Most of these studies point to the macro-economic benefits of intensified globalisation. In general, they tend to conclude that the negative impact of relocation of IT and business services on employment, and in particular on high-skilled jobs, is offset by two factors. First, delocalisation is still more prevalent in the lower-skilled segments of the traditional manufacturing industries, where it is an established management practice, than in the IT and business services. This was for instance a key finding of a study commissioned by the Dutch Ministry of Economic Affairs (2005:5). Second, employment growth in the domestic labour markets in the IT and business service sector is likely to outweigh the job losses in these sectors. Such growth also includes the inflow of jobs from abroad. The latter conclusion was drawn in research carried out in Denmark (Rambøll Management, 2005), the Netherlands (ter Beek e.a., 2005) and the UK (Abramovsky, e.a., 2004).

It is necessary, however, to note some limitations and nuances of these optimistic conclusions. The Danish study, for instance, concluded that the combined effects of inflows and outflows was resulting in changes in the qualification structure of the Danish labour market in favour of high-skilled jobs and was thus to the detriment of poorly qualified, unskilled workers. Furthermore, a lot of studies, in particular offshore outsourcing forecasts, are based on questions addressed to managers asking if they would consider outsourcing and offshoring activities (see for instance Bloch 2005, Cap Gemini 2005, Rambøll Management 2005, Ministry of Economic Affairs, 2005). It is not unlikely that such subjective assessments, based on intention rather than actual existing practice, may be biased by wishful thinking or by perceptions of what is the most socially desirable answer.

A number of academics and international organisations have also attempted to map at a global level the scope and impact of offshore outsourcing activities, notably in the IT and business services sectors. Mapping cross-border labour movements in business services and IT, including multi-country analyses, is, however, impeded by a number of definitional, methodological and statistical problems as well as a lack of systematic data collection (such as reliable firm level data). One problem is that analysing relocation, both domestically and abroad, is still much easier for goods and manufacturing than for services. In comparison with physical goods, services pose the additional problem of their abstract and immaterial nature (see for instance Kirkegaard, 2004). The European Commission (2005a) has summarised the different sources that can be used for this, along with their shortcomings. These include trade data, FDI data, firm-level surveys and input-output data. Alongside this study, the European Monitoring Center for Change (EMCC) issued a Status Report on this issue in 2004 in an attempt to underpin the debate with more evidence (Huws, Dahlmann, Flecker, 2004). Another initiative by the EMCC that contributes to tracking the impact of offshore outsourcing on the job market is the European Restructuring Monitor (ERM). Based on the reports of national correspondents monitoring and registering newspaper articles, this ERM has, since 2002, compiled lists of restructuring events in companies with more than 100 employees and analysed them by such variables as the type of restructuring, the industrial sector, the country, the number of jobs involved.

Despite these methodological and statistical problems, several studies have provides interesting insights into the offshoring and outsourcing of IT and business service activities. The authors of the EMCC report, Huws, Dahlmann and Flecker, drew similar conclusions for Europe as a whole as the national studies cited earlier. An analysis of European employment trends in ICT and related services revealed no evidence of net job loss between 2000 and 2003. With the exception of Denmark, there was net growth in all Member States. In some countries, in particular in the new Member States and most dramatically in the Czech Republic, a very rapid growth of jobs in these sectors was recorded. However the authors pointed out that these results could have been an effect of outsourcing from other sectors and might conceal job losses in other sectors (Huws, Dahlmann &Flecker, 2004:23).

According to ERM records, between 2002 and September 2007, 8942 jobs would have been lost in Europe as a result of offshoring, relocation and outsourcing in the

IT sector and Consultancy and Business Services sector. Compared to job loss related to other types of restructuring - such as internal restructuring, bankruptcy or mergers and acquisition - offshoring, outsourcing and relocations were not the most important reason for job losses accounting only for approximately nine per cent of total reported job losses.

A study undertaken in the framework of the WORKS[1] project measured shifts in employment in business functions throughout Europe based on occupational and sectoral data from the European Community Labour Force Survey (Geurts, Coppin, Ramioul, 2007). This analysis concluded that there had been an overall growth in jobs related to IT services of 1.2 million (an increase of 76%) in the old EU Member States between 1996 and 2004 and of 86.000 (+35%) in the New Member States between 1999 and 2004. This study did not provide evidence of geographical moves of occupations related to IT services between the old and the new Member States.

The OECD has also carried out several international studies of relevance here including an investigation of which IT-related occupations are likely to be susceptible to offshore outsourcing. In its 2004 study based on occupational data, the OECD concluded that about 20% of total employment could potentially be affected by ICT-enabled offshoring of services (Van Welsum & Vickery, 2004). The category 'potentially affected by offshoring' did not just refer to activities that might leave any given country but also to those that might enter it or be generated internally. In business services, financial services and research and development the proportion was considerably higher. The authors also concluded that the share of occupations making intensive use of ICTs potentially affected by offshoring in total employment had increased steadily in the EU 15 countries between 1995 and 2003, whilst it had declined in Canada and the US and increased only slightly in Australia during the same period. Building further on this, the OECD published a further study (Van Welsum & Reif, 2006) examining the relationship between the proportion of employment potentially affected by offshoring and other economic and structural developments. Countries with a large service sector, a growth in the share of ICT investment as a proportion of fixed investment and abundant human capital are those more likely to have a high share of employment potentially affected by offshoring. This study suggests that the offshoring of ICT-enabled services has not yet resulted in a loss of jobs which make intensive use of ICT. Eventually, the researchers conclude, the positive effects of offshoring will outweigh the costs.

Finally, another recent OECD study on 'moving up the value chain' (OECD, 2007) concludes that the advantages of globalisation are to be found in the improved competitive advantages related to a more efficient international division of labour. For some countries this implies a growing specialisation in high-tech and knowledge-intensive activities when specialisation in traditional manufacturing and mass production is no longer a viable option (OECD, 2007:9). The OECD concludes that, in the longer term, the main impact of globalisation will be on the composition of

---

1   WORKS stands for Work Organisation Restructuring in the Knowledge Society. This four-year, seventeen-partner project was launched in 2005 with funding from the European Commission under its 7th Framework Programme. See http://www.worksproject.be for further information.

employment rather than on the level (OECD, 2007, p.8) and concludes that ' despite the short-term losses of employment, most economic analysis shows that there are considerable long-term benefits to globalisation and further economic integration between countries' (OECD, 2007:118).

All these studies aim to quantify the globalisation phenomenon, and in particular the offshoring and outsourcing of IT and business service activities, in terms of macro-economic labour market effects. They tend to qualify the fear that only negative effects are to be expected from global1sation, with jobs lost through the relocation of activities offset by inflow and job growth. They conclude that there appears to be no massive job export to new Member States or to the Far East; other forms of restructuring still produce much labour market impacts and in the longer term from these market adjustments benefit competitiveness. Nevertheless, it can hardly be denied that jobs are indeed moving: even based on a limited and debatable recording method (newspaper articles), the ERM reports almost 9,000 jobs destroyed in five years. It should also be noted that not one of these sources denies that there are any negative impacts either. Considering the limitations of the data, we might legitimately suppose that the total impact of economic globalisation is not fully captured to date.

The gap between facts and fears; the contrast between macro and micro.

The gap between the fears, as measured by the Eurobarometer surveys, and the facts and figures, as mapped in all these studies, is an interesting phenomenon, deserving of more detailed consideration. To start with, it illustrates considerable tension between macro-economic and meso- or micro-economic approaches in their investigations and assessments of economic globalisation. Economic globalisation is assessed as beneficial or detrimental depending on the perspective: macro- or micro-economic; company or employee; source or destination region. There are several possible explanations for this gap. First, the obvious lack of reliable data for analysing the international employment flows related to offshore outsourcing is one reason why not only citizens but also policymakers often overestimate the effects of increased offshoring. Huws, Dahlmann, Flecker point out in their study that, because of the lack of reliable indicators, the current popular discourse on offshoring has been characterised by a somewhat hysterical tone : 'On the one hand, simplistic and scaremongering prophecies foretell large-scale job losses amongst the white-collar workforce of the developed world, whilst on the other optimistic win-win scenarios are presented in which the globalisation of the market for information services brings benefits both to developed and developing countries.' (Huws, Dahlmann, Flecker, 2004:1).

A second problem that is evident in most of the studies is that the aggregation level of the statistics used in the analysis can be decisive for the outcome. To state it simply: the more macro-economic the statistics, the more optimistic the outcome seems to be. These broad-brush results suggest that offshore outsourcing does not affect the aggregate level of employment overall, but nevertheless the process of sectoral restructuring that it triggers (or is triggered by) is found to be associated with significant employment flows from one sector to another (European Commission, 2005b). Most studies do acknowledge that at the meso (sectoral-) level and at the micro (enterprise) level the observed and expected macro-economic benefits are often difficult to accept when in the short term the only result that is recorded is job loss (or absence of job growth). The analyses at aggregate (national or EU-wide) levels typically disguise the qualitative shifts that are taking place underneath. At a Europe-wide workshop on 'the effects of relocation on economic activity: an EU perspective' concluded that ' the relocation of economic activities also entails risks in terms of employment losses and increased inequality that are likely to affect specific regions, sectors and low-skilled workers' . The conclusion that it is mostly lower skilled and unqualified jobs that are at risk, draws attention to the fact that both the depth of the analyses and the effectiveness of the policy conclusions would benefit from attention to the qualitative effects of offshore outsourcing, not just the quantitative ones (European Commission 2005b).

In addition to these problems it is not always easy to assess all the publications on their statistical reliability and validity. Conclusions that offshoring initiatives will grow in the future based on expressions of intentions may not be very likely either to give an accurate picture of trends or to contribute to a public opinion in favour of offshoring. Surveys that record intentions rather than actions are notoriously biased by what are considered to be socially desirable answers. However, the public audience will draw the conclusion remains that almost any job might be affected.

A final explanation for the gap between facts and fears is the contrast between the macro-level analysis and discourse and the micro-level experience of single relocation events, where the net job losses are clear and quantifiable. The time dimension plays a part in this. Collective redundancies related to the relocation of activities happen immediately, while any (macro-economic) benefits - in terms of competitive advantages, more growth due to improved productivity and innovativeness - are simply nice promises for the future. But they do not help the workers who have to look for a new job straight away and who do not have any reason to believe they themselves will benefit from any improved competitiveness. In addition, and more importantly in the context of this article, there may also be a contrast between the rather optimistic macro-level approaches and the day-to-day experiences of employees of companies involved in offshore outsourcing projects.

The main background for this latter argument is the observation that offshore outsourcing projects do not always run as smoothly and unproblematically as expected. These observations are backed up by statistics that show high failure rates in offshore outsourcing projects. Depending on the source, failure rates are estimated at between 40% and 50%. Gartner (2003) estimated in 2003 that 6 billion was wasted because of failed projects. Although figures from consultancy firms may be biased by a wish to sell advice, it is nevertheless evident that some companies do indeed have a very limited experience of offshoring and are unaware of how many organisational challenges arise and the full extent of the costs that occur in the process of planning to relocate part of their business. Even more convincing support for the proposition that such difficulties are underestimated is provided by case study research. When these include the views of employees, they can uncover a contrast between the success stories often presented in management handbooks and the promotional leaflets of consultants and real life experiences. In the next section we will focus in more detail on the some of the key findings related to success and failure that can be derived from case study research on offshore outsourcing in IT and business service activities.

Relocation of work: the illustrative power of worst practice cases

Two international research projects provide illustrations of factors that may explain the success or failure of offshoring and outsourcing projects. In 2001, four case studies were carried out in the Benelux region as part of the international research project EMERGENCE[2]. The focus of these case studies was on 'eWork', defined as information-processing work carried out at a distance with extensive use of computer systems and on the basis of telecommunication links. Each case study dealt with a trans-regional or cross-border relocation of eWork from a source location to a destination location. The case studies focused on work relocation in shared office-type premises (as opposed to relocation to individual home-based or mobile workers). The Benelux case studies included the offshoring of a credit card company back office, the outsourcing of a citizen's information point to a call centre; the offshoring to India of part of the software development for a high-tech product and the concentration in a shared services centre of the sales activities of a sports manufacturer.[3] In the WORKS project, the concept of the business function, originally developed in the EMERGENCE project, was also used as a window for understanding restructuring in companies in selected sectors and thus as the basis for further case studies, including a Belgian case study carried out in 2007 that investigated the offshoring of export administration from one site to a specialised shared services centre was investigated[4]. In both research projects, data collection was conducted at the workplace level using qualitative interview methods with management representatives as well as several employees and their representatives.

These five case studies clearly showed not only that outsourcing, and especially offshore outsourcing, projects may run less smoothly than expected, but also contained examples of failed projects, including one cases where the decision to outsource and relocate abroad was reversed and activities were brought back in house again. These cases, and in particular the less successful ones, demonstrate that what seems technologically and even organisationally feasible in the planning phase may encounter serious obstacles in the actual process of implementation. A first problem was the systematic underestimation of the costs of offshore outsourcing projects, an issue also attested in management handbooks on offshore outsourcing (Carmel & Tija, 2005; Robinson, Kalakota, 2005). These included one-off investments required to set the

---

2   EMERGENCE stands for Estimation and Mapping of Employment Relocation in a Global Economy in the New Communications Environment. Between 2000 and 2003, research partners in Australia, Austria, Belgium, Canada, Denmark, Germany, Hungary, Italy, Sweden and the UK, with associates and subcontractors in many other countries are undertaking a range of related research activities, full details of which can be found on http://www.emergence.nu.

3   The results of the case studies are described in detail in De Jonckheere, Ramioul, Van Hootegem (2003)

4   This case study is described in more detail in Ramioul (2007)

project up, including location search and partner choice and contract negotiation. In addition, managing remote working implies recurrent overhead and co-ordination costs (WTO, 2005:270; De Bruyn & Ramioul, 2006:20). As a result, project leaders faced higher losses than they had expected and had to recalculate returns on investment.

A second finding from the case studies was that there was a systematic underestimation by the management of the importance of the the the day-to-day experiences and tacit knowledge of employees for sustaining a smooth and uninterrupted production process and for solving the problems, both big and small, that tend to arise during the execution of the work (Kirschenhofer & Flecker 2002; Huws, 2003; Ramioul, 2004). The kind of knowledge needed for the day-to-day work mostly comes to the surface only in the context of reorganisations which entail a systematisation, codification and documentation of the entire range of work processes, tasks and work-related knowledge. This is a process that inevitably remains incomplete (Ramioul, 2007:10). Even in relatively standardised and well-documented work processes, unclear task demarcations, communication problems, incomplete knowledge transfer etc. may create bugs and hamper a 'seamless' work process over distance. Consequently, the period needed to transfer the work tended to be longer than expected, the learning period to train the new employees for the transferred tasks had to be more intensive than planned and the employees in the source company had to continue carrying out tasks after they were already supposed to have been transferred. It became increasingly clear that the relocation of work cannot simply be implemented overnight. On the contrary, it often appears to be a protracted learning process. This learning process is related especially to the need for a clear-cut division of work and the formalisation of knowledge, to requirements for elaborate and explicit communication procedures and practices and to the need to take into account the cultural aspects of co-operation over a distance.

The case studies also demonstrated the importance of regular meetings and systematic communication between all staff involved during the project implementation. Successful relocation seemed to be shaped by a climate of co-operation and trust between the employees at the source and destination locations and by a continuous transfer of knowledge and information. Such a co-operative atmosphere was created only if those concerned at the source location were actively involved in the decision-making and relocation process and if the relocation did not lead to a threat to their jobs and cutbacks in the content of their work.

Finally, these case studies made it apparent that the role of the employees of the source company often remains crucial and that the links between source and destination cannot be broken easily. The most common tasks that remained for workers in the original locations were providing general support for the employees working at the other end, quality control, prototype development, 'disaster management', training of remote employees and an playing active role in the transfer of the tasks and the knowledge.

Trade unions in Europe have been drawing lessons from the day-to-day experiences of their members at the workplace, the evidence from case study research and the published figures on outsourcing. Taken together, these have contributed to an increasing belief in union circles that, from the perspective of employees, failed offshore projects are worse than successful ones. The case studies from the WORKS and EMERGENCE projects provide graphic evidence of the extent to which employees involved in these project have to summon up reserves of loyalty and flexibility in a difficult company context of complex, and sometimes successive, restructurings. As a result, some unions have concluded that they too have a role to play in preventing disasters due to bad management. Trade unions in Europe are therefore becoming increasingly convinced that they need to gain a greater understanding of management outsourcing and offshoring strategies. This insight was one of the main drivers behind the Making Offshore Outsourcing Sustainable (MOOS) project, on which we now focus.

Responses of trade unions to offshore outsourcing

A shift from resistance to acceptance

The increased offshoring of activities and the growing awareness that 'offshore outsourcing is here to stay' (Rohde, 2005) is increasingly prompting trade unions and politicians in Western European countries to change their approach towards offshore outsourcing. In addition to the fact that unions too consider themselves to have a general interest in a macro-economic prosperous, growing and innovative economy, they also believe that badly managed or even failed offshore outsourcing may bring considerable tangible and intangible costs for the employees concerned.

In a presentation on offshore outsourcing for UNI-IBITS affiliates (Union Network International – Industry, Business & Information Technology Services), the UNI-IBITs head of department, Gerhard Rohde stated that with the growth of offshore outsourcing in IT and business services, it is not only managers and IT specialists who need new skills (such as complex project management skills, communications and inter-cultural sensitivity), but also employee representatives (Rohde, 2005). According to Mr. Rohde, they need firstly to understand the legal aspects of outsourcing contracts and of the impact on the workforce, secondly to build up awareness of which activities are liable to be outsourced in the future, thirdly to acquire expertise in assessing the risks and opportunities of offshore outsourcing projects, and finally to become competent in collaborating with employees and their representatives in destination countries as well as to try to develop the capability to negotiate with employers in supra-level bodies.

To support a proactive role in preventing failure and making offshore outsourcing socially and economically sustainable as well as to develop such new competences, the trade union movement needs a clear and pan-European union strategy as well as expertise and tools to advise, train and support employee representatives in the field. However, here too it seems difficult to reconcile the macro- and the micro-perspective. A shift from a protectionist and defensive position towards a proactive and offensive one, let alone towards active collaboration with the management, is not obviously attractive, especially to unions that are simultaneously confronted with an increase and acceleration in all kinds of company restructuring, including outsourcing and offshoring, and the related job losses, downward pressure on wages and working conditions, demands for flexibility and feelings of powerlessness and uncertainty.

A typology of union responses

The European Industrial Relations Observatory (EIRO, 2006:12 ff) carried out a European comparative study on the relocation of production. This demonstrated that trade unions in the EU apply a mix of different strategies to address offshore outsourcing processes. They group these into three main types.

The first approach can be labelled a restrictive and interventionist reaction, aimed at reducing the possibility of relocations. This includes, for instance, the demand to return public subsidies if activities are offshored, attempts to negotiate agreements committing the employer to maintain production at a certain location for a minimum number of years and demands aimed at ensuring that the social costs of offshore outsourcing, such as mandatory training or redeployment provisions, are fully reimbursed.

The second approach is the traditional union practice of promoting the role of negotiation and social dialogue at the firm level. Information disclosure and consultation procedures for the workforce are crucial to this approach, as well as negotiations to achieve collective agreements. This approach also promotes co-operation between the unions and the workforce in the different countries affected, together with the harmonisation of working conditions between these countries.

The third approach is more proactive. It is not explicitly directed at regulating the relocation of production but rather at fostering the development of activities and employment creation in high skilled sectors. This approach seeks to promote the development of sectors in which the country has a comparative advantage in comparison to other countries. In addition, in this approach, trade unions co-operate to a certain extent with the company management in order to reduce the negative social consequences of offshore outsourcing and to support training and innovation policies. This proactive position presupposes a participatory framework for a developed social dialogue at different levels. The importance of each approach in the overall union strategy varies from one country to another and from one union to another depending on the economic and institutional context as well as the characteristics of the relationship between the social partners. In practice, elements of all three approaches are present in the positions of most unions and a comprehensive union strategy draws on actions from each of them.

However, strategies to address the effects of globalisation are not only deployed at a national level, or at the level of particular industrial sector or within (transnational) companies. Both national unions and international trade union associations are having to develop new types of international collective action as a reaction to the increasing global organisation of capital and management. In his overview of recent labour movement trends, Kelly (2005: 297) identifies three main forms of international union action: solidarity action with groups of striking workers; mobilisation in conjunction with other social movements targeted plants of particular companies in developing economies (e.g. clean clothes campaigns); and mobilisations focused around international agencies such as the World Trade Organisation (for instance in alliance with the anti-globalisation movement). International unions also engage in trying to organise the employees of relocating companies in developing countries. The efforts of UNI-IBITS to organise IT and business service employees in India is an example of such a strategy (Karin Hirschfeld, 2005). This article focuses on one particular union project which provides an interesting illustration of the shift in union strategies towards a more proactive response to globalisation. This is the MOOS project which was set up with the aim of developing a better understanding of how offshore outsourcing projects are designed and implemented at the company level and giving effective support to employee representatives to enable them to contribute to the economic and social sustainability of these projects.

The MOOS Project: towards sustainable offshore outsourcing

The MOOS project started in December 2004 and was commissioned by the European Social Fund of the EU. The project involved the white collar, professional unions of six European Member States (Belgium, Denmark, France, Germany, Sweden, and the Netherlands) and one research institute (Higher Institute for Labour Studies, Katholieke Universiteit of Leuven, in Belgium). UNI-IBITS, the international white collar union for IT professionals, coordinated the project.

The objectives of the MOOS project were threefold. First, it aimed to inform employee representatives about the underlying dynamics, scope and impact of offshore outsourcing. Second, it aimed to collect more information in these countries about offshore outsourcing initiatives in the knowledge that employee representatives are often well placed to know about pending restructuring initiatives within their companies, region and country. Third, it aimed to provide tools for employee representatives to help them anticipate offshore outsourcing processes in the company and find ways to develop a strategy to render the offshore outsourcing processes more socially sustainable from an employee perspective in both the source and the destination country. While managers have an increasing number of tools at their disposal to assist them with offshore outsourcing, employee representatives have not. It was hoped that MOOS's role in helping employee representatives become better informed might contribute to limiting the failure rate of offshore outsourcing initiatives in the belief that it is also in the interest of the workers in the source company that problems should be resolved and failure prevented. Apart from the impact of offshore outsourcing on jobs, functions, working conditions, wages etc., which form the traditional bargaining agenda for unions, there are also other concerns related to the ways that the day-to-day organisation of work impacts on the quality of working life and the quality of production, that imply that workers can not just stand aside and watch or protest.

The key objectives and principles that the MOOS project wanted to address were: involvement and participation of employees and their representatives; no unilaterally imposed changes; avoidance of compulsory redundancies;

protection of the terms and conditions of employment for existing employees; effective redeployment of existing employees displaced by the introduction of offshoring; the right to training, assistance and support if alternative employment is necessary; reinvestment of the savings from offshoring with a share of the financial savings made by offshoring to be invested in employee skill development, to increase the adaptability and employability of workers; and core labour standards to be observed in offshore destination countries, including those relating to collective organising and bargaining. This package includes many of the more traditional trade union demands, as well as elements of the proactive approach.

To achieve these objectives, the MOOS project developed a range of tools and instruments targeted at employee representatives, such as a website (www.moosproject.be) and a handbook on offshore outsourcing complemented with training material and seminars to build the capacities of employee representatives to enable them to contribute to the day-to-day management of offshore outsourcing projects in their organisations.

The MOOS handbook (De Bruyn & Ramioul, 2006) was designed to involve employee representatives in their employers' strategy on outsourcing and in the assessment of the feasibility of the plans and their implementation. It thus combined information with guidance.

The handbook treats all stages of a 'typical' offshore outsourcing process. Starting from the initial informal stages when the idea is first mooted by management, it deals with the bidding process, due diligence procedures, pilot projects, contract negotiations, the definition of Service Level Agreements and other contractual aspects, up to the monitoring of the implementation and the final evaluation. The active involvement of employee representatives at every stage is elaborated as a 'check-list' with key principles of appropriate employee involvement and action.

Five main steps are distinguished. First, the importance of anticipation of offshore outsourcing plans is stressed: 'what are possible signs and indicators that the company may have plans to outsource? what jobs are suitable for outsourcing and vulnerable? What might be the motives and drivers of the firm and how can these be assessed?'. Second, employee representatives are encouraged to develop a proactive approach by means of offshore outsourcing agreements and social plans.

A third part of the handbook focuses on developing a proactive approach to the anticipation of problems and failure, a so-called 'risk assessment'. This risk assessment includes an evaluation of the possible goals that the company wants to achieve with offshore outsourcing (cost reduction, expansion of activities, close to market strategies etc.) and guidance on how to assess whether the business model chosen is indeed the best answer. In addition a comprehensive overview is included of all the possible (and often overlooked) costs related to offshore outsourcing, both one-off costs (location search, contract negotiation, and training) and recurrent costs (monitoring, communication, travel...). It also addresses organisational, human related, cultural and other 'intangible' dimensions that are generally decisive for the final outcome of an offshoring project. Practical tools, such as an 'efficiency test' and templates are provided, along with best practice examples of offshore outsourcing agreements.

A fourth chapter focuses on the implementation of the offshore outsourcing project, with a discussion of issues related to the tendering process and the selection of the destination. Finally, the negotiation process is discussed: aspects of the transition process, service level agreements, the monitoring of the transfer and the established collaboration and eventually an evaluation of the whole process, including the assessment of the role of the social dialogue.

A dedicated page on the MOOS website was also developed in order to provide additional information about national and international regulations that are relevant for outsourcing and to enable updates. The site also includes a framework for negotiation, taking account of all possible consequences for the employees and based on UNI principles.

Conclusions

There remains a considerable gap between, on the one hand, the positive messages about globalisation that are expressed in a lot of macro-economic studies, and, on the other, the day-to-day reality of how offshore outsourcing projects are implemented in companies. The first stresses both the limited overall impact on employment levels and the expected benefits in terms of competitiveness and productivity. Employees, by contrast, are confronted with redundancies, neglected tacit knowledge that risks beng lost, increasingly complex working environments, communication and information problems and other negative effects. In addition to the obvious downward pressure on their wages and working conditions, the employees that are affected also have to deal with the insecurity and stress that are typically generated in organisations undergoing restructuring.

Within this context, the aims of the MOOS project may be called ambitious. One aim was to explicitly address the issue of offshore outsourcing at the company and workplace level, a level that is often underestimated in the public debate but that touches directly on the consequences for those primarily affected. Further, the project wanted to bring about a shift from a protective and defensive attitude against globalisation towards a more proactive approach and to develop tools that allow employee representatives to contribute to successful offshore outsourcing projects. Raising awareness about future relocations, increasing their expertise in anticipating risks and failures and strengthening negotiation and consultation rights were the most important ingredients of this strategy. The main message behind the project was that offshoring and outsourcing can be acceptable management strategies if rules and procedures are applied correctly and if the restructuring process is managed in a sustainable way, with a balanced and fair involvement of the interests of all stakeholders in the organisation.

Although the tools were developed interactively with inputs from the unions at all levels and seem likely to be widely adopted, it is still too early to assess the extent to which they have actually led to changes in the agreements reached in offshore outsourcing situations and, even more importantly, to assess the impact of such agreements on actual practices within companies. In its focus on the company level, the project has put some new issues on the agenda but also left some important questions unanswered.

First, it must be asked to what extent employees are convinced by the argument that cooperating with the employers will make it possible to manage offshore outsourcing to their benefit, and, more generally, can such responses from trade unions contribute to a shift in attitude from a fear of globalisation to a proactive approach aiming at sustainable work for all.

Second, it is still not clear how the ambitious ideas of influencing the offshore outsourcing process can be reconciled with mundane realities that form the daily business of employee representatives. What is their room for manoeuvre in processes which are often guided by macro-economic and global rationales?

Third, it is necessary to ask what role is left for national regulation and industrial relation models in a globalised economy? How do national contexts impact on the opportunities for employee representatives to influence offshore outsourcing processes?

A fourth challenge is how to reconcile the interests of employees and their representatives in source countries with those of their counterparts in destination countries?

A final underlying question, not dealt with explicitly in MOOS, is of crucial importance: will globalisation affect the strength of the labour movement, locally, nationally or internationally? Some grounds for a rather optimistic answer to this question are offered by Kelly (2005:298). On the one hand, he points out that 'institutions and politics matter'; national differences in labour rights and protection and in workers' rights and conditions under similar global competitive pressures clearly demonstrate that states and institutions still enjoy a considerable degree regulatory discretion. On the other hand, he points to the inherent contradictions of capitalist globalisation, including the fact that its expansion inevitably goes hand in hand with the expansion of working classes and hence with organised labour movements (Kelly, 2005:299). Another contradiction is the increased vulnerability of globally organised production processes to disruption caused by collective action (Kelly, 2005:300). The lengthening of value chains, resulting from the growth in offshoring and outsourcing of a variety of business activities contributes to the increasing interconnectedness of production and labour processes and a growing interdependency of regions around the globe. Collective action - or any kind of disruption - in one link of the chain, especially where there are regional instabilities, is likely to affect the effective functioning of the whole chain. The case study findings from failed or nearly-failed offshore outsourcing projects presented briefly in this article seem to suggest that employees play a decisive role in the practical implementation and effectiveness of economic globalisation. Without their co-operation, it cannot succeed.

© *Monique Ramioul and Tom de Bruyn, 2008*

REFERENCES

Abramovsky, L., R. Griffith & M. Sako (2004) *Offshoring of Business Services and its Impact on the UK Economy*, AIM Research: Oxford

Bloch, L-K. (2005) 'Offshoring creates jobs', summary of the study *Jobskabelse gennem globalisering*, note provided for the MOOS project committee, Stockholm. June 2005

Cap Gemini (2005) 'Outsourcing Pulse Survey'. Accessed on 18 April 2005 from http://www.capgemini.com/resources/news/outsourcing_survey_results/

Carmel, E. & P. Tjia (2005) *Offshoring Information Technology. Sourcing and Outsourcing to a Global Workforce*, Cambridge: Cambridge University Press

De Bruyn, T. & M. Ramioul (2006) *Offshore Outsourcing. A Handbook for Employee Representatives and Trade Unionists, Geneva:* UNI-IBITS

Dejonckheere J., M. Ramioul & G.Van Hootegem (2003) *Jobs on the move - Benelux case studies in relocating eWork,* Leuven: HIVA-Katholieke Universiteit Leuven

European Commission (2005a) *The EU Economy Review. Rising International Economic Integration. Opportunities and Challenges*, Brussels: European Commission

European Commission (2005b) 'Summary Conclusions', DG-ECFIN Workshop, *The Effect of Relocation on Economic Activity: An EU Perspective,* Brussels, 21 June 2005, ECFIN/E(2005) REP53517

European Industrial Relations Observatory (2006) *Relocation of Production and Industrial Relations.* Accessed on 1 March 2007 from http://www.eiro.eurofound.ie/2005/11/study/tn0511101s.html

European Restructuring Monitor (2007). Accessed on 1 October, 2007 from http://www.eurofound.europa.eu/emcc/erm/index.php

Gartner (2005) 'Gartner Says Companies Must Invest in New Skills and Staff to Benefit from the Move to Outsourcing. Shortage of Skills to Manage IT Outsourcing Partnerships Poses Critical Threat to European Business', Gartner Press Release, 1 October 2003

Geurts K., L. Coppin & M. Ramioul (2007) 'Tracing employment in business functions. A sectoral and occupational approach', WORKS Project report D9.2 *The transformation of work?* Part 1. Accessed on 1 October 2007 from http://www.worksproject.be/Subgroup_2_proj_reports.htm

Gorter J., P. Tang & M. Toet (2005) *Verplaatsing vanuit Nederland (Relocation from the Netherlands)*, CPB document n° 76, Den Haag: Centraal Planbureau

Hirschfeld K. (2005) 'IT professionals forum in India: organisation at a crossroad', Berlin', Ref. 03-2005/0011, unpublished paper, Geneva: UNI

Huws U. et al (2003) *When work takes flight: final report of the EMERGENCE project*, IES Report 397, Brighton: Institute for Employment Studies

Huws U., S. Dahlmann & J. Flecker (2004) *Status Report on Outsourcing of ICT and Related Services in the EU*, Dublin: European Foundation for the Improvement of Living and Working Conditions

Kelly J. (2005) 'Labor Movement and Mobilization', *The Oxford Handbook of Work & Organization,* Oxford: Oxford University Press:283-304

Kirkegaard, J.F. (2004) 'Offshore Outsourcing - Much Ado About What', *CESifo Forum*, Vol 2, No. 5:22-29

Kirchenhöfer S.& J. Flecker (2002) *Jobs on the move: European case studies in relocating eWork,* IES Research Report 386 , Brighton: Institute for Employment Studies

Ministry of Economic Affairs the Netherlands (2005) *Vision on Relocation, the nature, extent and effects of relocating business activities*, Research Series, The Hague: Ministry of Economic Affairs

OECD (2007) Staying competitive in the global economy. Moving up the value chain, OECD report, Paris: OECD

Rambøll Management (2005) 'Opportunities and consequences of globalisation for the Danish labor market – A regional perspective', unpublished paper, Copenhagen: Rambøll Management

Ramioul M., U. Huws & S. Kirschenhofer (2005) *Offshore outsourcing of business services,* Dublin: European Foundation for the Improvement of Living and Working Conditions - European Monitoring Center of Change

Ramioul M. (2004) 'Delocalisatie in de informatie-economie, mogelijkheden en grenzen: illustraties van goede en slechte praktijken (Relocation in the information economy:illustrations from good and bad practices)' in G. Van Hootegem & B. Cambré B (eds), *Over Werkt(t) in de actieve welvaartstaat,* Leuven:Acco:57-75

Ramioul M. (2007) 'Global value chain restructuring and the employment relationship', ISA Conference *New challenges in work and employment,* Montréal, 28-30 August 2007

Rohde G. (2005) 'Opening Session', *First international MOOS conference*, Paris, 10 February 2005

Robinson, M & R. Kalakota (2004) *Offshore Outsourcing. Business Models, ROI and Best Practices, Alpharetta:* Mivar Press

Sofres, T.N. (2003) *Globalisation. Flash eurobarometer* 151b, Brussels: European Commission

Ter Beek H.M., H.S. Dekker, J.W.M. Mevissen & H.A.Weening (2005) *Offshoring in de Nederlandse ICT: grenzeloze kansen (Offshoring in the Dutch ICT: opportunities without boundaries?)* Research carried out by Regioplan Beleidsonderzoek commissioned by Raad voor Werk en Inkomen, Den Haag

TNS Opinion & Social (2005), *Standard Eurobarometer* 63 Spring 2005, Public opinion in the European Union, Brussels: European Commission

Van Welsum D. & G. Vickery (2004) *Potential offshoring of ICT-intensive using occupations,* Paris: OECD

Van Welsum D. & X. Reif (2006) *The share of employment potentially affected by offshoring - An empirical investigation,* Paris: OECD

World trade Organisation (2005) 'Offshoring services: recent developments and prospects', *World trade Report 2005, Exploring the links between trade, standards and the WTO.* Accessed on 15 February 2006 from http://www.wto.org/english/news_e/pres05_e/pr411_e.htm:265-302

South African trade unions and globalisation:

going for the 'high road', getting stuck on the 'low road'

Marlea Clarke and Carolyn Bassett

Marlea Clarke *is a post-doctoral fellow in the Labour Studies Programme at McMaster University in Canada and a research associate of the Labour and Enterprise Policy Research Group at the University of Cape Town in South Africa.*
Carolyn Bassett *is an assistant professor at the School of Social Sciences at York University in Toronto in Canada.*

ABSTRACT

In this paper, we assess the South African labour movement's engagement with globalisation in the 1990s and its implications for labour politics in the following decade. Drawing on extensive archival research and interviews with key informants, we show that, although the labour movement had become committed to a 'high road', post-Keynesian restructuring vision by 1993, its representatives failed to pursue that vision consistently in the economic policy negotiations that preceded the historic 1994 democratic election. In fact, labour delegates actually agreed to several policy changes that were more in line with a 'low road', neo-liberal approach, with dramatic implications for workers in some sectors. The inability of labour's engagement with globalisation to benefit the working class has led to a long search for a new basis for union strategy.

Introduction

In the 1980s and 1990s, unionists and researchers looked to South Africa for inspiration. Like workers' movements in Brazil, South Korea and other industrialising economies with authoritarian governments, South Africa's working class mobilised against incredible odds and was able to realise significant industrial and workplace gains while playing a pivotal role in broader processes of political change. In contrast to the decline in union density, membership and organisational strength experienced by unions elsewhere, South African unions grew in size, strength and political significance during the 1980s and early 1990s. Indeed, the Congress of South African Trade Unions (COSATU), the country's largest labour federation, seemed to offer a way forward for working class politics in an era of globalisation that other movements around the world could look to for inspiration and guidance (Moody, 1997; Munck, 2002). Moreover, the election of a sympathetic government in the country's first democratic election in 1994 seemed to promise that labour would retain considerable influence in reshaping the economy and society, compared to the more conservative transitions seen in countries like Brazil (Cardoso 2002).

Yet, precisely at the time when people were celebrating the breakthroughs of 'social movement' unionism in South Africa, the search for effective ways to operate on the new terrain where politics was being 'normalised' ran into roadblocks. As we shall see, COSATU steadily moved away from its social movement unionism approach and tried to use newly established tripartite forums to advance its worker-centred vision for socio-economic change – a vision that was increasingly shaped by the post-Keynesian 'progressive competitiveness' approach advocated by the labour-aligned Industrial Strategy Project (ISP). Although much has been written about the labour movement's role in the transition and its subsequent political marginalisation in the post-apartheid period (Adler & Webster, 1995; Von Holdt, 2000; Webster & Buhlungu, 2004), few have examined how COSATU engaged with globalisation and the implications of its approach for the policy framework, the labour market, and labour's ability to organise and represent those most negatively affected by economic restructuring. We argue that labour representatives interpreted globalisation as trade and investment liberalisation, and engaged with these challenges associated with global market integration in the early 1990s in a way that proved to be a major constraint on labour politics in the following decade, limiting the labour movement's ability to deal with the impact of economic reforms in the post-apartheid period.

Three central claims are advanced First, COSATU's focus on social partnership to promote global competitiveness was fraught with problems and pitfalls. The strategy itself – what we have termed a 'high road' restructuring vision (based on a post-Keynesian approach) – was too narrow and inadvertently accepted the deepening of labour market segmentation. Even if this strategy had been successful, only a fraction of unionised workers would have benefited, and it would have been largely irrelevant, or even harmful, to workers in sectors that were vulnerable to foreign competition, those that were not unionised, and the marginally employed or unemployed. Second, the policy-making process was problematic and resulted in the labour movement accepting key compromises. As will be outlined below, labour representatives agreed to several policy changes that were more in line with the 'low road' neo-liberal approach they claimed to be counteracting with their post-Keynesian proposals, with dramatic implications for workers in vulnerable sectors. Third, COSATU's involvement in tripartite forums under a social partnership framework limited the union movement's ability to challenge globalisation and represent those most affected by economic restructuring. Its leaders' eagerness to secure access to, and participate in, policy processes led them to prioritise technical approaches over continuing to build an engaged, broadly-based movement.

As we shall see, COSATU quickly became aware of the limitations of its strategy and began to develop different approaches and policies – some rooted in past practices of social movement unionism – but an alternative strategy has been slow to emerge. The last section of this paper will examine recent developments that suggest that COSATU is decisively moving away from its social partnership approach and focusing on rebuilding the labour movement in order to better challenge neo-liberal globalisation. These changes are significant in a context where new opportunities – but also new dangers – may be arising, associated with the government's renewed proposals for a developmental state that incorporates organised labour within its vision. Moreover, there are lessons for other unions and working class organisations as they, too, seek new strategies for progressive working class politics under globalisation. This is particularly the case in other industrialising societies, like Brazil and Argentina, where labour has also played a significant political role and where the possibility of joining a 'developmental state' project has been mooted in recent years under more sympathetic governments (Chibber, 2004; Etchemendy & Collier, 2007; Beynon & Ramalho, 2001). South African unions failed so dramatically because they focused on attempting to reach a consensus plan to co-manage capitalism with representatives of capital and the state, rather than taking the needs of their membership and the working class more broadly as their starting point. In future, unions in industrialising developing countries would be wise to recognise what South Africa's unions have now accepted and ensure that they do not prioritise consensus, or economic growth, ahead of employment creation, good wages and working conditions, and the provision of basic public services to improve the living conditions of the majority.

Debating labour strategy under globalisation

The neo-liberal restructuring of the globalisation era has presented dilemmas for labour that have been widely recognised both in practice and in theory (Ross, 2000; Frege & Kelly, 2003; Therborn, 1984). The retreat of labour, whether measured in terms of union density, membership, capacity to organise new constituencies of workers or policy influence, has become a central theme in the literature on the industrialised countries. Increasingly, organised labour has been portrayed as a victim of the vicissitudes of global capital rather than as an agent with the potential to shape the nature of restructuring.

Despite the seeming disempowerment of workers under globalisation, some authors have posited labour strategy options that could improve the socio-economic outcomes for the working class. Two approaches are of particular interest. Some authors have advocated post-Keynesian policies as offering a way for states to reconcile high wages with global economic competitiveness – a high-tech, high-wage, high-road strategy. Direct and indirect state involvement in investment decisions, with labour unions on board (to secure their consent to limit income growth), has been the cornerstone of this approach (Arestis, 1996). The 'high-road', post-Keynesian, 'progressive competitiveness' policy framework has been roundly criticised, however, by some analysts as an inappropriate strategy for labour because its policy goals were not designed to further workers' interests, but rather to improve the functioning of capitalism (Albo, 1994; Zuege, 1999; Panitch, 1994; Gindin, 1997).

While the 'progressive competitiveness' approach focused on effective policies to engage with globalisation, the alternative approach centred on union purposes, structures and practices. Both led to a general consensus: the re-building of the union movement was of pressing importance. Researchers and unions in Britain, Canada, Australia and other industrialised countries have now begun to focus on union renewal strategies (Fairbrother & Yates, 2003). Although some proposals have limited their focus to membership expansion, others have undertaken a more rigorous examination of union strategies and purposes, and have called for a reorientation of union activity towards social movement unionism. Some unions and researchers have gone so far as to suggest not only that this type of unionism is more effective than the traditional 'service model', but that it is the only type able to counter the effects of neo-liberal globalisation on workers and their communities (Moody, 1997).

This focus on union renewal and social movement unionism has generated renewed interest in some of the highly mobilised labour movements of the global South, such as those in South Africa and Brazil. Gay Seidman's work on social movement unionism has explored the similarities between these two geographically disparate movements. She defined social movement unionism as 'an effort to raise the living standards of the working class as a whole, rather than to protect individually defined interests of union members' (Seidman, 1994: 2). The concept of social movement unionism captures labour's role as a social and political actor in struggles around housing, transportation and various municipal services, and the fusion between workplace and community-based struggles in apartheid South Africa.

The importance of this fusion between labour organising and broader social struggles and movements has been highlighted by Moody (1997) and Ronaldo Munck (2002). Moody emphasises the broader relevance of rejuvenating unionism world-wide in the face of the assaults of globalisation, claiming that 'successful unionism in today's integrated world must be social-movement unionism' (1997: 205). Panitch (2000) concurs that it is more essential than ever for labour to focus on building a broadly based movement that focuses on developing the democratic capacities of the working class to demand radical changes instead of attempting to co-manage capitalist restructuring.

Curiously, before union renewal strategies in industrialised countries were launched, and before much of this scholarly material had been published, the political context in South Africa had already begun to change, affecting COSATU's commitment to social movement unionism. The legalisation of the African National Congress (ANC) in 1990 and the introduction of other political reforms resulted in the ANC quickly moving to exert its leadership over the broad anti-apartheid movements. Though legalisation of the ANC and majority rule had been among the main objectives of the union movement, these developments also meant that they had to find a new approach suitable for the transitional and post-apartheid situation of labour. And, as will be discussed below, a range of other political reforms and substantial changes to the industrial relations system ran parallel to the legalisation of the ANC, offering organised labour a voice in policy-making.

In a dramatic departure for the federation, COSATU's leadership turned in the direction of a so-called 'high-road', post-Keynesian, 'progressive competitiveness' approach, whereby labour's new role would be to devise and negotiate new strategies for capitalist restructuring. At the time, this approach was perceived as enhancing COSATU's influence in the rapidly changing policy environment (Habib, 1997). COSATU's leadership and academic advisors were inspired by the Australian social-democratic experiment. Johann Maree (1993:46-47) argued that:

'The Australian Accord [between the Australian Labour Party and the Australian Confederation of Trade Unions] demonstrates to South African trade unions *what can be achieved by corporatist agreements under the appropriate conditions, but also some of the pitfalls to avoid. It shows that unions can enter into such arrangements as the senior partner with the state and that it does not imply a domination of labour by capital. The Australian unions also set examples of how to enter into co-operative relations with employers without compromising either their autonomy or rank and file participation. They have done so by developing their own industrial strategies by drawing on experts while, at the same time, ensuring extensive consultation with the rank and file to ensure that the experts remain both representative of and accountable to the rank and file of union membership.'*

Adler and Webster were among the leading academics in this debate, arguing that institutionalised policy negotiations and social movement unionism were at least potentially complementary, and, indeed, that concertation could push social movement unionism to a new level (Adler & Webster, 1995). Webster (1996:3) suggested that

'the innovative part of South Africa's response to neo-liberalism [has been] the crucial role of the [COSATU-SACP-ANC] Alliance in acting as a "left pressure" on the ANC. This dynamic, where labour is powerful both on the streets and in the centres of power, was described as a process where COSATU is both "inside and outside the state".'

Although Adler and Webster noted a growing gap between the leadership and the base in COSATU in the early 1990s, and anticipated that labour leaders would face pressure to prioritise economic development ahead of workers' needs, they nonetheless remained optimistic that the progressive potential of the trade union movement would remain alive. As we show below, similar optimism played out among labour leaders themselves, at least at the national level, in the first half of the 1990s, until COSATU began to move away from the co-management strategy in 1996-97.

Several writers have argued that labour has been marginalised from the economic policy process (Buhlungu, 2005; 2002; Bassett, 2005). There is much evidence to support this claim, especially during the ANC's first five years in power. However, we believe that this presents an incomplete picture of labour's engagement with economic restructuring, especially the situation prior to 1994. To focus only on labour's marginalisation in the policy processes misrepresents COSATU as a victim of neo-liberal globalisation, rather than an actor that participated in the restructuring decisions that soon affected workers. Certainly, in South Africa, as elsewhere, one of the main effects of neo-liberal globalisation has been a weakening of the organisational, economic and political effectiveness of unions. However, an analysis of labour's participation in developing economic restructuring proposals reveals the complexities of labour's struggle in a rapidly shifting political and economic environment.

The remainder of this paper focuses on these issues by uncovering the direct involvement of COSATU and other labour federations in several policy decisions centred on the tripartite National Economic Forum (NEF), where labour representatives put forward proposals for a post-Keynesian economic programme and where they participated in and supported key decisions that put South Africa firmly on the road to neo-liberal restructuring. The specifics of the policy process within the NEF have received surprisingly little attention in the academic literature on the transition and that on labour politics. Here, we draw on extensive archival research on internal policy proposals, minutes and reports as well as interviews with some of the key participants to show that, early in the economic restructuring policy process, the labour delegates were not excluded from the key decisions by the state and capital – they were active agents and collaborators. We also utilised interviews with labour leaders and participant observation in the critical late 1990s period, as well as published materials, to document the growing disillusion among labour activists with the achievements of the economic policy negotiations and the search for new strategies to reassert working class politics, including some efforts to re-establish the tattered social movement unionism of the earlier era[1]. Our conclusion reflects on the broader lessons not only for trade unionism under globalisation in South Africa, but also in similar industrialising economies such as Brazil and Argentina.

Social dialogue, globalisation and the economic forums

The non-racial trade unions seldom engaged in policy dialogue with the apartheid government before the late 1980s. Instead, these unions focused on building strong workplace structures while also taking up a range of broader social and economic issues facing the working class. This social movement unionism approach that had characterised the black trade union movement in the 1970s was maintained when COSATU was formally launched in 1985.

Although the federation remained committed to social movement unionism, COSATU began to change its approach to policy issues in 1988, when itmobilised against proposed amendments to the Labour Relations Act that would have undermined a decade of gains. The unions forced business and the government to involve them in developing a new legal framework for industrial relations. The agreement reached, and the process involved, were significant breakthroughs for the unions, beginning to shift policy formulation outside Parliament to bilateral and tripartite processes (du Toit et al., 1998:15).

The initiation of democratic negotiations in the early 1990s inspired further efforts to influence the economic programme by engaging with government and business

---

1   Carolyn Bassett spent 1996 and 1997 undertaking dissertation research in Johannesburg. She viewed primary documents (especially minutes, policy proposals and position papers) from the NEF, NEDLAC and the member organisations at the NEDLAC offices, additional COSATU documents at the National Labour and Economic Development Institute (NALEDI) resource centre, and government documents in the government document repository at the University of the Witwatersrand library. She interviewed more than fifteen key participants in the process, including labour representatives (including Mark Bennett and Martin Nicol); academics who supported the labour delegation (Stephen Gelb and James Heinz); NEF and NEDLAC staff (Lael Bethlehem, Jayendra Naidoo and Shan Ramburuth) as well as engaging in dozens of informal discussions with people familiar with the processes. Marlea Clarke undertook fieldwork in South Africa (primarily Cape Town) for her dissertation as well as related research labour market research between 1997-2003. She also carried out archival research at NEDLAC and the COSATU NALEDI archives, and interviewed approximately 30 labour leaders and relevant government officials, including Neil Coleman and Kenneth Creamer of the COSATU Parliamentary Office; senior labour leaders Ebrahim Patel and Connie September, lawyer Paul Benjamin and NEDLAC staff Philip Dexter and Wendy Dobson. She also had the opportunity to learn (off the record) from numerous informal discussions with labour leaders and government officials. Both authors have remained in touch with contacts in South Africa and have made periodic short trips for research and conference purposes.

(Baskin, 1993; Von Holdt, 1993). Unions turned their attention to economic and industrial policies and to broader issues of workplace and economic restructuring, which required them to 'engage' with globalisation in a new way. During protests against a new Value Added Tax (VAT) in 1991, COSATU demanded that the government establish a macro-economic policy-negotiating forum (SALB, 1991). Trade unionist Ebrahim Patel (1993) claimed that this forum would allow labour to help shape policies rather than just fighting their effects. After months of discussions, labour and business agreed to create the National Economic Forum (NEF) in March 1992, which would consider monetary, fiscal, trade and industrial policy.[2] Government was invited to join, which it agreed to do by the year's end (Patel, 1993). The three member constituencies agreed that delegates would secure mandates from their constituencies before seeking consensus on policy issues[3]. COSATU believed that it could use the NEF to forestall neo-liberal restructuring prior to majority rule and extend the arena of democratic decision-making and the power of the working class. Labour leaders thought that these new institutional spaces would regularise their interactions with the state and capital, and that capital would be forced to play by the same rules, which would limit and channel its power (Baskin, 1993).

In December 1994, a few months after the ANC came to power, legislation created the National Economic Development and Labour Council (NEDLAC), which succeeded the NEF and the National Manpower Commission (responsible for labour market policy issues). The NEDLAC legislation gave the forum legal status, government funding, a permanent secretariat, and a mandate to consider all proposed labour legislation and all significant changes to social and economic policy (South Africa, 1994b). NEDLAC maintained the NEF's membership basis, adding a 'community' constituency to some of its policy deliberations. The establishment of NEDLAC meant that labour's direct participation in economic policy-making was institutionalised in the post-apartheid governing regime.

The election of the ANC created new opportunities and new challenges for labour in the forums. The opportunities resulted from their alliance with the government around a common restructuring vision. The Reconstruction and Development Programme (RDP), which had been developed by the ANC, the South African Communist Party, COSATU and allied organisations in 1993, became the ANC's electoral platform (ANC, 1994). Rhetorically, at least, the RDP remained a common programme in the post-election period. The legislation that established NEDLAC called on the institution to 'mobilise the entire South African society behind these objectives of the RDP' (South Africa, 1994a). The challenges were rooted in the ambivalence of the ANC to NEDLAC, which had been expressed as early as 1993, when ANC leaders raised objections to the scope of the NEF's powers (Friedman & Shaw, 2000), and in

---

2   Labour market policy remained in the National Manpower Commission, a government advisory body that the non-racial labour federations joined in 1993.

3   The labour delegation was comprised of three non-racial trade union federations that together accounted for about half of the country's unionised workers. In addition to COSATU, the National Council of Trade Unions (NACTU) and the Federation of South African Labour (FEDSAL, also known as the Federation of Salaried Staff), which is now called the Federation of Unions of South Africa (FEDUSA) participated. About one half of unionised workers were either members of independent (non-federated) unions or of race-based unions, or both, and were therefore excluded from NEF/NEDLAC.

some of the weaknesses within the alliance around policy issues that began to surface in the years following the election. Further, liberalisation and other forms of neo-liberal restructuring had already been initiated by the previous regime and, to a certain extent, were endorsed by the ANC. The election of the ANC, therefore, did not guarantee that labour's post-Keynesian vision of restructuring would be supported and advanced by the new government.

Labour's 'high road' global restructuring vision

COSATU succeeded in creating the economic policy forum before it had fully developed the content of labour's restructuring program. Once at the NEF, labour delegates proposed an economic restructuring vision that emphasised state-business-labour partnerships to make South African industries more globally competitive. As this section shows, this new, 'high road', post-Keynesian labour vision promised benefits only to a narrow section of the working class, who, by and large, were already relatively secure in their labour force positions, while reducing the employment security of a substantial segment of workers.

Traditionally, organised labour had emphasised job retention, job creation, better wages and workers' rights. COSATU's late-1980s Living Wage Campaign insisted that all workers should receive a reasonable living wage to cover basic food, housing, transportation and educational costs for themselves and their families (Baskin, 1991). The campaign also demanded job security, centralised bargaining, an end to privatisation and stronger labour market regulation, including an end to temporary and casual work and sub-contracting, and elimination of the racial wage gap. However, these kinds of demands were difficult to put forward in the forums – they were designed for public campaigns and grassroots mobilisation rather than for negotiation with business and state representatives.

COSATU began to develop economic restructuring proposals for the negotiations at a special conference in 1992, which recommended a two-tier approach to industrial restructuring: basic goods industries for the domestic market, and a 'cutting edge', highly competitive export-oriented sector (COSATU, 1992). Domestic restructuring using training and investment – rather than wage cuts – to increase productivity and international competitiveness would be followed by trade liberalisation and export promotion. This approach embraced capitalism and global integration, but also good working conditions and social stability – a post-Keynesian approach. Patel (1994) described it as the 'new unionism', reflecting a shift from consumption issues to investment strategies and their implications for the labour market.

Growth and investment were further emphasised in the NEF. Seeking a suitable language and style of engagement, labour turned to sympathetic policy professionals in the Macro-Economic Research Group (MERG) and the Industrial Strategy Project (ISP), several of whom sat as labour delegates at the NEF. It was through these relationships that a handful of prominent senior COSATU unionists became champions of post-Keynesian industrial restructuring. Although COSATU remained opposed to deregulatory proposals from business for new labour legislation, labour's proposals were shaped by the ISP's post-Keynesian assumptions that certain forms of flexibility were both acceptable and desirable. Many of labour's policy recommendations at the NEF were derived directly from MERG and ISP documents, even when these conflicted with long-standing labour objectives.

According to the ISP's analysis, South Africa's deficiencies could be traced to the decline of the manufacturing sector under the import substitution industrialisation programme of the apartheid regime. Therefore, the ISP (1994) proposed a managed trade and industrial strategy with specialised manufacturing in 'higher value-added' areas, utilising selective temporary protection while sectors with long-term competitive potential built up their capacity. They also recommended training, improved work organisation, and enhanced technological capacity to improve productivity, with lower wages in some sectors (Joffe, Kaplan, Kaplinsky & Lewis, 1995). A consistent theme in labour's ISP-based recommendations was that capitalism functioned inefficiently in South Africa, so the goal of economic reform was to make firms more competitive in national and international markets. This implied that successful economic transformation should be judged by market criteria, not social criteria.

Job creation had been central to COSATU's vision, but when the ISP found that employment creation was incompatible with manufacturing competitiveness, jobs were sacrificed (ISP 1994). Even though employment creation was usually mentioned in the introduction to labour's proposals, which were based on the ISP approach, there was seldom any further reference to the employment implications (NEF, 1992; 1993b; 1994). The ISP dropped the goal of building basic needs industries for the domestic market, saying that liberalising this sector would benefit low-wage consumers more, a position that had negative implications for job quality and quantity.

The strategy labour put forward at the NEF, which emphasised the 'high-road' vision of managed competitiveness and abandoned the commitment to social protection and manufacturing for the local market, would benefit only a portion of COSATU's own membership and the broader working class[4]. Although COSATU did not acknowledge this, the strategy was destined to reinforce a segmented labour market benefiting that small group of unionised workers in core sectors of the economy that were likely to become globally competitive, while reinforcing the marginalisation of the informal, temporary and casual workforce. Unionised male workers in the most secure and competitive industries were in the best position to benefit from enhanced international competitiveness and training to improve their productivity, while other unionised workers, especially black women workers in vulnerable manufacaturing

---

4   The post-Keynesian vision was designed to benefit those manufacturing workers employed in sectors that would be amenable to productivity improvements associated with higher levels of training and technology, in order to become more competitive in terms of price and quality on international markets. Only a small portion of the workers represented by COSATU – and in the South African labour force more generally – met these criteria. By their nature, service sector workers, ranging from retail to the public sector, were not included in the vision. Nor were workers in clothing, textiles and footwear, sectors that would realise few productivity improvements through training and new technologies, likely to benefit. Moreover, the main impact of new technologies and training on sectors like mining, food, beverage and other natural resource-based sectors would be job loss. Even acknowledging that there would be some workers who would benefit from post-Keynesian restructuring who were not represented by COSATU, we can conclude from this analysis that the number to benefit would be a relatively small portion of the total labour force and would be those workers who were already in a relatively privileged position.

sectors, would face unemployment and were seldom candidates for training because their industries were the least likely to become globally competitive. By allowing South Africa's international competitiveness to become the main goal, labour abdicated its social justice and transformation agenda. Although reading the ISP program alongside traditional labour programmes like the Living Wage Campaign and the recommendations arising from COSATU's 1992 labour policy convention demonstrates that the ISP's recommendations contradicted many traditional labour objectives, their proposals nevertheless shaped labour's recommendations at the NEF and NEDLAC for several years.

The tendency to rely on experts at the NEF coincided with a breakdown in the mandating and report-back processes within COSATU. Researchers Chris Lloyd and Stephen Rix (1995) found that a core group made decisions without proper debate within the movement, at times committing COSATU to policies whose orientation was precisely the opposite of the wishes of the membership. An internal study conducted in 1993 found that worker-leaders, women and local organisers were not participating sufficiently in policy development, which negated democratic decision-making and mandating and led to a weakening of campaign structures (Patel, 1993). Not surprisingly, COSATU members, and working people more generally, never fully accepted the trade-offs the labour delegation had made at the NEF in anticipation of developing a new growth model, particularly when the *quid pro quo* of training and new jobs did not come to fruition. Job creation and retention remained a strong priority with many unions and workers.

The failure of the vision

Although COSATU helped to create the NEF in pursuit of a post-Keynesian vision, the labour delegation failed to insist on this approach in the policy negotiations. Instead, they allowed the government to set the agenda in a number of areas, winding up merely negotiating details, which led them to agree to policies that virtually foreclosed their high-road vision. This meant that, in practice, labour promoted a form of neo-liberal global integration that placed even greater segments of the working class in a highly precarious situation.

Perhaps the most significant example of labour's concessions in policy negotiations was the government's 1993 proposal to liberalise tariffs. The government wanted trade liberalisation to become the core of an overall industrial restructuring strategy (DTI, 1993; Naudé, 1992). The position of the labour delegation, strongly influenced by the ISP, generally supported the rationalised tariff structure. Their industrial policy submission recommended exposing domestic producers to international competition because they 'recognise[d] the high-powered, productivity-enhancing incentives that flow from market relations' (NEF, 1993b). COSATU explained:

'We have to address the challenge of restructuring our industrial economy. We cannot resort to high levels of protectionism since in an increasingly integrated world economy the co-existence of large disparities between domestic and international prices creates a political economy that is not viable and is inimical to the interests of the working class.' (COSATU, 1993)

Instead of simply liberalising tariffs, the unions wanted to develop an active industrial strategy in which industrial restructuring support measures preceded tariff liberalisation.

However, COSATU's post-Keynesian approach was hijacked by the 'emergency' nature of the negotiations leading to the revision of South Africa's GATT offer. The labour delegation allowed the government to set the agenda, timetable and terms for discussion. The basis for discussion was the government's 1990 offer to the Uruguay Round of GATT, and the GATT's response to the offer, which demanded substantial tariff reductions and the elimination of extensive quantitative restrictions and export subsidies (Hartridge, 1993). The government insisted that business and labour should make their comments on the GATT proposal within five weeks of bringing it to the NEF (DTI, 1993). The perceived urgency prevented consideration of how to support domestic firms, industries and workers in adjusting to the liberalised tariff regime by promoting industrial restructuring, job creation and job retention. It also limited the extent to which forum delegates could consult with their constituencies. The government must have known, at least for several months, about the impending GATT deadline, but chose not to place the proposals on the agenda sooner, thus limiting both the policy discussion and participation in that discussion.

Securing agreement on the GATT offer strengthened the hand of certain actors within the state and the private sector (especially the mining, mineral and related companies) to promote industrial restructuring via trade liberalisation rather than a state-guided process. Yet there was no outcry from the trade unions: negotiator Ebrahim Patel accepted that the urgency of the GATT offer prevented broader consultations (NEF, 1993a). Labour's willingness to expedite the deal meant that trade liberalisation went ahead before any accompanying industrial restructuring program – on which there was little consensus – was in place.

In contrast with its inability to shape trade and industrial policy in the ways it had initially envisioned, COSATU had far more success in realising its demands for labour law reforms. The ANC met the labour movement's insistence that new labour legislation should create a more co-operative industrial relations system with an increased role for organised labour, while also promoting economic growth and international competitiveness. New laws marked a major advance for organised labour[5]. COSATU played a critical role in shaping the new regulatory framework and was a strong force in the newly established tripartite labour institutions.

Despite labour's success in advancing its demands in new labour laws – especially in comparison with its ability to defend workers' interests in trade policy and other areas of economic reform – the resulting regulatory framework still had significant loopholes and weaknesses, largely due to the government's concessions to pressures from the national and international business community for increased labour market flexibility.

---

5   The new Labour Relations Act (LRA) formalised and codified organisational rights, laid a basis for worker participation in the workplace, granted workers a meaningful right to strike (without fear of dismissal), introduced a new dispute resolution system, provided strong support for collective bargaining and extended coverage to most workers. The new Basic Conditions of Employment Act (BCEA) improved employment conditions for many workers and extended rights and protections to some workers who had previously been excluded from legislative protection.

A key weakness in the framework was that protection was limited to those workers in 'standard employment' (full-time, permanent work with one employer) (Clarke, 2004; 2006). Self-employed workers such as homeworkers and owner-drivers (self-employed truck drivers), task-based workers and all informal workers fell outside the definition of 'employee' in the new laws and were therefore not protected. Furthermore, even though the Basic Conditions of Employment Act formally included most casual workers, many temporary and fixed-term contract workers were effectively excluded since benefits were structured on the basis of a model of full-time, continuous employment (Clarke, 2004; 2006). Indeed, even Paul Benjamin, one of the drafters of the new statutes, has acknowledged that these laws have failed to protect the most vulnerable workers: the informal, temporary and casual workers (interview, July 23, 2003). These weaknesses, plus extensive flexibility provisions in the laws, have proven to be especially significant for vulnerable workers when combined with other aspects of economic restructuring that have increasingly encouraged employers to favour unprotected and unregulated forms of employment, such as informal, temporary and casual work (Clarke, 2006). The rise in unemployment and various forms of casual and temporary work has meant that a large and growing percentage of the workforce falls outside regulatory protection and union organising.

Faced with this growth in unemployment, informalisation and casualisation, it soon became apparent that support for trade liberalisation did not extend very deep within the labour movement. Few of the broader membership knew that labour delegates had committed to the GATT offer on their behalf, and many were actively opposed to it, calling for South Africa not to 'join' or 'sign' GATT (Lloyd & Rix, 1995). This was particularly the case for workers and union leaders within the manufacturing sectors that were most vulnerable to competition from imports, such as clothing, textiles and 'white goods.' Protests against the tariff reduction process grew when trade liberalisation accelerated in the absence of effective industrial support measures, resulting in more job losses in vulnerable sectors after 1994. It was an embarrassing moment for COSATU when the trade minister revealed that labour representatives at the NEF had consented to the GATT deal less than two years earlier.

Soon after this, the ANC government confirmed its commitment to neo-liberal global integration (and its rejection both of interventionist, post-Keynesian approaches and of growth through redistribution) with the announcement of its economic restructuring program, Growth, Employment and Redistribution (GEAR). One of GEAR's primary aims was to attract foreign investment, which the government saw as key to reviving growth. Therefore the emphasis on state-led development and redistribution in the RDP was replaced with a focus on trade and market liberalisation, debt reduction, spending cuts, and the privatisation of state assets and public utilities – including water, electricity and waste management at the municipal level. GEAR ushered in a period of heightened tensions between COSATU and the ANC (Webster, 2001; Buhlungu, 2005; Bassett & Clarke, 2008). By now it was apparent that labour's earlier promotion of 'high road', post-Keynesian-inspired global competitiveness had permitted the introduction of the very neo-liberal approach that they had attempted to forestall. As we shall see in the next section, the impact on workers has been severe.

South African workers and globalisation

Global integration and economic liberalisation have contributed to the 'job crisis' in the country, and created a distinct set of 'winners' and 'losers' in the post-apartheid labour market. Unionised black workers in full-time, permanent employment in core sectors of the economy are amongst the 'winners', due to improved labour and social rights, collective bargaining protections and contractual benefits. Training processes put in place by new labour legislation and strengthened collective bargaining in some sectors have meant that many full-time unionised workers in skilled occupations within the public and industrial sectors have had their skills upgraded, earned real wage increases and realised significant improvements in a range of employment benefits.

The strong auto industry provides one example. Vehicle exports grew nine-fold between 1994 and 2004. By 2005, the automotive industry – including the manufacture, distribution and servicing of vehicles and components – was the third-largest sector in the economy, accounting for nearly 7% of exports and contributing 7% to GDP (DTI, 2005). Rising production and improved collective bargaining agreements resulted in secure, stable employment with rising wages and benefits for many auto workers, with skilled workers benefiting especially. A three-year agreement signed in 2004 between the National Union of Metalworkers of South Africa (NUMSA) and the Automobile Manufacturers Employers Organisation (AMEO) provided for secure, stable employment with rising wages as well as benefits that included new study assistance schemes and full wages for four months' maternity leave. However, such 'winners' in global economic restructuring were far outnumbered by the unskilled and semi-skilled workers who saw their wages and working conditions decline or under threat (Woolard & Woolard, 2005). Tariff reform, public sector restructuring (largely through privatisation), and workplace reorganisation put downward pressure on wages and working conditions in many sectors (Clarke, 2006; Godfrey et al, 2003; Kenny, 2003). For example, public sector restructuring through privatisation, outsourcing and subcontracting pushed many workers into poorly-protected jobs in the private sector. In agriculture, marketing boards and price stabilisation measures were abolished to increase competitive pressures on the sector, while new labour standards were extended to farm workers without effective protection of their jobs, resulting in retrenchments and the growth of poorly paid and unprotected casual and temporary employment (du Toit & Alley, 2001; Ewert & Hamman, 1996).

Within manufacturing, tariff reduction had a particularly dramatic impact on the clothing and textile industries. Intensive tariff liberalisation in the mid 1990s led clothing manufacturers to rely increasingly on imported cloth, and domestic textile industries suffered Clothing firms responded to the more competitive environment by outsourcing and sub-contracting more of their production to unregistered (informal) factories and to small home-based operations. Retailers, meanwhile, began sourcing clothing directly from small, informal clothing producers as well as taking advantage of the lower tariffs to increase clothing imports from China and other low-wage regions. Overall, formal employment in the clothing, textile and footwear sectors declined by an estimated 64,000 jobs between January 2003 and June 2006 (Kriel, 2006). These job losses were only partially compensated by a rise in informal, home-based work. In all, the sector saw a decline in both employment quality and quantity.

The impact of liberalisation and flexibilisation has been devastating for many workers and communities, leading to rising inequalities, pervasive poverty, and a deepening jobs crisis. Job insecurity is rife and the gains initially won by labour are now being eroded, with mounting employer offensives cutting into union membership and power. Some of the country's mainstream economists have recently acknowledged the negative impact of liberalisation on many sectors, evident in the spread of unemployment and unregulated and unprotected employment to 38.3% of total employment (Bhorat & Hinks, 2006:9). It was found in 2004 that only 40% of the economically active population (and approximately one-third of economically active Africans) were employed in full-time occupations (Barchiesi, 2004). From this perspective, the growth of casualised, flexible work has been a central aspect of liberalisation and globalisation, not a reflection of the failure to incorporate a large segment of the population into globalisation.

This outcome was not unprecedented, but labour's embrace of globalisation as a strategy to improve the material situation of workers was destined to reinforce segmentation because it protected and benefited a declining core of relatively skilled workers, while accelerating downward pressure on the wages and working conditions of many other workers and reinforcing the marginalisation of informal, temporary and other precarious workers. Rising unemployment, and the expansion of various forms of precarious employment, has affected the labour movement itself, both in terms of declining membership levels and in highlighting the need for new strategies to organise and represent an increasingly fragmented working class.

Signs of a new response from labour

Beginning in 1996, labour's policy proposals began to turn away from advocating global economic competitiveness and towards demands for higher levels of social protection. However, as already indicated, this gradual shift in union policy had little impact on government policies and the processes of economic restructuring that were under way. And, although COSATU attempted to develop a more independent trade union position in cooperation with other labour organisations, the first new initiative reasserted labour's priorities within a post-Keynesian model:

'First, we need a series of active industrial policy measures to improve efficiencies and the performance of companies. Then, we need a pragmatic programme which lowers tariffs carefully, and not faster than required under the terms of the General Agreement on Tariffs and Trade. Simultaneously – not afterwards – we need to put into place a set of social adjustment programmes which will absorb, retrain and then place into new jobs those workers who are displaced by restructuring. ... The trade union movement accepts the need to open our economy, but we require a process that is carefully managed and sequenced in order to avoid job losses.' (COSATU, NACTU & FEDUSA, 1996)

Labour remained in NEDLAC, but began using this forum to assert policies that would defend workers against the ravages of liberalisation, in conjunction with campaigns and strategies that reflect a much more defensive perspective on jobs and globalisation than in the 1993-1996 period. This new approach has contributed to the marginalisation of NEDLAC, but the government had effectively abandoned the forum as a policy-making institution by 1996 in any case (Bassett, 2004). Strikes and protest actions against casualisation and job losses have been on the rise in recent years, punctuated by a general strike in 2006, a further sign that labour has begun to challenge the global restructuring agenda rather than attempting to engage with it. One of the specific initatives to protect their members' positions, especially workers in the clothing and textile industries, has been the Proudly South African campaign, which marks a shift in union responses to globalisation away from the push for a post-Keynesian strategy to a more protectionist and defensive approach.

More recently, COSATU has begun to re-think its orientation, strategies and approach. Although the union movement has continued to embrace the social partnership model, despite its failure and the waning influence of unions on both government and business, the last several years have seen a slow move back towards linking labour with community struggles. Alongside this shift, labour's policy proposals have moved more into line with traditional worker demands. For example, the People's Budget campaign, developed by COSATU in conjunction with the South African Council of Churches and the South African NGO Coalition, focused on redirecting government spending towards addressing poverty directly with policies that meet basic needs, create quality jobs, help the majority to acquire assets and skills, support democratic, participatory governance, and protect the environment (PBC, 2005). The call for a Basic Income Grant (BIG) similarly emphasised reducing poverty by providing a small monthly grant to all citizens (COSATU 2003b). The federation's Toward 2015 programme identified job creation, better pay and reduced inequality as labour's most important economic policy goals (COSATU 2003a).

In addition, the federation has started re-focusing on organising and mobilising vulnerable workers and has initiated new campaigns to challenge directly the restructuring linked to neo-liberal globalisation As in union renewal initiatives elsewhere, COSATU has begun to examine its structures, strategies and purpose with the aim of strengthening and rebuilding the union movement. For example, for the first time since COSATU was formed, organisational reforms became a key focus of debate at the federation's sixth national congress in 1997. Virtually all the recommendations on strengthening the federation's structures put forward by a union-appointed research committee, the 'September Commission', were adopted. The congress also adopted recommendations regarding the launching of an organisational renewal campaign, including proposals to organise causal workers. Two years later, the federation launched its Jobs and Poverty campaign as one way to challenge the ongoing job losses, high levels of poverty and growing inequality associated with restructuring. This campaign remains in place, with the federation outlining new actions in May, 2006.

Accompanying their reconsideration of the benefits of globalisation for workers, and resulting revisions to their policy framework, unions are beginning to shift their attention away from 'high politics' back to community issues that respond to the impacts of restructuring at a local level in working class communities, resulting in new forms of organising around the country. One indication of this shift is the federation's increased attention to rebuilding its relationship with other civil society organisations, especially the new community-based groups that began organising around a range of socio-economic issues in the late 1990s. The renewed focus on working with social movements to address unemployment, poverty and inequality culminated in a Jobs and Poverty Conference in 2007. These moves suggest that COSATU is, perhaps, finally and decisively moving away from the framework of engaging globalisation by trying to transform economic processes and policies from 'within', and instead shifting back towards a more defensive, community-based approach characteristic of social movement unionism.

Conclusion

In this paper, we have examined the bumpy road COSATU and other labour federations have followed in seeking to engage with globalisation. At first entranced with the idea that globalisation could be shaped to the benefit of South African workers, the federation failed to pursue this path consistently and instead made policy concessions that rendered its approach unfeasible. The results were soon apparent – though some workers benefited, many experienced the impact of globalisation in the form of informalisation, casualisation, unemployment, dislocation and poverty. But the significance of this case study relates to more than poor policy choices – it is about the reorientation of a union movement around a social partnership model that failed to deliver, and the slow process of rebuilding towards the social movement unionism that once was. The South African case demonstrates what theorists of labour strategy like Leo Panitch (2000) have argued: that trade union politics must be rooted in the needs of the working class (however seemingly unfeasible) rather than a desire to co-manage capitalism, especially based on a consensus with capital. The unprecedented challenges that globalisation presents for workers should not obscure longstanding trade union dilemmas associated with building a movement that genuinely represents and empowers workers and seeks to incorporate the working class as a whole into its political project. The temptation to be drawn into co-management schemes may be stronger in industrialising societies because the need for economic growth convinces labour leaders that they must prioritise economic development over specific worker demands, but in most cases the risks of doing so are actually higher because they exacerbate trends towards income polarisation and casualised work – precisely the building blocks for neo-liberal global integration. The question of how to develop an effective trade union response to globalisation cannot easily be answered, but the experiences of South Africa's unions should nonetheless serve as a cautionary tale to other labour movements in similar economies.

© Carolyn Bassett and Marlea Clarke, 2008

REFERENCES
Adler, G. & E. Webster (1995) 'Challenging Transition Theory: The Labor Movement, Radical Reform, and Transition to Democracy in South Africa', *Politics and Society*, 23.1:75-106
ANC (1994) *Reconstruction and Development Programme*, Johannesburg: Umanyano Publications
Albo, G. (1994) 'Competitive Austerity and the Impasse of Capitalist Employment Policy', in R. Miliband & L. Panitch (eds), *Socialist Register, 1994*, London: Merlin
Arestis, P. (1996) 'Post-Keynesian Economics: Towards Cohesion', *Cambridge Journal of Economics*, 20
Bassett, C. (2004) 'The Demise of the Social Contract in South Africa', *Canadian Journal of African Studies*, 38.3

Bassett, C. (2005) 'Labour and hegemony in South Africa's first decade of majority rule', *Studies in Political Economy*, 76

Bassett, C. & M. Clarke (2008) 'The Zuma Affair, labour and the future of democracy in South Africa'. *Third World Quarterly*, 29.4 [forthcoming]

Buhlungu, S. (2005) 'Union-Party Alliances in the Era of Market Regulation: The Case of South Africa', *Journal of Southern African Studies*, 31:4: 701-717.

Barchiesi, F. (2004) 'Class, Social Movements and the Transformation of the South African Left in the Crisis of "National Liberation"', *Historical Materialism*, 12.4:327-353

Baskin, J. (1991) *Striking Back: A History of Cosatu*, London: Verso

Baskin, J. (1993) 'The Trend towards Bargained Corporatism', *South African Labour Bulletin*, 17 (3):64-69

Benjamin, P. (2003), Interview, Cape Town, July 23

Beynon, H. & J. Ramalho (2000) 'Democracy and the Organization of Class Struggle in Brazil', in L. Panitch and C. Leys (eds), *Socialist Register 2001*, London: Merlin

Bhorat, H & T. J. Hinks (2006) *Changing Patterns of Employment and Employer-Employee Relations in post-Apartheid South Africa*, Cape Town: Development and Policy Research Unit (DPRU)

Buhlungu, S. (2002) 'From "Madiba Magic" to "Mbeki Logic"', In S. Jacobs and R. Calland (eds), *Thabo Mbeki's World*, London: Zed:179-198

Buhlungu, S. (2005) 'Union-Party Alliances in the Era of Market Regulation: The Case of South Africa', *Journal of Southern African Studies*, 31.4:701-717

Cardoso, A. M. (2002) 'Neoliberalism, Unions, and Economic Security in Brazil', *Labour Capital and Society*, 35.2

Chibber, V. (2004) 'Reviving the Developmental State? The Myth of the National Bourgeoisie', in L. Panitch & C. Leys (eds), *Socialist Register 2005*, London: Merlin

Clarke, M. (2004) 'Ten Years of Labour Market Reform in South Africa: Real Gains for Workers?', *Canadian Journal of African Studies*, 38.3

Clarke, M. (2006) *'All the Workers'? Labour Market Reform and Precarious Work in Post-Apartheid South Africa, 1994-2004*, PhD Dissertation, York University, Toronto

COSATU (1992) 'Economic Policy in COSATU: Report of the Economic Policy Conference,' March 27-29

COSATU (1993) 'Trade Unions, Economic Development and Industrial Policy', Input Paper to CGIL, CUT, COSATU Conference, September 15-16

COSATU (2003a) 'Consolidating Working Class Power for Quality Jobs – the Toward 2015! Programme', 8th National Congress, Johannesburg, September

COSATU (2003b) 'Coalition for a Basic Income Grant', Press Statement, December

COSATU, NACTU & FEDUSA (1996) 'Social Equity and Job Creation: the Key to a Stable Future', Johannesburg, May

DTI (2005) *Current Developments in the Automotive Industry 2004*. Retrieved August 17, 2005 from http://www.thedti.gov.za/midp/automotives.htm

DTI (1993) 'South Africa's Tariff Offer in Terms of the Uruguay Round of Multilateral Trade Negotiations', Presented to NEF, July

Du Toit, A. & Alley, F. (2001), *The Externalization and Casualisation of Farm Labour in Western Cape Horticulture*, Unpublished Research Report, Cape Town: Centre for Rural Legal Studies

Du Toit, D., D. Woolfrey, J. Murphy, S. Godfrey, D. Bosch & S. Christie (1998) *The Labour Relations Act of 1995*, Cape Town: Butterworth

Etchemendy, S. & R. B. Collier (2007) 'Down but not Out: Union Resurgence and Segmented Neocorporatism in Argentina (2003-2007)', *Politics and Society*, 35.3

Ewert, J. & J. Hamman (1996) 'Labour Organisation in Western Cape Agriculture: An Ethnic Corporatism', *Journal of Peasant Studies*, 23 (2/3)

Fairbrother, P. & C. Yates, (eds) (2003) *Union Renewal and Organising: A Comparative Study of Union Movements in Five Countries*, London: Continuum Publishers

Frege, C.M. & J. Kelly (2003) 'Union Revitalization Strategies in Comparative Perspective', *European Journal of Industrial Relations*, 9.1

Friedman, S. & M. Shaw (2000) 'Power in Partnership? Trade Unions, Forums and the Transition', in G. Adler & E. Webster (eds) *Trade Unions and Democratization in South Africa, 1985 – 1997*, New York: St. Martin's Press

Gindin, S. (1997) 'Notes on Labour at the End of the Century: Starting Over?' *Monthly Review* 49.3

Godfrey, S, M. Clarke & J. Theron with J. Greenburg (2003) 'On the Outskirts but Still in Fashion: Homeworking in the South African Clothing Industry', Cape Town: Institute of Development and Labour Law Monographs, University of Cape Town

Habib, A. (1997) 'From Pluralism to Corporatism: South Africa's Labour Relations in Transition', *Politikon*, 24.1

Hartridge, D. (1993) 'What are the Future Implications for South African Trade Policy of Continued Membership in GATT?' Conference on *South Africa's International Economic Relations in the 1990s*, March 30

Industrial Strategy Project (1994) 'Industrial Strategy for South Africa: the Recommendations of the ISP', *South African Labour Bulletin*, 18.1

Joffe, A, D. Kaplan, R. Kaplinsky & D. Lewis (1995) '*Improving Manufacturing Performance In South Africa: Report of the Industrial Strategy Project*', Cape Town: University of Cape Town Press

Kenny, B. (2003) 'Labour Market Flexibility in the Retail Sector: Possibilities for Resistance' in T. Bramble & F. Barchiesi (eds) *Rethinking the Labour Movements in the 'New South Africa'*, Burlington: Ashgate: 168-183

Kriel, A. (2006) 'Morris' job data not authoritative', *Business Report* [online edition], October 11. Retrieved February 15, 2007, from www.busrep.co.za/index.php?fSectionId=553&fArticleId=3480005

Lloyd, C. & S. Rix (1995) *Unions and Democratic Institutions*, Johannesburg: NALEDI

Maree, J. (1993) 'Trade Unions and Corporatism in South Africa', *Transformation*, 21

Moody, K. (1997) *Workers in a Lean World*, London: Verso

Munck, R. (2002) *Globalisation and Labour*, London: Zed

Naudé, S. (1992) 'Blueprint for Prosperity', Speech presented at the *Blueprint for Prosperity* Conference, South Africa. October 8

NEF (1994) 'Unmandated Labour Submission on Supply Side Measures', Cape Town, May

NEF (1993a) 'Report of the National Economic Forum Plenary', Johannesburg, July 5

NEF (1993b) 'Labour Submission to National Economic Forum re Industrial Policy', December 9

NEF (1992) 'Labour Submission to the LTWG', Johannesburg, February

Panitch, L. (1994) 'Globalisation and the State', in R. Miliband & L. Panitch (eds), *Socialist Register 1994*, London: Merlin

Panitch, L. (2000) 'Reflections on a Strategy for Labour', in L. Panitch & C. Leys (eds), *Socialist Register 2001*, London: Merlin

Patel, E. (1993) 'New Institutions of Decision-Making: The Case of the National Economic Forum', in E. Patel (ed), *Engine of Development?*, Cape Town: Juta

Patel, E. (1994) 'The Role of Organised Labour in a Democratic South Africa' in E. Patel (ed) *Worker Rights*, Kenwyn, South Africa: Juta

PBC (2005) 'People's Budget 2006-2007', Johannesburg: NALEDI

Ross, G. (2000) 'Labor Versus Globalization', *Annals of American Political and Social Science* 570

Seidman, G. (1994) *Manufacturing Militance*, Berkeley, University of California Press

South Africa (1994a) *Government Gazette* #16126, volume 354, December 2

South Africa (1994b) 'White Paper on Reconstruction and Development'. *Government Gazette* #16085, Office of the President, November

South African Labour Bulletin (1991) 'National General Strike: "It's more than VAT, it's the entire economy" Interview with Jay Naidoo', 16.2

Therborn, G. (1984) 'The Prospects of Labour and the Transformation of Advanced Capitalism', *New Left Review*, I.145

Von Holdt, K. (1993) 'The Dangers of Corporatism', *South African Labour Bulletin* 17.1

Von Holdt, K. (2000) 'From the Politics of Resistance to the Politics of Reconstruction? The Union and "Ungovernability" in the Workplace', in G. Adler & E. Webster (eds), *Trade Unions and Democratization in South Africa, 1985-1997*, Johannesburg: Witwatersrand University Press

Webster, E. (1996) 'COSATU: Old Alliances, New Strategies', *Southern Africa Report,* 11.3.
Webster, E. (2001) 'The Alliance Under Stress: Governing in a Globalizing World', *Democratization,* 8(1):255-274
Webster, E & S Buhlungu (2005) 'Between Marginalisation and Revitalisation? The State and Trade Unionism in South Africa', *Review of African Political Economy,* 31.100
Woolard, I. & C. Woolard (2005) *Wage Dispersion in South Africa: Household Survey Evidence, 1995-2003,* Working Paper, Pretoria: HSRC
Zuege, A (1999) 'The Chimera of the Third Way', in L. Panitch & C. Leys (eds), *Socialist Register 2000,* London: Merlin

Solidarity across cyberspace:

Internet campaigning, labour activism and the remaking of trade union internationalism

Bruce Robinson

Bruce Robinson *is an Honorary Research Fellow in the Informatics Research Institute at the University of Salford in the UK.*

ABSTRACT

Global communication through the Internet has provided new possibilities for trade union solidarity action across national boundaries. Email campaigns are one form of this. Taking the example of an email campaign in support of imprisoned Eritrean trade unionists, this paper examines the social organisation and information flows underlying such campaigns. These throw light on the effectiveness of such actions, their capacity to overcome inequalities in access to ICTs and current debates on the role of the Internet in the remaking of trade union internationalism managing to develop a certain social power.

Prologue - cybersolidarity in action

Three Eritrean trade union leaders were arrested and illegally held on March 30th and April 9th, 2005. News of this emerged six weeks later via the international trade union federations to which their unions were affiliated. The Geneva-based International Union of Food, Agricultural, Hotel, Restaurant, Catering, Tobacco and Allied Workers' Associations (IUF) made a call to protest to the Eritrean government.

The campaign was picked up by the trade union news service Labour Start from the website of the IUF and a link provided among the day's news stories. Another link urged visitors to 'Act Now!', leading to the text of a letter to the Eritrean government calling for their release that could be dispatched with the addition of some minimal personal information. These letters were forwarded to Eritrean embassies round the world. At the same time, details of the campaign were sent to the 31,000 subscribers to Labour Start's e-list with a link to the 'Act Now!' page.

The campaign was taken up by other organisations and over 5,000 emails were sent within a week (1,500 in the first 14 hours) through Labour Start and other websites taking a news feed from it. The US Campaign for Labor Rights and the Stop Killer Coke campaign sent it off to their e-lists – one of those arrested worked at Coca Cola. The UK campaign 'No Sweat' picketed the embassy in London. UK Coca Cola workers and their union, the GMB, gave support. The umbrella international union federation, the ICFTU, took up the case with the International Labour Organisation. While it did not lead to the freeing of the trade unionists, Labour Start received feedback indicating that the action had certainly been noticed by Eritrean embassies.

Introduction

While other campaigns may have been more successful in reaching their aims or attracted more participants, the Eritrean campaign throws a spotlight on a number of issues of interest from the viewpoint of researchers and labour activists. This paper examines the operation and effectiveness of such campaigns and puts them in the context of the broader issues concerning the implications of globalisation, the Internet and networked activism for labour.

The Eritrean email campaign was one example of what we shall call 'cybersolidarity' – Internet-mediated action in support of trade unions or groups of workers involved in disputes with employers or the state. An email campaign is only one form of cybersolidarity. Other forms include 'info war' or 'hacktivism' where the information assets of a target are attacked over the Net (Walker, 2002). The most recent example is a mass picket organised by the international white-collar trade union confederation UNI of IBM's site in the virtual reality world of Second Life in support of Italian IBM workers in dispute. It succeeded in disrupting a meeting of IBM executives and forcing IBM to close down large parts of its $10 US million site to outsiders (UNI, 2007). Boycott campaigns, such as that in support of Coca Cola workers in Columbia, have also been built through the Internet. Online fundraising to support workers is another means of showing solidarity – for example, an appeal through the Working Families Network of the US AFL-CIO raised $180,000 US in a few weeks for striking Safeway workers in California (Newman, 2005).

This paper will focus on the organisation and working of email cybersolidarity campaigns and use this analysis to assess their effectiveness and value in trade union action. It will focus on the relationships between, and roles of, participants in the action and the information flows between them. This permits a more detailed analysis of the mechanics of Internet use by labour activists and can provide an underpinning for the more general and widely-considered issues of trade union use of the Internet. By incorporating an informational dimension and a concern with social organisation, it also points to the value of a cross-disciplinary approach which analyses the interaction of information systems, social movements and organisational forms and structures (Lucio, Martinez & Walker, 2005).

The material used is largely drawn from documentation publicly available on the World Wide Web or received by the author as a participant in labour-oriented e-lists and email actions since the mid-1990s. Some of this material is ephemeral in that it is removed from public access as one campaign follows another[1]. Of particular value have been the regular reflections by Eric Lee of Labour Start on the effectiveness of various activities undertaken through that web site.

A brief history will first indicate the development of union use of the Internet. Email campaigns will then be contextualised in terms of a number of issues raised in the academic literature before a more detailed analysis is carried out in terms of the social organisation and information flows that make them possible.

---

1   Material relating to the Eritrean campaign can be found at http://www.labourstart.org/cgi-bin/dbman/db.cgi?db=2005&uid=default&view_records=1&sb=4&so=descend&labstart_jump=1&keyword=eritrea

.

The pre-history of cybersolidarity

The drive towards using the Internet as a vehicle for international trade union solidarity has not, on the whole, come from within the formal structures of trade unions themselves, which have tended to be conservative in their use of ICTs. Rather, it has depended on a process of convincing unions, their members and supporters of its value. Pioneering efforts can be traced back as far as the early 1970s (Lee, 1997) and the first practical demonstration of the potential of open computer-mediated communication (CMC) came when Marc Bélanger set up Solinet, a computer conferencing and email system, for the Canadian Union of Public Employees in 1985. Solinet did not merely disseminate information but allowed union members to set up conferences on topics of interest and to freely interact with one another (Bélanger, 1994; Taylor, 2001). However, the decisive breakthrough – in Europe and the USA, at least – came in the mid to late 1990s. Alongside the pressure towards international action from globalisation and the increased availability of, and familiarity with the technology, two factors were particularly important.

The first was advocacy and support from a number of people with a political commitment to the trade union movement who were also enthusiastic about using ICTs for its goals. They proselytised for the use of the Internet and began to create institutions ranging from websites to training centres which could support this activity. The Labour Telematics Centre in Manchester, US Labornet, which produced a number of internationally affiliated imitators, Labor Tech conferences on use of the new media and ICTs, Eric Lee's (1997) book on trade unions and the Internet (which preceded his own Labour Start site), and the Cyber Picket Line directory all began to encourage and develop trade union interest in the Internet during this period.

There were also a number of high profile industrial disputes which demonstrated the immediate practical value of CMC. The 1996-8 Liverpool dockers' dispute showed its value in setting up acts of solidarity across national boundaries, making it possible to evade the local constraints of strict anti-union laws and organise face-to-face meetings and action across the world. It also provided the spur to the setting up of UK Labournet (Bailey, 1997; Renton, 2004). The ICEM's international campaign against the Bridgestone tyre company showed how it was possible to mobilise individuals internationally in cyberspace and to use the technology to wage 'information warfare' in pursuit of a trade union dispute (Herod, 1998; Walker, 2002). The South Korean general strike of 1996-7 used the Internet to build support around the world.

Activities in this period laid the basis for the growth of a 'net-internationalism'. Cybersolidarity has developed under the enabling power of the technology and widening access to it which has occurred since the 1990s, alongside the development of globalised capitalism and resistance to it.

Theorising cybersolidarity: four research areas

Cybersolidarity is a multi-faceted phenomenon: a form of action involving trade unions; action across space, potentially on a global scale; a form of cyberactivism and social movement; and a complex structure of human activity mediated by information flows. Each of these related and converging aspects throws up questions of relevance to an understanding of cybersolidarity.

Trade unions and the Internet

The implications of Internet use can vary widely according to the differing organisational contexts within which this use occurs (Bennett, 2003). Trade unions existed long before the Internet and their structures and ideology affect how their members take up new forms of communication (Lucio Martinez & Walker, 2005). Thus while pro-labour activism shares many features with broader cyberactivism – the development of activist networks and the use of ICTs in support of a social movement – it has a number of specific features that are important (Bailey, 1999).

Lee (2004c:81) has noted that 'probably the final obstacle to a new global unionism will be the conservatism of the unions themselves. There are few institutions in civil society as conservative as the trade unions' and this is reflected in attitudes to the adoption of ICTs. While they are mass membership organisations, those in control have often been reluctant to share information and potentially open themselves up to criticism from the ranks, or to provide a platform that could be used for unofficial organisation within the unions (Newman, 2005).

A suspicion of the technology may also have reflected a period in the 1980s where new technologies were seen as a weapon of employer offensives on the shopfloor or as something that was not the concern of unions beyond the processing of membership records and dues. Now the increased pervasiveness of computer and communications technology means that few unions lack some sort of presence on the Internet. While some unions and international federations have been innovative, union use of the Internet all too often reflects a model of top down information dissemination that Waterman (2001b) characterises as a use of 'ICT as instrument (faster, cheaper and further-reaching), not as cyberspace (another kind of space with unlimited possibilities for international dialogue…).' The web presence of unions often revolves around the union, not the worker, both in terms of content and by reflecting the existing organisational structures (Lewis, 2002). There has also been a widespread failure to keep up with developments in the technology, which means many unions remain stuck at the level of 'first generation' use of the Internet (Lee, 2007; Newman, 2005).

The spread of the Internet encountered a trade union movement on the defensive. Globalisation and the shift in industrial production to countries of the South has led to the development of labour movements in many of those countries with large differences in their degree of solidity and recognition, while facing those in the North with decline (Monck, 2002). A renewed emphasis on trade unionism with an international dimension is consequently widely recognised to be necessary.

Further, the impact of neo-liberal globalisation has led to a questioning of traditional strategies, such as US business unionism, and pressure for more open and flexible forms which are often identified with a social movement unionism that both allies itself with and learns from other radical social movements (Robinson, 2002; Waterman, 2001b). In this view, if union internationalism is to be adequate to the challenges of globalisation, it must go beyond the traditional structures of international federations, May Day celebrations and periodic calls for solidarity in major disputes filtered down through union structures. Moody (1997:248) argues that 'without dismissing the entire official structure of international organized labor, it is clear that another level of international activity is needed that involves the ranks and workplace activists from the start', which means that 'international solidarity is not carried out primarily by top union leadership and union functionaries … but at local and intermediate levels of the union' (Nissen, 2002:265), which are also more innovative in their use of ICTs (Lee, 2004c).

The role of the Internet in the reconstitution of labour internationalism is now widely recognised but its precise contribution and potentialities are still the subject of debate. Hodkinson (2001) asks 'Will the new union internationalism be a "net-internationalism"?'. His negative response focuses both on political and social obstacles to internationalism *per se* and on what he sees as the limitations of the Internet, particularly global inequalities in access. In contrast, Castells simply dismisses the potential of labour internationalism because he believes labour is exhausted as an emancipatory force as a result of its 'desocialisation' and 'individuation' (Castells, 2000:505-6; Waterman, 1998). Waterman (2001a) and Monck (2002), accept much of Castells' analysis of the 'network society' but dispute his conclusion, arguing that unions themselves should take on the network form typical of Internet activism. Still others believe that ICTs can at best be a useful supplement to more traditional forms of international union solidarity (e.g. Renton, 2004). Most optimistically, Lee (2007) argues that cybersolidarity itself 'can tip over into a massive resurgence of trade union internationalism at a global level.'

How far then are cybersolidarity actions part of an effective remaking of trade union action in the face of globalisation? How do they support trade union internationalism?

Trade union action and the global digital divide

The impact of the Internet on trade unions is not uniform but reflects broader inequalities. The term 'digital divide' has been coined to describe inequalities in access to and use of ICTs, both within and between nations. The latter – the 'global digital divide' – is clearly an obstacle for trade unionists seeking to make links across the world. Can this be overcome?

The Eritrean campaign spanned the global digital divide. Eritrea comes 149th in the world for Internet users, according to UNCTAD, and was the last country in Africa to be connected to the Internet. Only one trade union federation in Eritrea has an email address (one of the 9,500 Internet users there in 2003), and African unions generally face major problems in exploiting ICTs, mostly endemic to their societies – such as the absence of infrastructure and their cost – with others more specific to unions such as a lack of resources and competing priorities (Bélanger, 2001). Yet, despite this technological gap, the Eritrean campaign was taken up by individuals and organisations across the globe. How far then can activist networks then provide a way round the absence of direct access to technology?

Cybersolidarity as Internet activism

Despite the peculiarities of trade union use of the Internet, cybersolidarity remains a form of cyberactivism (McCaughey & Ayers, 2003), dependent on the commitment and participation of individuals in activist networks who identify with its goals.

In summing up the motivations of ' Internet-worked social movements' inspired by the consequences of globalisation, Langman (2005) notes four 'mediations between injustice and adversity, which are often far removed from personal experience, and actual participation in a social movement.' They are: '(1) information and the way it is framed; (2) a personal identity that is receptive to this information; (3) a structural location that is conducive to activism; (4) linkages or ties with networks of social actors with similar concerns.' Miller (2004) further points to the need for a collective identity to underpin social movement mobilisation.

The rooting of cybersolidarity in a pre-existing trade union movement points to an identity and location that can underpin specific campaigns. However, this does not address Langman's points (1) and (4): the relationship between the provision and framing of information and the creation and maintenance of a constituency of networked actors. How is information gathered and presented to potential participants in such a way as to encourage them to act? How and to what extent do these Net-based actions then become an active factor in the dispute they are intended to support?

If Langman is right, the underlying social organisation and information flows play important roles in defining the effectiveness and transformational power of campaigns. By examining this structure and its implications we can begin to address some of the broader issues raised above. Anchoring an informational analysis in a consideration of the social and organisational relationships avoids the danger of seeing information as a reified entity that acts or flows independently of human action.

Our analysis of email campaigns therefore takes the form of identifying the actors involved in different aspects of the action and the information flows which link and coordinate them in pursuit of an overall goal.

Our focus is on Labour Start as the most wide ranging and technologically innovative site[2].

The social and informational structure of cybersolidarity

There are three major groups of actors necessarily involved in a cybersolidarity action: the protagonists in the labour dispute; the intermediaries concerned with supplying the information about it and setting up and monitoring the action; and the respondents who take part in the action. Each acts in a distinct way in response to an initial triggering event and, although their actions are coordinated to serve a single goal, the differences between them and how these are overcome are central to defining the implications of this form of action.

The first of these groups consists of the protagonists. An act of solidarity starts naturally with a triggering event such as the imprisonment of trade unionists in Eritrea. The instigators may be the state, employer, a union organisation or a group of workers. The triggering event is place-based, though it may occur across a number of physical

---

2   A brief history of Labour Start can be found in Lee (2007)

locations. From the viewpoint of the cybersolidarity action two groups provide the overall framework through their position in the dispute:

The first of these groups is made up of the subjects: those in whose support the action is taken. They may be those directly calling for the action or the call may come from an organisation that supports them (in our case, the IUF). It is worth noting that the subjects of the call may have no direct involvement in it and only become aware that the action has been taken after the fact.

The second group is made up of the targets: those the action seeks to influence – in our case the Eritrean government. This may be more than one organisation across a wide range: a company, state organisation or government, employers' organisations, even sometimes trade unionists themselves.[3] They are not necessarily those most immediately involved in the dispute. It may, for example, be more effective to urge a multinational to intervene with a sub-contractor to resolve a dispute than to seek to influence the sub-contractor directly. The targets will typically be unaware of the action until they begin to receive emails or faxes.

The protagonists typically enter the cybersolidarity action at its start and its end. The action is initiated by or on behalf of the subjects through a call for support; the target receives the flow of information generated by the action and the action ends when it is felt that it will no longer bring about useful pressure on the target.

The subsequent course of a cybersolidarity action depends crucially on a range of intermediaries who structure and initiate the information flows that underlie the action and who define and present the action to those who take part in it. These intermediaries have several functions which are conceptually separable, although in practice they may be carried out by the same people.

The first function is acting as an information source that provides the link between the triggering action and the organiser of the online action. This need not be done by those directly involved – which suggests the digital divide need not be an obstacle here. It can be an organisation to which they belong or which supports them – in the case of Eritrea, the international union federation to which their unions belong.

Other sources include media reports, other labour activists and volunteers directly recruited by the website to act as reporters. For example, China Labor Report, based in New York, has sources providing information inside China, which has enabled them to run very precisely targeted email campaigns. Labour Start has a network of correspondents who have volunteered to provide Labour Start with current news stories from different countries or sectors. Labour Start also enables any user of the web site to submit stories or information not found elsewhere on the site.

A second role is that of information gatherer. This role consists of bringing together information and making it available for presentation on the Net. This may be an automated process, as when websites are scanned for items that may relate to trade union issues. Alternatively, individuals may have responsibility for covering particular countries or industries in order to ensure thorough coverage, as with Labour Start correspondents.

---

3   Often messages of support are sent to workers in dispute to encourage them in their action rather than to influence an employer or government.

At this stage, the basic information is available but the call has yet to be presented in a form to which anyone can respond electronically.

Networkers make up the next category of intermediaries. These are the people who run the websites, e-lists or other online mechanisms for campaigning. They form the key link between those who request a campaign and those that respond to it. The term networkers, which we borrow from Waterman (see Herod, 1998), does not do justice to the range of functions they undertake, which include: maintaining the infrastructure that enables the dissemination of the information and the campaigning, such as web sites, e-lists; collating, editing and making the information available in an easily accessible form; initiating, monitoring and backing up the campaigns; and building and maintaining a constituency of potential participants in campaigns.

The overall control of cybersolidarity actions is in the networkers' hands in that they decide what information to make available through their net resources and which calls to take up as appeals for action. Several factors are involved in these decisions. One is the origin of the call for support and its relationship to the subjects of the action. Labour Start takes the position that a call should come from an official trade union organisation (Lee, 2003). Eric Lee goes further: 'The best campaigns are the ones run with the full support both of the local union (…), sister unions in the same sector in different countries, as well as the global union federation' (Lee, 2004a). In contrast, Labour Net UK places emphasis on 'contributions and reports from rank and file trade unionists, although we also welcome contributions from trade union organisations' (LabourNet, n.d.), recognising that workers in dispute may also be in conflict with union structures (as was the case with the Liverpool dockers). This difference is also reflected in the audience to which they aim to appeal.

Labour Start also tends to select campaigns around issues of workers' rights, rather than privatisation or wages, believing that they have a broader appeal (Lee, 2004a).

Other considerations emerge from the need to build a constituency that uses a site regularly and is prepared to take part in actions. Alongside concerns about information quality and timeliness, are others which include avoiding bombarding readers with so many appeals that they are less likely to read and act upon them.

At this stage, the information is presented in a form that both gives the background to the dispute and the pro-forma letter that, on Labour Start at least, can be edited before being sent.

Up to now, our analysis has been concerned with the flows of information and forms of action that enable a cybersolidarity action to take place. We now move to those directly involved in taking the suggested action - respondents. Here questions of a personal identity that is receptive to the information and a structural location that is conducive to activism become important in forming the basis for joining a network and responding to calls to take action.

In the case of trade unions, there is a pre-existing ethos of solidarity and internationalism and organisational identities as trade unionists that can be appealed to. These ideas do not lose their importance as a means of collective identity because of the individualistic nature of Internet use. Rather, users bring their social identities, including such norms, into the virtual collective (Brunsting & Postmes, 2002; Kendall, 1999).

It is possible for networkers to orient their web sites to appeal to such pre-existing identities and exploit them as an aid to mobilisation (Robinson, 2003). Labour Start promotes itself as the place where 'trade unionists start their day on the Net.' The site contains little that seeks to convince people to join a union but rather sees its role as servicing existing trade unionists in terms of information, campaigns and technology. Such an identity is not one that emphasises the differences between general secretaries and rank and file members, as with Labour Net UK.

With a couple of mouse clicks, it is possible to find the information and send the letter to a prescribed recipient. Yet, however well a web site appeals to a collective identity and however easy it is, involvement in online campaigns is ultimately an individual decision taken in response to a particular appeal. The extent of responses to particular campaigns may vary considerably, not always in proportion to the inherent importance of the issue (Lee, 2004b). Participants do not have any necessary incentive to move from one campaign to the next. Rather the very ease of participating means that email campaigning requires less consistent or deep commitment than a more long-term campaign. The incorporation of the individual into the network remains limited and, in deciding whether to participate in a given campaign, s/he may be swayed by other considerations such as time, 'compassion fatigue', or the geographical closeness and familiarity of the dispute (Lee, 2004b).

Assessing campaigns

It is only when respondents act that the flow of information is transformed into pressure on a target and re-enters the arena of the real world dispute that triggered the action. The subsequent impact of cybersolidarity action on the outcome of an industrial dispute is very difficult to assess. There are two measures of success (Lee, 2005). The first depends on the impact of the whole action on the dispute. Assessing this depends on feedback from the direct participants, whether they are the subjects of the action or the targets. This might not give a true picture of the real impact of the action and it is difficult otherwise to ascribe a precise assessment of its role in the overall outcome of a dispute (e.g. the winning of a strike). Accordingly in only a few cases out of 24 victorious disputes supported by online campaigns does Lee (2006) give details of precisely how the online campaign contributed to the end result.

The second measure assesses how far the action has served to mobilise respondents to take part in it. This is a quantitative measure based on the number of emails sent in response to a call. The wide range of responses to different campaigns points to each respondent deciding on every campaign separately and as an individual.

There is no necessary correlation between the two measures of success – a consequence of the structure of cybersolidarity action as outlined. Lee contrasts the Eritrean campaign (high mobilisation but no result) with a low mobilisation, highly focused but successful campaign for the reinstatement of workers at a hotel in the Bahamas (Lee, 2005) – one of several successes at hotels. It is possible that certain types of target – e.g. those concerned with brand reputation or potential consumer reaction – are more susceptible to email campaigns than repressive governments.

Action by proxy

The social and informational structure outlined here shows that email solidarity action is in some sense action by proxy. For the respondents who act in it, it is mediated by the form in which the information is presented to them by the website or other means of transmission. The subjects of the action are not directly present at this stage and may not be, or only minimally, in the whole process. This has some advantages: it means that the absence of direct access to the Internet or possession of the technology need not be an obstacle to obtaining support by means of it. All that is necessary is that a call for support gets out somehow. To this extent, cybersolidarity can overcome the digital divide. It is also a necessity when, as in our example, the subjects of the action sit in jail or are otherwise unable to act freely.

Nevertheless there are obvious disadvantages to this. Control of the action is in the hands of the networkers rather than those directly affected by the outcome of the action. Mostly this does not lead to problems as the networkers take steps to keep contact where possible and to ensure that the action corresponds to the wishes of those directly involved, even if expressed indirectly. There is however a potential of conflicts of interest here. The ability of networkers to choose news and select which campaigns are taken up as actions also lays them open to accusations of favouritism or censorship.

The structure outlined here is not the only way in which action can be taken in support of trade unionists through the Internet. For example, there are open forums and many-to-many e-lists which have different methods of operation from the centralised one-to-many model embodied in email campigns. However there are some general lessons that can be drawn from these campaigns for trade union use of the Internet.

Conclusions: liberating flows and grounded forces

Net-internationalism is already a fact of life and can have an impact on the outcome of industrial disputes on a wide geographical scale. Cybersolidarity is helping to shift trade union internationalism from something undertaken by remote international organisations, or periodically in major disputes, to a continuing concern, bringing home (literally) the day to day reality of trade union battles across the world and permitting every trade unionist with access to an Internet connection to be actively involved. This already marks a step towards the direct links between concerned labour activists, whether within or outside existing union structures, that Waterman (2001) sees as crucial to 'a new labour internationalism.' A cybersolidarity action occurs across spatial scales that were not previously easily accessible to the actors, 'opening up the landscape and making the connections between workers in different parts of the globe visible' (Herod, 2003, 509). Beyond the easy availability of the information, it is the speed, timeliness and ease of Net-based email actions that distinguish them from earlier forms of solidarity. At one level, sending an email is little different from signing a paper petition, but it would hardly be possible to get together a petition with 5,000 signatures from around the world and deliver it to Eritrean embassies within a few days of learning about the imprisonment of trade unionists in a distant country.

However there is little evidence that trade union use of the Internet has become something widely considered by employers, at least outside certain highly consumer-sensitive industries such as tourism. Place-based legal and social conditions still play a dominant role in industrial disputes, though creative use of the Internet may enable trade unionists to evade local restrictions (Grieco & Bhopal, 2005). Unless it results – accidentally or deliberately – in damage to the target's information resources or infrastructure, a cybersolidarity action does not have the direct effect on the target that place-based solidarity actions such as a sympathy strike, a human picket line or a refusal to handle an organisation's goods can have.

Lee (2007) acknowledges that, as well as victories to which Labour Start has contributed, 'most such campaigns fizzle out and disappear with no such results.' The individual nature of the response means that it does not have the collective cohesion and power of place-based actions. A virtual presence is not a substitute. This is recognised by those who organise Internet actions: Lee (2004a) notes that 'the most successful online campaigns feature strong offline elements as well, including picket lines and other protests. They are not exclusively online'.

Reaping the potential benefits of cybersolidarity requires the active creation and maintenance of a socio-technical infrastructure, human networks and new spaces that bring them together, not by the replacement of grounded place-based action but by its augmentation. This occurs by drawing respondents, whose physical location does not matter, into an online space where they can be encouraged to support particular campaigns.

Davies (n.d) notes that it is 'extremely rare for online campaigning and "virtual" associations to be entirely divorced from traditional, offline, place-based and face-to-face campaigns.' So the physical remoteness of respondents and subjects in a cybersolidarity action need not be an obstacle to subsequent face-to-face interaction, as when No Sweat invited representatives to the UK and subsequently organised a trade union delegation to Mexico following a cybersolidarity action undertaken in support of workers on strike at a subcontractor for Nike in 2001 (Carty, 2001). Virtual action in cyberspace can also serve to provide the spark that leads to place-based action (as with the pickets over Eritrea).

This an example of what Aoyama and Sheppard (2003:1152) describe as the 'dialectics of geographic and virtual space... meaning that neither is reducible to the other; dialectics, inter alia, of specificity and universality, of liberating flows and grounded forces, and of the contrasting logics of distance and proximity'.

Cybersolidarity has the potential to open up new horizons of labour solidarity by marrying liberating flows of information and new forms of social connection through the Internet with the grounded forces and methods of action more traditionally used in trade unionism. Particular 'e-forms' (Greene, Hogan & Grieco, 2003) of activity emerge alongside tried and tested methods. Net-internationalism does not replace place-based action but becomes a weapon alongside it through which it can become more effective.

© *Bruce Robinson, 2008*

REFERENCES

Aoyama, Y. & E. Sheppard (2003). 'The dialectics of geographic and virtual space.' *Environment and Planning* A 35:1151-1156

Bailey, C. (1997) *Towards a global labournet.* Accessed September, 2005 from http://www.lmedia. nodong.net/1997/article/w4-2e.html

Bailey, C. (1999) *The Labour Movement and the Internet.* Accessed September, 2005 from http:// www.amrc.org.hk/Arch/3401.htm

Bélanger, M. (1994), *SoliNet: A Computer Conferencing System Designed for Trade Unions.* Accessed October, 2007 at http://www.net4dem.org/cyrev/archive/issue1/articles/SoliNet/SoliNet2.htm

Bélanger, M. (2001) *The Digital Development of Labour Organisations in Africa.* Turin: ILO International Training Centre, Turin

Bennett, W.L. (2003) 'Communicating Global Activism.' *Information, Communication and Society*, Vol 6, No 2:143-168

Brunsting, S. & T. Postmes (2002) 'Social movement participation in the online age: Predicting offline and online collective action', *Small Group Research*, Vol 33, No 5:525-554

Carty, V. (2001) 'The Internet and grassroots politics: Nike, the athletic apparel industry and the anti -sweatshop campaign.' *TAMARA: Journal of Critical Postmodern Organization Science,* Vol 2, No 1:34-48. (Also at: http://www.zianet.com/boje/tamara/issues/volume_1/issue_1_2/2Carty_Nike_corp_predator.htm)

Castells, M. (2000) *The Rise of the Network Society,*Oxford: Basil Blackwell

Davies, W. (no date) *Trade Union Movement and the Internet; Lessons from Civil Society,* London: IPPR

Grieco, M. & M. Bhopal (2005) 'Globalisation, collective action and counter-coordination' *Critical Perspectives on International Business,* Vol 1, No 2/3:109-122

Greene, A. M., J. Hogan & M. Grieco (2002) *E-collectivism: Emergent Opportunities for Renewal.* Accessed May, 2003 from http://www.geocities.com/e_collectivism/papers/madrid.html

Herod, A. (1998) 'Of Blocs, Flows and Networks; The end of the Cold War, cyberspace and the geo-economics of organized labor at the fin de millenaire', O Tuathail, Herod & Roberts (eds) *An Unruly World? Globalization, Governance and Geography,* London: Routledge

Herod, A. (2003) 'Geographies of Labor Internationalism', *Social Science History,* Vol 27, No 4:501-23

Hodkinson, S. (2001) *Problems@Labour: Towards a Net-Internationalism?* Accessed August, 2005 from www.globalstudiesassociation.org/conference1papers/Problems1.doc

Kendall, L. (1999) 'Recontextualizing "Cyberspace": Methodological Considerations for On-Line Research.' In S. Jones (ed) *Doing Internet Research,* Thousand Oaks & London: Sage Publications: 57-74

LabourNet UK (n.d.) *What is LabourNet?* Accessed August, 2005 from http://www.labournet. net/whatis.html

Langman, L. (2005) 'From Virtual Public Spheres to Global Justice: A Critical Theory of Internetworked Social Movements', *Sociological Theory,* Vol 23, No 1:42-74

Lee, E. (1996) *The Labour Movement and the Internet: The New Internationalism,* London: Pluto Press

Lee, E. (2003) Personal communication

Lee, E. (2004a) *How to win an online campaign..* Accessed October 1st, 2005 from http://www.ericlee. me.uk/archive/000094.html#more

Lee, E. (2004b) *Why we don't give: Online donations and international solidarity.* Accessed October 1st, 2005 from http://www.ericlee.me.uk/archive/000077.html

Lee, E. (2004c), 'Towards Global Networked Unions', in Munck, R. (Ed.) *Labour and Globalisation: Results and Prospects,* Liverpool University Press, Liverpool

Lee, E. (2005) *Building International Solidarity, One Campaign at a Time.* Accessed October 1st, 2005 from http://www.ericlee.me.uk/archive/000117.html#more

Lee, E. (2006) *Global campaigning: Beyond protest emails and solidarity messages* Accessed October 1st, 2007 from http://www.ericlee.info/2006/02/global_campaigning_beyond_prot.html

Lee, E. (2007) 'LabourStart and Trade Union Internationalism: At the Tipping Point?' *Labor History,* Vol. 48, No.1:73-79

Lewis, P. (2002) 'Unions and the Web: Where to Now?', in Shostak, A. (Ed.) *The Cyberunion Handbook: Transforming Labor through Computer Technology*, Armonk, NY: M. E. Sharpe

Martinez Lucio, M. & S. Walker (2005) 'The networked union? The Internet as a challenge to trade union identity and roles.' *Critical Perspectives on International Business*, Vol 1, No 2/3:137-154

McCaughey, M. & Ayers M.D. (eds) (2003) *Cyberactivism: Online Activism in Theory and Practice* London: Routledge

Miller, B. (2004) 'Spaces of Mobilization: Transnational Social Movements', C. Barnett & M. Low (eds) *Spaces of Democracy*, Thousand Oaks & London: Sage Publications: 223-246

Monck, R. (2002) *Globalisation and Labour: the new 'Great Transformation'.* London: Zed Books

Moody, K. (1997) *Workers in a Lean World: Unions in the Globalized Economy*, London: Verso

Newman, N. (2005) 'Is Labor Missing the Internet Third Wave?', *Working USA: The Journal of Labor and Society*, Vol. 8:383-394

Nissen, B. (2002), 'Concluding Thoughts: Internal Transformation?', in Nissen, B. (ed.) *Unions in a globalized environment: changing borders, organizational boundaries and social roles*, Armonk, NY: M. E. Sharpe

Renton, D. (2004?) *The means to fight globalisation? Using the Internet to support rank-and-file trade unionism.* Accessed September, 2005 from http://www.dkrenton.co.uk/research/edgepaper.htm

Robinson, B. (2003) 'Building a constituency for online activism: the Labour Start experience.' *Workshop on Social Movement Informatics*, Leeds Metropolitan University, 2003

Robinson, I. (2002) 'Does Neoliberal Restructuring Promote Social Movement Unionism? US Developments in Comparative Perspective', in Nissen, B. (ed.) *Unions in a globalized environment: changing borders, organizational boundaries and social roles*, Armonk, NY: M. E. Sharpe

UNI (2007) *IBM Union Protest: Second Life.* Accessed September, 2007 from http://www.union-network.org/uniwebmasters.nsf/slibm?openform

Walker, S. (2002) *To Picket Just Click It! Social netwar and industrial conflict in a global economy*, Leeds Metropolitan University School of Information Management, IMRIP, 2002-1.

Waterman, P. (1998) *The Brave New World of Manuel Castells: What on Earth (or in the Ether) is going on?* Accessed September 2005 from www.antenna.nl/~waterman/castells.html

Waterman, P. (2001a) 16 *Propositions on International Labour (and Other?) Networking.* Accessed August 2005 from http://www.lmu.ac.uk/ies/im/people/swalker/labournetworking/pw16props-31-5-01.htm

Waterman, P. (2001b) 'Trade Union Internationalism in the Age of Seattle', in Waterman, P. & Wills, J. (eds), *Place, Space and the New Labour Internationalisms*, Oxford: Blackwell

ACKNOWLEDGEMENTS

An earlier version of this paper was presented at the 2006 IFIP Working Group 8.2 conference on 'Social Inclusion: Societal and Organizational Implications for Information Systems' in Limerick, Ireland. The proceedings were published by Springer Verlag. Thanks to Eric Lee for his help in answering my questions.

The Movement for the Abolition of Child Labour as an Example of a Transnational Network Movement

Patrick Develtere and An Huybrechs

Patrick Develtere is the General Director of the Higher Institute for Labour Studies at the Catholic University of Leuven.
An Huybrechs is the Advocacy Project Coordinator for the International Planned Parenthood Federation European Network.

ABSTRACT

With the advent of a global network society, movements and social organisations acquire a new place and space in development. A wide range of actors, including international non-governmental organisations and transnational coalitions, are reacting in a variety of ways to new domestic and global challenges. Separated from traditional social movements, such as trade unions, new forms of collective action have emerged on the international scene which can be described as 'transnational network movements'. This paper discusses the differences in ideology, practice, and organisation between traditional social movements and these new network movements, using the movement for the abolition of child labour as an example. The history of this movement, the actors involved and its repertoire of actions illustrate clearly that transnational network movements are very dynamic and open environments in which a wide variety of national and international organisations and movements, as well as institutions, corporations and individuals, can choose their own level of involvement whilst managing to develop a certain social power.

Introduction

During the International Labour conference of June 1999, the Worst Forms of Child Labour Convention (No 182) was accepted unanimously. This Convention calls on all countries and parties involved to take immediate action to prohibit the worst forms of child labour[1]. This achievement was the provisional climax of a global movement fighting for the swift eradication of child labour. The Convention was ratified more quickly than any other since the International Labour Organisation (ILO) was launched in 1919. In less than three years, it was ratified by 132 states, including many developing countries. By the end of 2007 no fewer than 165 countries had ratified the convention.

---

1   The worst forms of child labour are defined as comprising: all forms of slavery or practices similar to slavery (sale and trafficking of children, debt bondage, serfdom, forced or compulsory recruitment of children for use in armed conflict); the use, procurement or offering of children for prostitution or the production of pornography; the use, procurement or offering of a child for illicit activities (including drug trafficking) and work which, by its nature or the circumstances in which it is carried out, is likely to harm the health, safety and morals of children (ILO, 2001).

This demonstrates that the movement for the elimination of child labour has managed to accumulate enough power to register the exploitation of children as a reprehensible concept in the official international norm system. This can be seen as a first important step in the eradication of a practice that still remains widespread.

In this paper the movement for the eradication of child labour will be used as an example to study the emergence of a particular form of collective action that is increasingly occurring on the international scene, the transnational network movement. First, the concept will be further explained. Then, the particular history of the movement for the abolition of child labour, as well as the variety of actors involved and its diverse repertoire of actions will illustrate how a transnational network movement differs from other forms of transnational collective action and social movements.

Transnational network movements

Transnational collective actions, involving non-governmental organisations (NGOs), social movements, media groups and others, have become a very important factor in global politics. They have become as much part of the international scene as the international and intergovernmental institutions and transnational companies (Olesen, 2005; Sikkink, 2005) as can be seen by the very visible and vocal role these new global and NGOs have played in the many international conferences organised by the United Nations over the last decade. As Khagram et al., among others, have argued in a recent publication on this phenomenon, the first objective of these transnational pressure groups is to create international norms, to reinforce them, and to implement and monitor them (Khagram et al., 2002). Their common aim has been described as being to create an alternative world order and to civilise global society (Waterman, 2001).

Transnational collective actions occur in many forms and are carried out by a variety of actors. International NGOs and transnational coalitions, for instance, play a key role in present day transnational collective actions. But, as we argue in this paper, empirically and theoretically they have to be distinguished from transnational social movements and the emerging transnational network movements.

International NGOs are indeed the first kind of civil players we see on the global scene. They have been around for a very long time. The term covers a wide range of organisations, of which churches are likely to be the oldest examples. International organisations of trade unions, employers and farmers also belong to this group. These are in fact international federations of national organisations. However, the most visible non-government organisations on the international scene are now multinational organisations such as Oxfam International, Care International, Greenpeace, Amnesty International or Human Rights Watch. It is noteworthy that most of these Big International NGOs (BINGOs) originated in the industrialised world. A typical feature of these international non-government organisations is their hierarchical, federal international structures. The individuals involved are allocated their place in the international non-governmental organisation through their own national organisation. The strategic and target-oriented approach of these international non-government organisations also deserves note.

Another way of carrying out transnational collective actions is through transnational coalitions, in which several national and international organisations consciously attune their strategies to maximise their influence by operating co-operatively. Often, these coalitions are of a temporary nature, with a limited agenda and a limited set of activities linking into an international campaign. The participation and mobilisation of individuals in many of these transnational actions still takes place through national organisations. The Jubilee 2000 campaign for the abolition of Third Word Debt is a case in point. Apart from a number of churches, this campaign was supported by a wide range of national and international civil society actors: NGOs, national and international trade union organisations and other social movements. International coalitions have become an increasingly important phenomenon in the international arena since the mid 1970s. At a time when the free market was heralded as a panacea for development problems, they managed to present the 'human rights' approach as a morally superior alternative. With their 'communicative power' (Dryzek, 1999), a deep knowledge of their subject and their emotional involvement with the victims of the dominant development model, they have succeeded in pushing issues onto the international political agenda, helping to define problems and hence contributing to their resolution.

The power play on the international forum has been studied extensively in the literature on transnational social movements (e.g. Diani & McAdam, 2003; McAdam et al., 1996; Tarrow, 2002). This is indeed a third kind of transnational collective action. Under certain conditions transnational collective actions can develop into transnational social movements. In this paper, transnational social movements are defined as collective actions carried out on a continuous basis with the participation of a specific and well-defined group of actors, driven by a more or less coherent and explicit ideology, and supported by at least some form of institutional entity. One transnational social movement that has gained momentum over recent years is the World Social Forum. The World Social Forum is 'an open meeting place where social movements, networks, NGOs and other civil society organisations opposed to neo-liberalism and a world dominated by capital or by any form of imperialism come together to pursue their thinking, to debate ideas democratically, to formulate proposals, share their experiences freely and network for effective action'. Since the first world encounter in 2001 in Porto Alegre (Brazil), it has taken the form of a permanent world process seeking and building alternatives to neo-liberal policies'. This self-definition as a permanent transnational movement is referred to in its Charter of Principles, the WSF's guiding document (World Social Forum, 2001).

The World Social Forum is also characterised by plurality and diversity and is non-confessional, non-governmental and non-party. It declares that its aim is to facilitate decentralised coordination and networking among organisations engaged in concrete action towards building another world, at any level from the local to the international, but it does not intend to be a body representing world civil society. The World Social Forum emphasises that is neither a group nor an organisation.

For our argument it is important to note that the World Social Forum, as a prime example of an transnational social movement, is a civil society movement, has a coordinating body, organises regular meetings and a has a common ideological platform or charter. Alongside the rise of transnational social movements, another form of collective actions has appeared on the international scene: transnational network movements. These network movements differ from traditional social movements in terms of practice, ideology, and organisation, as Table 1 shows.

Table 1: International NGOs, Transnational Coalitions, Transnational Social Movements and Transnational Network Movements

	International NGO	Transnational Coalition
Prime identity	Social organisation	Coalition
Participation	National members or affiliates	Civil society organisations and movements, individuals, corporations, government agencies, international agencies
Practice	Participation and commitment on a continuous basis (until membership expires)	Participation and commitment on temporary (as long as agreed upon by parties involved) and regular basis
Ideology	Coherent ideology and vision on a broad range of issues right from the start; common search for adaptation	Coherent ideology and vision on specific issue right from the start; common search for adaptation
Organisation	Formal, hierarchical, federal international structure	Non-hierarchical, decentralised; minimal formal and institutional entity

	Transnational Social Movement	Transnational Network Movement
Prime identity	Social Movement	Network
Participation	Civil society organisations and movements as well as individuals	Civil society organisations and movements as well as individuals; corporations, government agencies, international agencies
Practice	Participation and commitment on continuous and regular basis	Participation and commitment on temporary and irregular basis
Ideology	Pluralist but common investment in ideological coherence	Pluralist right from the start. Not in search of coherent ideology
Organisation	Minimal central and decentralised formal and institutional entities	No central or decentralised formal and institutional entities or coordinating bodies

source: Develtere and Huybrechs, 2008

Unlike transnational collective actions and social movements, transnational network movements are, in our opinion, less rigidly organised. They cannot be reduced to one or a few international non-government organisations or to a single particular coalition; nor are they guided by some form of institutional entity. Network movements are very dynamic, open and pluralist environments in which organisations, but also individuals, can choose their own level of involvement. There is no need for direct, streamlined and co-ordinated interaction between the participants. Yet, between them, they define the issue they are concerned with, without endeavouring to achieve a single coherent, consistent vision of it. The movement is able to encompass a wide spectrum of diverse analyses and opinions. In combination, they bring their topic into the spotlight. Together, they develop a discourse. Together, they often create tensions and highlight contradictions in the system. This is how they manage to develop power, without any single organisation (or coalition of organisations) playing a central part in drawing up the strategy and tactics. The participants are often mobilised in a virtual and ad hoc manner, rather than according to a pre-set plan. As Juris – who uses the term 'networked social movements' to refer to both transnational social movements and network movements – rightly points out, they are shot through with internal differentiation and contestation (Juris, 2004). But this does not make the power of their influence less real. The new information technologies offer a new, efficient, material basis for these movements. If we agree that the new social architecture of society rests to a large extent on networking (Castells, 1997, 2000), then it must be admitted that network movements have the potential to become pretty powerful players. Their dispersed nature means that they are well equipped to tackle the other networks (such as those of regulatory authorities, companies, the media, the world of finance or organised religions) operating on the global scene. As Castells put it, what we see is a 'networking, decentered form of organisation and intervention, characteristic of the new social movements, mirroring, and counteracting, the networking logic of domination in the information society' (Castells, 1997).

These features of transnational network movements are illustrated in the movement for the abolition of child labour, which has managed in barely two decades to put the eradication of child labour onto the international agenda. An analysis of its history, the parties involved, and its repertoire of actions shows how the collective actions of various parties, despite incoherence in ideology, organisation, and practices, have still managed to play powerfully on the present day international stage.

The emergence of a network movement

Describing the origins of a movement is a near impossible task. Should we begin with someone who has done something significant, with someone who has said something important, with a conference, or with a new law? The movement for the abolition of child labour arguably has its roots in the inter-war period when the Forced Labour Convention No. 29 (1930) was adopted by the International Labour Organisation at its annual conference. Later, in 1973, the same international organisation adopted the Minimum Age Convention No. 138. This Convention fixes the minimum age for employment at 15. Children between the ages of 13 and 15 are allowed to do some light work, as long as it does not interfere with their education, their health or development. The Convention also determines 18 as the minimum age for dangerous work. The problem with this Convention was that it only paid attention to the formal economy and that it only drafted a few very general guidelines.

The current movement for the abolition of child labour was not directly inspired by these Conventions, but formed part of a triple development which took place from the 1980s on. Firstly, the human rights approach emerged, in the footsteps of Nobel Prize winner A. Sen (2000), who argued that poverty should not be seen simply as a problem in its own right, but should be regarded as a deprivation of fundamental rights and freedoms. Child labour illustrates the power of this argument. Both as a cause and as a result of poverty, child labour can be viewed as a prison depriving children of all rights and freedoms, stunting their potential to develop.

A second development seized on by the movement against child labour was the emerging idea of a socially-corrected economic globalisation. In this context, child labour is regarded as a very important example of the 'race to the bottom' which obliges developing countries in particular to try to compete in ever worsening working conditions in the context of ever-fiercer competition in international trade. Protagonists of a socially corrected economic globalisation dismiss this phenomenon.

The third development is related to the so-called 'multi-stakeholder principle' based on the premise that big social problems should be prevented and resolved through the co-operation of a range of different stakeholders. Child labour in this view is seen as a problem issue that should be tackled through the concerted efforts of regulatory authorities, companies, trade unions and other civic entities.

These inter-related developments can be seen in context in several events. In 1985, five non-government organisations founded Child Workers in Asia with the goal of acting together against the exploitation of children in the region. They aimed to set the agenda in relation to this problem, both at local and international levels. Furthermore, they wanted to ensure that children would be able to participate in formulating programmes and policies on this issue.

In 1989, the UN adopted a Convention on the Rights of the Child. This Convention attracted wide-ranging political support. With more than 190 ratifications, this Convention is the most universally supported human rights instrument. The Convention explicitly refers to the issue of child labour. In paper 32, reference is made to the right of children to be delivered from 'economic exploitation and from performing any work that is likely to be hazardous or to be harmful to the child's health or physical, mental, spiritual, moral or social development'.

In the meanwhile, in North American and, later, European trade union circles a debate was initiated on the need for social clauses in international trade law (van Roozendaal, 2002). Proponents of this approach wanted to insert a clause which would become an integral part of GATT (the General Agreement on Tariffs and Trade) and, later, the World Trade Organisation, triggering a penalty system every time a commercial party manufactured goods in contravention of fundamental working conditions standards. At the most basic level of argument, social clauses were considered to be instruments that would prohibit unfair competition based on a disregard for workers' rights. Going beyond this, some searched for a more positive approach to social clauses, with a special focus on supporting efforts to abolish social abuses.

The 1990 World Summit for Children put the emphasis on the universal rights of children (UNICEF, 2000). A great deal of attention went into detailing the violation of these rights in the case of child workers. Inspired by these discussions, the German government was the first to allocate resources for the International Programme on the Elimination of Child Labour (IPEC) of the International Labour Organisation in 1992.

Initially, six countries took part. Unexpectedly, the programme was very successful, both with donor countries and developing countries.

Not only did the discussion on social clauses, unfair competition and the exploitation of children lead to fierce debates in both North and South, but it also led to a range of innovatory initiatives. In 1992, Reebok International Ltd introduced a company policy aiming to abolish the use of child labour in the production of Reebok products.

During the same period, a powerful lobby emerged from the American consumer and trade union movement, calling for a boycott on clothes and textiles from Bangladesh, where child labour was prevalent. In 1993, American senator Tom Harkin, a Democrat from Iowa, introduced the Child Labour Deterrence Act in the Senate. The purpose of the Act was to stop the employment of children below the age of 15 in the production of processed goods and mining products for the American market. These proposal caused shockwaves in several countries that had become dependent on supplying the American market for textile and items of clothing. Bengali manufacturers sacked approximately 50,000 children below the age of 14 from their factories. For many, however, this was a move from the frying pan into the fire, since they had no alternative means of economic survival. This occasioned the now famous negotiations between the Bengali government, the American embassy, the Bangladesh Garment Manufacturers and Export Association, UNICEF and the International Labour Organisation. The Memorandum of Understanding signed in 1995 by the latter three entities stipulates that Bengali textile factories are prohibited from taking on children younger than 14, but also that no child should be sacked without being given access to education.

In 1995, the Indian government issued a leaflet with the heading 'Meet Jalil Ahmed Ansari. Successful owner of a carpet manufacturing unit. And former "child labourer"'. The aim was to demonstrate that child labour does not necessarily seal an irreversible fate for life, and that in India even children from this deprived group may become upwardly mobile.

In the mid 1990s, the first voluntary labelling initiatives were instigated by non-government organisations, export promotion agencies and exporters. In September 1996, the International Federation of Football Associations (FIFA) announced an agreement with three international trade union federations concerning a code of labour practice. In future, goods carrying the FIFA logo would have to meet certain criteria, including a prohibition on their being produced by children.

In the meanwhile, the network of non-government organisations and movements fighting for fair trade, the observation of terms and conditions of employment and the abolition of child labour expanded and diversified. In Europe, the Clean Clothes Campaign gained considerable ground, with the active input of NGOs and professional associations. In India, child workers and their supporters were involved in several demonstrations. On 17 January 1998, a Global March against Child Labour set off. Hundreds of thousands of people marched in dozens of countries in national demonstrations to demand the abolition of child labour. The march was organised by a global coalition of international NGOs and international trade union organisations, supported by national committees set up for the occasion. The committees were made up of local NGOs, trade unions, women's movements, action groups on children's rights and various other civil society groups. The mission of the march was 'to mobilise world-wide efforts to protect and promote the rights of all children, especially the right to receive a free, meaningful education and to be free from economic exploitation and from performing any work that is likely to be damaging to the child's physical, mental, spiritual, moral or social development'. The march, which could be followed in the national and international media and which had their support, culminated in the participation of several dozen child workers and hundreds of militants at the International Labour Conference in June 1998 in Geneva. On the agenda was a first discussion of the new Worst Forms of Child Labour Convention. After a second discussion on the subject in 1999, the Conference adopted the convention. The convention states that 'Each Member which ratifies this Convention shall take immediate and effective measures to secure the prohibition and elimination of the worst forms of child labour as a matter of urgency' (Article 1).

This historical sequence of events illustrates the wide repertoire of actions and parties involved in the movement for the abolition of child labour. When examining the parties and actions of this transnational network movement in more detail, differences in practice, ideology, and organisation become apparent.

The parties involved

The parties involved in the movement for the eradication of child labour always intended to create a broad network of individuals and institutions that would provide the necessary norms and control mechanisms to eradicate child labour once and for all. For this reason, the network movement systematically sought to enlist new elements (individuals and institutions) and to use them as a lever to achieve this objective. This short historic overview has already pinpointed the main protagonists of the movement. It will already be obvious that they share the same broad aim of abolishing child labour, but not always based on the same concerns; nor do they follow the same strategies.

The NGOs are without doubt one of the most prominent parties involved. The local and international NGOs are most consistent in offering the children involved and their parents a chance to articulate their problems. Most of them harbour a constructive, albeit critical, view of the other protagonists. Many of the NGOs have as their primary goal the defence of the rights of the child, but their outlook may differ substantially. The 'abolitionists' want the immediate and total abolition of the exploitation of children. The 'gradualists' favour a step-by-step approach, expressing concern for the rights of children as workers.

Up to now, trade unions have also played a crucial role in the network movement (Fyfe & Jankanish, 1997; ILO, 2000; Develtere & Huybrechts, 2006). With their international contacts extending beyond those of the NGOs, they have been even more successful in forcing the debate on the eradication of child labour into international debating chambers. At national level, however, they had to get through the filters of national industrial relations and political economy, which determine their power relationship with authorities and employers. It is this context which explains, for instance, the motivation of the American trade union federation AFL-CIO for opposing child labour on the grounds that it constitutes unfair competition with US workers. Furthermore, trade unions are based on a membership system. The theme of child labour may consequently involve some difficult internal debates. For instance, the trade unions for bidi workers (cigarette rollers) in India or Bangladesh do not represent the children who do this tedious job but often their fathers or uncles who have the contracts with the middle-men or buyers, people who actually stand to gain from the current situation remaining unchanged. However trade unions' close links with workers do also open up new opportunities for campaigning. For example, the Brazilian Confederation of Agricultural Workers (CONTAG) uses its rural radio stations to inform its members and the rural population of the dangers to children of toxic chemicals.

Employers' organisations have also played a critical role by raising political awareness and politically mobilising people against child labour. Many international organisations of employers are actively promoting a strategy of corporate social responsibility and even ethical business practice, encouraging their members to develop practices to encourage conformity with international norms for working conditions and sustainable development. In this context, abolishing child labour is a higher priority than any other social objective.

Consumer organisations, by contrast, have introduced a strong ethical dimension into their operations, with a strategy of 'naming and shaming' manufacturers and retailers of goods that are produced with child labour. At the same time, they have made the movement for the eradication of child labour aware that purchasing power can be converted into social power. Activities like those of the Clean Clothes Campaign have demonstrated that Western companies are often verysensitive with regard to their image.

Legislators have also played a very prominent role from the beginning. We have already referred to the unexpected consequences of Harkin's Bill in the United States, as an example of policies that aim to impose sanctions against countries that allow child labour in the production of clothing and textiles. In Belgium, Member of Parliament Dirk Van der Maelen took the legislative initiative to protect a few fundamental social rights by the creation of penal provisions that make breaches, including the failing to observer the minimum age for labour, universally punishable. In Brazil, a Parliamentary Front for the Rights of Children and Adolescents has been set up. To date, these parliamentary initiatives have mainly played a promotional role, raising levels of awareness. The same can be said of resolutions, norms and declarations adopted by regional and international bodies.

The mass media have played an important role as catalysts. For several months, the Global March against Child Labour in 1998 received prime time attention from CNN and other global and national channels. Some media tended to focus on the sensational aspect of the issue, presenting children as victims. Others willingly agreed to play a part in campaigns and strategies for change. For instance, the police and an NGO in Nepal, launched a campaign designed to raise awareness of the sexual exploitation and trafficking of children. Several media channels became actively involved in this campaign.

The international organisations to which these predominantly national players belong have given the movement for the eradication of child labour a transnational dimension. These international organisations themselves mainly work transnationally, addressing the other international organisations (as opposed to national or regional bodies) in such a way that a debate opens up between them, resulting either in co-operation or in a reaction against them. This has produced some results, including a host of agreements between international organisations. One example is the agreement reached in 1999 between the International Union of Food, Agricultural, Hotel, Restaurant, Catering and Allied Workers' Association (IUF) with the International Tobacco Growers' Association for the eradication of child labour in the tobacco industry. In many cases, the international umbrella organisations made up of NGOs, trade unions, members of parliament, governments and media have themselves instigated or forced action from their national representatives. Since the early 1990s, many national organisations have found it impossible to ignore the campaign for the eradication of child labour. The most important international institutions involved in this global network movement have been the International Labour Organisation, UNICEF, Oxfam International, ActionAid and the international trade union organisations.

Developments in the repertoire of actions

Social movements tend to adopt fairly well-defined models of action. Depending on their objectives, ideology and strategy, they opt for a limited range of action models, such as demonstrations, strikes, lobbying, media campaigns or self-help initiatives. These models of collective action are discussed with the membership, and planned as much as possible in advance. Since part of the intention is to perpetuate the movement and to give it a visible place in the national social, economic and political system, the action model also becomes a sort of display board, with a rather repetitive character.

Network movements, however, and particularly transnational network movements, do not build up their repertoire of actions in the same way. Their action models are shaped by a very dynamic interaction between different national and international actors, with scope for rapid changes over time.

For instance, the movement for the eradication of child labour started out with a wide spectrum of ad hoc projects in which children were removed from their workplaces and given an alternative education. Over time, attention focused more particularly on children subjected to the worst forms of labour: children in prostitution, children who were trafficked, child-slaves and children in armed conflicts. The projects responded to these awful situations by removing children from them. The plight of children working in bad conditions, exposed to chemicals, dust, fumes, falling objects and dangerous machinery also came into focus, triggering a search for ways to improve their working conditions. From the 1990s on, these more target-oriented projects became increasingly integrated into national programmes, with the participation of a range of national parties such as governments, employers, trade unions and NGOs. Since the adoption of ILO Convention 182, the focus of these programmes has become even narrower. The so-called 'time-bound programme approach' is used to reach very specific objectives, for instance the eradication of child labour in specific economic sectors (such as mining, the textile industry and waste disposal). Several countries have also incorporated the campaign to eradicate child labour into their national poverty reduction programmes or their strategies for reaching their Millennium Development Goals, thereby treating it as part of a much wider approach.

The mobilisation of public opinion has always been a strong factor in the movement for the eradication of child labour. But, even here, major changes in both content and form have taken place over a very short period of time. Originally, the mobilisation of public opinion was mainly aimed at Western consumers and governments, designed to convey the message that the very existence of child labour demonstrated how social conditions in the global economy were deteriorating in a downward spiral and that countries involved in such abuses should be punished. This was quickly followed by a further phase, in which the movement targeted global public opinion, including that in the South. Here, the message was that child labour was a violation of human rights and that, furthermore, child labour was ethically, socially and economically unjustifiable. The alternative to child labour was education. The Global March against Child Labour in 1998 has undoubtedly been the most important lever in the formation of global public opinion on this issue. The active mobilisation of citizens in a global project with very high visibility was instrumental both in building support and in demonstrating the scale of this support. Since then, the emphasis has returned to the national level, although this action was co-ordinated at internationally. The Global Campaign for Education is the main advocate of the message that the eradication of child labour can (only) be achieved if education is offered as an alternative. In addition to the Global March (which has now become an international NGO), this campaign is supported by several other international NGOs including Oxfam International, ActionAid, World Vision and Social Alert, as well as the International Trade Union Confederation.

In parallel with this campaign, consumer groups and trade union movements have developed a strategy aimed at convincing consumers that other people's business is also their concern. Through petitions, media campaigns and negotiations with manufacturers of goods made in poor working conditions (in a broad approach typical of this sort of campaign), the Clean Clothes Campaign has shown that buying power carries a lot of weight. The campaign has convincingly demonstrated that manufacturers and traders are not only responsible for the existence of child labour but also for maintaining poor working conditions and terms of employment, as well as the violation of workers' rights. This has led to some concrete achievements: some companies and sector organisations have even developed their own codes of conduct. Already, by June 2000, the Organisation for Economic Co-operation and Development (OECD) was able to list no less than 210 of these codes of conduct, most of which refer to the prohibition of child labour. These codes are, however, by no means perfect. According to the Clean Clothes Campaign, most fall far short of meeting all the campaign's targets. Important omissions include a failure to recognise fundamental workers' rights such as the freedom of association and collective bargaining, the absence of discrimination, a safe and healthy working environment, limitations on working excessive hours and minimum wages. Furthermore, the codes are generally vague and difficult to interpret and the responsibilities of the companies involved is not always clearly defined. The campaign also reproaches the transnational companies that have agreed to these codes for refusing to undergo independent monitoring and control. For this reason, a few initiatives have recently been set up jointly by NGOs, trade unions, public authorities and employers' organisations to take things a stage further. The Ethical Trading Initiative in the United Kingdom is one such example. This involves a pilot project designed to test out and compare different control models.

In order to reassure consumers that no child labour takes place, NGOs and governments are considering the development of special labels in a number of cases. In 1994, for instance, the Rugmark certification programme was set up in India. The Rugmark label – a smiling carpet - can be found on the back of carpets produced and sold by companies that allow their factories to be inspected with regard to the use of child labour in the production process. Other examples are the Kaleen labelling programme launched by the Indian Carpet Export Promotion Council in 1995, the STEP programme developed by Swiss NGOs and the Care and Fair programme set up by German carpet traders. The Brazilian Abrinq Foundation uses a different approach, awarding some companies, particularly those operating in the sugar and sports goods industries, the title of a 'Child-Friendly Company'. In 1997, Baden Sports started to label the footballs it imported from China with the phrase 'certified: no child or slave labour used on this ball'. Critical academics also stepped in to present the results of research that showed under which conditions social labelling can have a positive outcome and impact (Sharma et al., 2004).

A characteristic of these initiatives is that they rely on corporate ethics, being based on voluntary measures and a great deal of self-regulation. Within the network movement for the eradication of child labour, some parties wish to take the issue further than this, arguing that a global human rights regime should lay down enforceable laws and responsibilities that correspond with these ethical principles. Organisations like the International Council on Human Rights Policy defend an international legal system based on the principles of responsibility and indemnification through compensation and rehabilitation when someone suffers a loss (Howen et al., 2002). This would apply, for example, when children are forced to work in ways that inflict physical, moral and social damage. This international legal system would still have to be implemented at a national level but would no longer only apply to the countries involved, but also to individuals, organisations and companies. A first step in this direction came with the introduction of international procedures to verify whether states adhere sufficiently to their international obligations with regard to human rights, and whether they make appropriate checks on citizens or companies on their territory to enforce these rights. The Human Rights Commission set up by the United Nations, the International Labour Organisation and the North American Free Trade Agreement (NAFTA) have already set up purpose-made procedures for this purpose. However, to a large extent, preference is still given to weak and quasi-legal instruments which do not have legally binding force, often describes as 'soft international law'. An example of this is supplied by the Global Compact Initiative launched by the Secretary-General of the United Nations in July 2000. This initiative is intended as a forum, whose participants are asked to underwrite nine principles relating to human rights, working conditions and sustainable development.

This account demonstrates that the repertoire of activities used by the movement for the eradication of child labour can be seen as having followed a trajectory from 'opposition' to 'proposition'. In the first few years, the emphasis lay on the bad conscience and character of those who used or tolerated child labour. Over time this evolved in the direction of the development of a new, more co-operative approach, whereby those involved in the movement make proposals for policy measures to alleviate child labour altogether or abolish it altogether.

Conclusion

In recent years the elimination of child labour has featured strongly on the international agenda and become recognised as a high-profile issue where campaigning efforts have produced significant results (ILO, 2004) Although the movement for the eradication of child labour is still very young , it has nevertheless managed to contribute significantly to this new understanding and interpretation of the phenomenon of child labour and possible ways to tackle it. The NGOs, social movements, journalists, companies, academics, and national and international public servants who have contributed to this movement form a moral community that has defined the problems of child labour and raised it as an issue. Studying the movement for the eradication of child labour can thus help us to develop an overall understanding of the recent phenomenon of transnational network movements. By contrast with traditional social movements, these network movements are much more pluralist, since they attract a commitment not only from civil society organisations but also from governmental and intergovernmental agencies and even from private companies, all of whom identify themselves as part of this movement. To the extent that they do so, they can be regarded as equal and alike, although they are conscious of the reality that they are also unequal and unalike in many respects, and remain involved in antagonisms and conflicts amongst themselves.

It is therefore no surprise that a network movement like the one studied here is by definition ideologically pluralist as well. Its members accept divergent and conflicting ideas about the causes and effects of child labour as well as about responsibilities and strategies. In addition a range of different, sometimes incongruous, patterns of action co-exist concerning projects and programmes, the mobilisation of media and public opinion, initiatives to label and certify good practice, and national and international legislation. Involvement in this kind of movement is a long-term commitment for some, but only a temporary engagement for others.

The co-existence of these differing approaches has, of course, a serious impact on the power relations within such a movement. More than in any other kind of international social organisation or movement, global co-operation and networking is based on decentralised, informal and horizontal relationships. Typically, this kind of movement has no headquarters; no single institutional entity; no uniform decision-making procedure; no coherent ideology; no fixed mechanisms for participation; and no single website which all the protagonists of the movement can refer to and where they can present a converging view.

Nevertheless, the movement for the abolition of child labour has shown how, in the new social architecture of society that is increasingly reliant on networking, transnational network movements have the potential to become powerful players, well equipped to make their presence felt on the international stage. The campaign against child labour has demonstrated that they are able to challenge and interact with the other networks (for instance of authorities, companies, media, financial organisations or religions). The fact that the Worst Forms of Child Labour Convention, formally adopted in Geneva in 1999 during the General Conference of the International Labour Organisation, has become the most rapidly ratified ILO Convention ever graphically illustrates the power of this transnational network movement.

In general, it can be observed that the number of transnational network movements is increasing and is likely to continue to do so in the foreseeable future. Other issues that have evolved into transnational network movements, including the campaigns against female genital mutilation and against land mines, have evolved into transnational network movements. Many of these transnational network movements seem to have developed around ethical issues and include the promotion of an alternative global society.

Unfortunately little or no research has been carried out to produce concrete evidence of the real impact of this kind of movement for the people concerned (in our case, child workers). Nor can we firmly establish a causal relation between the existence and dynamics of this movement and the recent announcement by the ILO that the number of working children in the 5-14 age group decreased by 20 million between 2000 and 2004 (Fyfe, 2007). What is clear is that this network movement appears to have achieved in a short space of time what the trade union movement, acting alone, failed to achieve over many decades. This suggests that involvement in such movements, despite their many contradictions and limitations, might offer a fruitful way forward for trade unions in the future, as one part of a multi-pronged strategy for curbing the worst excesses of the multinational corporations.

© *Patrick Develtere and An Huybrechs, 2008*

REFERENCES

Castells, M. (1997) *The Power of Identity*, Cambridge, Massachusetts:Blackwell
Castells, M. (2000) *The Rise of the Network Society*, Cambridge, Massachusetts: Blackwell
Develtere, P. & A. Huybrechts (2006) *Trade Unions and the Fight against Child Labour: Review of Policies and Practices*, Working Paper 16, Leuven: Centre for Global Governance Studies
Diani, M. & D. McAdam (2003) *Social Movements and Networks: Relational Approaches to Collective Action*, Oxford: Oxford University Press
Dryzek, J. (1999) 'Transnational Democracy', *The Journal of Political Philosophy 7* (1): 30-51
Fyfe, A. & M. Jankanish(1997) *Trade Unions and Child Labour: a Guide to Action*, Geneva: International Labour Office
Fyfe, A. (2007) *The Worldwide Movement against Child Labour: Progress and Future Directions*, Geneva: International Labour Office
Howen, N. & D. Petrasek (2002) *Beyond Voluntarism: Human Rights and the Developing International Obligations of Companies*, Versoix: International Council on Human Rights Policy
ILO (2001) *Eliminating the Worst Forms of Child Labour: an Integrated and Time-Bound Approach*, Geneva: International Labour Organisation

ILO (2000) *Trade Unions and Child Labour: Children out of Work and into School – Adults at Work*, Geneva: International Labour Organisation

ILO (2004) *Investing in every child: an economic study of the costs and benefits of eliminating child labour*, Geneva: International Labour Organisation

Juris, J. S. (2004) 'Networked Social Movements: Global Movements for Social Justice', in M. Castells (ed), *The Network Society: A Cross-cultural Perspective*, Cheltenham: Edward Elgar:341-362

Khagram, S., J.V.Riker & K. Sikkink (2002) *Restructuring World Politics: Transnational Social Movements*, Minneapolis: University of Minnesota Press

McAdam, D., J.D. McCarthy & M.N. Zald (eds) (1996) *Comparative Perspectives on Social Movements: Political Opportunities, Mobilising Structures, and Cultural Framings*, Cambridge: Cambridge University Press

Olesen, T. (2005) 'Transnational Publics: New Spaces of Social Movement Activism and the Problem of Global Long-Sightedness', *Current Sociology* 53 (3):419-440

Sharma, A., R. Sharma & N. Ray (2004) *Child Labour in the Carpet Industry: impact of social labelling in India*, New Delhi: Institute for Human Development

Sikkink, K. 2005. 'Patterns of Dynamic Multilevel Governance and the Insider-Outsider Coalition', in D. della Porta and S. Tarrow (eds), *Transnational Processes and Social Movements*, Lanham, MD: Rowman and Littlefield:151-74

Sen, A. (2000) *Development as Freedom*, New York: Anchor Books

Tarrow, S. (2002) 'From Lumping to Splitting: Specifying Globalisation and Resistance', in J. Smith & H. Johnston (eds), *Globalisation and Resistance: Transnational Dimensions of Social Movements*, Lanham, MD: Rowman and Littlefield:229-49

UNICEF (2000) *Beyond Child Labour, Affirming Rights*, Geneva: UNICEF

Waterman, P. (2001) *Globalization, Social Movements and the New Internationalisms.*, London & New York: Continuum

World Social Forum (2001). Retrieved on December 23, 2007 from http://www.ifiwatchnet.org/?q=en/node/3921

ACKNOWLEDGEMENTS

The authors would like to thank the participants of the international conference *A World for All? The Ethics of Global Civil Society*, organised by the University of Edinburgh in 2005, as well as the anonymous peer reviewers, for their valuable comments on this paper.

Review article:

reflections on international labour studies in the UK

Peter Waterman

Peter Waterman, *formerly a Senior Lecturer at the Institute of Social Studies in The Hague, Netherlands, is an independent research and writer specialising in labour and internationalism.*

ABSTRACT

Reflecting personally on the contribution of the UK to international labour studies over the past forty years and his own role in this history, Peter Waterman reviews some recent publications and websites from both inside and outside the official trade union movement. These are:

Tony Pilch (ed) *Trades Unions and Globalisation,* London: Smith Institute. 86 pp. ISBN 1-905370-14-8

Sheila Cohen, *Ramparts of Resistance: Why Workers Lost Their Power and How to Get it Back,* London: Pluto, 248 pp. ISBN 13-978-0-7453-1529-4 (pb)

Ronaldo Munck, 2006. *Globalisation and Contestation: The Great Counter-Movement,* London: Routledge. 176 pp. ISBN-10 0415376564

Angela Hale and Jane Wills (eds). *Threads of Labour: Garment Industry Supply Chains from the Workers' Perspective,* Oxford: Blackwell, 288 pp. ISBN-10: 1405126388

Paul Mason, *Live Working or Die Fighting: How the Working Class Went Global,* London: Harvill Secker. 304 pp. ISBN 978-0-436-20615-3

NewUnionism http://www.newunionism.net/

Union Ideas Network http://www.uin.org.uk/

> '*A new idea that blossoms in Britain is not a British idea except for the time that it takes for it to be printed. Once launched into space by the press, this idea, if it expresses some universal truth, can also be instantaneously transformed into an internationalist idea.*'

(José Carlos Mariátegui, 1986-1923)

Introduction: two cheers

Two cheers for the newest international labour studies and resources from the UK.

Many Britons might wish to ask what 'universalism' might humanly and effectively mean in our post-modern and post-postmodern times. But Little Britain, curiously, *has* had some kind of initiating role in the production of international labour studies and resources – and not only on the 'emancipatory left' (which is where I like to place myself). Having been involved with the 'New International Labour Studies' (NILS) in the 1970s and 1980s, and published the *Newsletter of International Labour Studies* (also NILS) through the 1980s, I was also a reluctant witness to their decline, as the twin *tsunamis* of globalisation and neo-liberalism struck unions and labour studies worldwide. None of the major labour movement traditions of the previous period, whether Communist, Social-Democratic or Populist (Radical-Nationalist), had in any way prepared unions for this. With such temporary exceptions as Poland, South Africa, South Korea and Brazil, the forward march of labour was not so much halted as reversed.

The decline of international labour studies was marked in the UK at that time by the failure of a planned Zed Press series to take off from a promising start, as well as by the collapse of the monthly *International Labour Reports,* based in the UK's de-industrialising North. Many activist international labour specialists migrated, one of them literally, to what he expected to remain the social-democratic island paradise of New Zealand. Other activists abandoned their little lifeboats to return to the trade union *Titanic,* playing here the role of organisers, advisors, or freelance consultants, often quite impressively.[1] British projects dating from the post-1968 period, such as the Coventry Workshop and the Leeds Trade Union and Community Resource and Information Centre (combining labour, community and internationalist activities) also went into decline. Clearly there remained exceptions, but these were small voices crying in a political and academic wilderness.[2] Others, still committed to international social protest, moved in the direction of the 'new social movements' in general or feminism in particular. Or they began reconsidering the international labour movement as a potential part of some kind of new global process. I was one of these Britons, though an expatriate one. So was Ronaldo Munck, an 'inpatriate' of the British Isles, my one-time collaborator and occasional interlocutor.[3] I do not wish to overstate the depths of the decline, nor the extent of the recovery. But I would like to note my pleasure at what has been coming to my attention, in padded envelopes or down the virtual pipeline to my computer screen.[4]

I would also like to note that, although the term 'international labour studies' could include international studies of production, of work and workers, I have used it here to mean international studies of labour as a community, culture or class, as a

---

1   One of these is Celia Mather, a former editor of *International Labour Reports* (ILR), who has played this role both for traditional trade unions and for the new labour networks. See, for example, her excellent handbook for women workers in the global clothing industry (Mather, 2004). Others are the two founders of ILR, Dave Spooner and Stuart Howard. The first became a leading figure in the International Federation of Worker Education Associations, the second in the International Transport Workers Federation.

2   One of these has to be the quarterly *International Union Rights*, currently, I think, the only autonomous international labour solidarity magazine in the world. In both style and appearance the UK-based magazine is reminiscent of *International Labour Reports.* But the origins of IUR lie not in the shopfloor internationalism of the 1970s-80s but in the sclerotic World Federation of Trade Unions (see below). As the WFTU followed the downward path of its Communist-bloc sponsors, its labour rights network – coordinated in the UK by Tom Sibley - broke away and gave birth to this magazine and associated activities. It is my impression that IUR has been becoming simultaneously more open, more relevant and more radical, whilst showing little if any relationship to the new global justice and solidarity movement. It has a broad left Editorial Board. It deserves closer attention.

3   I draw here, and elsewhere in this review, on an autobiography underway as well as earlier reviews (Waterman, 1998; 2004a; 2004b; 2004c). Compare Munck (2002; 2003).

4   In case anyone should consider that I disregard the newest international labour studies resources from outside the UK, I would like to note here some of these: *Global Labor Strategies* (Kloosterboer 2007), *Prol-Position, The Big Sell-Out, International Association of Labour History Institutions 2007, Asia Monitor Resource Centre, No Border Network, New Labor Forum,* and *Streetnet International.* To these I think one should add studies of national-immigrant relations, or 'internationalism in one country', most advanced probably in the USA. An example would be Ness, 2005.

movement, in terms of self-organisation, and as a form of protest by workers against their condition and a demand for something *more* or something *other*.[5]

Anti-Globalisation Creep

Tony Pilch's *Trade Unions and Globalisation* collection, has the kind of literal name, and staid yet glossy appearance that one might expect of an establishment production. The establishment it represents, is that of 'social partnership' – i.e. a capitalist partnership between corporations, the state and the unions. It bears these marks also in the contributed texts. But what strikes me is the extent to which it is also marked by the kind of language that NILS (the school) and NILS (the newsletter) were speaking two decades ago. Again, I do not wish to exaggerate this. Insofar as new notes *are* struck by certain contributors, they represent some kind of anti-globalisation creep or infection and hardly challenge the national or international social partnership frame that shapes the collection.

In keeping with traditional unionism and labour studies, *Trade Unions and Globalisation* simply *assumes* a national frame of reference, with its two non-UK chapters being – by chance or choice – by holders of the national passport. Contributions are thus made by two New Labour members of the British government or parliament, three top officials of national trade unions, the General Secretary of the European Trade Union Confederation (ETUC), and one academic writing on China.

This range of participation is predictable, and so, too is much of the content, from the self-congratulatory contributions of the politicos to the self-serving chapter by the Human Resource Director of BAE Systems – a major British producer and exporter of weapons. BAE employs 100,000 worldwide, of whom just 32,000 are in the UK. This context explains the balance between its anxiety and need to keep the minority UK workforce satisfied which seems to underlie what is in many ways a model of the partnership structure and consultation process typical of the 1970s and 1980s [6]. The success of this marriage of convenience is hinted at by the donation of one page, within the author's ten, to a group of junior partners, top union representatives who endorse this MNC manager's understanding of globalisation and his general world view. There is no mention, though, that BAE, is currently better known in the UK, the Gulf, and the USA as the subject of press accusations of corrupt business practices, allegedly carried out with the collusion of the British government. The role of the junior partner in such a marriage is likely to be a limited, complicit and often silent one.

Unfortunately, the chapter by the union-employed General Secretary of the ETUC is similarly marked by what might be a termed a 'subordinate-partner syndrome'. The ETUC is a confederation of national European trade unions of all backgrounds – Social-Democratic, Christian-Socialist and Communist. The major point of reference in the contribution by John Monks is the European Union itself, its competitive position, its

---

5   This is why I do not here consider the undoubtedly pioneering work of Ursula Huws (2003), which is certainly both aware of and relevant to understanding the new global world of work. The book of Huws on the 'cybertariat' does occasionally touch on consciousness and protest, but what it is primarily concerned with is the complex nature and implications of a new kind of labour. It is, of course, essential reading in this field.
6   This would seem to be a limitation of even the most recent European analyses and proposals for worker participation or economic democracy. See the review of the *New Unionism* site below, and Kester (2007). Yet challenges to what is produced and how it is sold – as well as various other 'managerial prerogatives' is a rising labour and social concern, as suggested, again, by the review of Hale and Wills below.

internal market, its technological progress and, of course, its social peace. Although he refers in passing to the shock of the French (and, hey, Dutch!) 'No' to the European Constitution, Monks fails to mention that, in its loyalty to a Europe of its own imagination, the ETUC (and its Dutch affiliate!) had urged workers to vote 'Yes' to this!

Readers may by now be wondering where the good news referred to in my introduction is hiding itself. Actually, I feel it is possibly concealed within the Monks piece, insofar as he criticises 'the illusory internationalism of the International Monetary Fund and the World Bank' (52). This is a step forward from the traditional international union practice, which has long been one of *polite dialogue* with these promoters of labour movement auto-destruction - as well as with the World Trade Organisation. Monks goes further:

'There is an urgent need for a genuine Europe-wide debate. Fundamental changes in our internal economic and social policies cannot be dictated by the considerations of the traditional political economy. Recent history in the EU shows that trade and globalisation questions are now of wide-ranging public concern [...] We need a debate on the 'new capitalism' that is emerging, driven by global rootless capital.' (57)

These are fighting words. Unfortunately, however, his address is to a Europe of 'rights-based values' (53), presented as morally superior to the Chinese in their nefarious 'offensive in Africa' (55). Not only is this Europe a morally superior entity, it is also one embodying will and power. Does this raise echoes not only Jacques Delors but of British social-imperialist Joseph Chamberlain?

Fortunately, this is not the best (from an emancipatory point of view) union effort in this publication. Derek Simpson is General Secretary of Amicus, the UK's largest union of 'manufacturing, technical and skilled persons', itself a merger of several others, and currently involved in creating further mergers or partnerships with other unions nationally and internationally:

'The platform for creating multinational unions is larger domestic trade unions and solidarity agreements with our international counterparts. Amicus and the Transport and General Workers' Union are beginning this process, now creating the UK's biggest union. We have signed solidarity agreements with super-unions in Europe and the American unions, the Machinists and the United Steel Workers. I believe it is possible to have a functioning, if loosely federal, multinational trade union organisation within the next decade.' (33).

Fortunately, again, Simpson is not simply talking in terms of calculable size and speculative reach; he also refers to the necessity of reinvigorating the union image, of developing a 'culture of activism', of becoming 'embedded in local civil society', here referring to a labour-community alliance in London's historical immigrant worker centre, the East End, and noting how this has

'Successfully targeted people whom trade unions have found particularly hard to reach – mostly female, ethnic minority and migrant workers and agency staff.' (34).

Simpson further talks of what social geographers might call 'multi-scalar' union action against global corporations, of links between workers and consumers transnationally, and of unions recognising the new kinds of work and workers – particularly female, young, ethnic minorities and part-timers - often to be found in private services, retail and distribution, hospitality and leisure. The language on communication and on civil society coalitions is similarly assertive:

'[T]he communications advances associated with globalisation can assist us. Robust organising strategies are being made possible and being democratised through the use of global technologies – fax, email, cheap travel, blogs etc – which can be used to spread workers' experiences across the world simultaneously, and can be adopted as readily by trade unions as by global corporations [...W]e have to deploy all the expertise and resources available to maximise... leverage. This may depend on the building of powerful on-going as well as ad hoc coalitions with other groups, be they faith organisations, student networks, shareholders, consumers or charities – either at global, national or local level, or all levels.' (38)

This is the evidence for what I have called anti-globalisation creep in the international and national unions. I use the term 'creep', rather than 'leap', since, for all its assertiveness, this is taking place within traditional union structures and in terms of its specific benefits to these. One could also argue that there is here some adoption of 'social-movement-unionism-speak', insofar as elements can be identified here of a critical discourse about union transformation going back twenty years (Waterman 2004b). Saying so is not to claim some posthumous victory for this discourse. But it does suggest that we might say of the union organisations, as Galileo, under the Inquisition, is supposed to have whispered about the earth, *eppur si muove* (and yet it moves).

The sore thumb in this small, but evidently rich, collection has to be the piece by academic Jude Howell on Chinese workers and unions. This is a balanced and informative article. Unfortunately, in this company, it may be read as another contribution to the 'New Yellow Peril' discourse presently spreading amongst unions and workers both in the North (particularly America) and the South (including Southern Africa). Howell has no illusions about the present role of the All-China Federation of Trade Unions (ACFTU), as a transmission belt and shock absorber. She suggests, however, that globalisation will provide the ACFTU with 'opportunities to engage with the international trade union movement and understand how a trade union could effectively represent workers' (48). There is here a Eurocentrist assumption that Northern unions provide a model that is both adequate at home and appropriate for export. The emergence of China as a major industrial producer and centre of the world's working classes raises rather more complex issues. Nationally the question is what forms growing labour protest in China actually takes. Internationally the question surely is how the international labour, and global justice and solidarity movements can effectively and positively relate to such struggles[7].

Perhaps the best one can conclude of this book is that it reveals the British trade unions with one foot still firmly in a passing phase of capitalist and state development, whilst one toe of the other foot explores the new world of work, workers and global solidarity.[8]

---

7   For which see http://laborstrategies.blogs.com/global_labor_strategies/2007/05/ why_labor_can _a.html

8   It would be nice if one could report that European unions - or at least Left unionists in Europe

A Surfeit of Roots

Ramparts of Resistance: Why Workers Lost Their Power and How to Get it Back, by Sheila Cohen, falls into two parts, the first mostly historical, the second more conceptual and strategic. It concentrates on labour protest since 1968 in the UK and the USA. This structure means that the book is bi-national rather than even international, let alone globally focused or informed. However, the historical half of the book provides us with a lively reminder of the upsurge of such struggle in 1968-74 and the following period, of the Reagan-Thatcher counter-attack of the early-1980s, of 'class warfare in the 1990s', and of the ups and downs of the period marked by the 'Battle of Seattle' (1999). From the beginning, Sheila Cohen argues for 'putting workplace-based rank-and-file organisation at the head of strategic discussion' (1). Insofar, however, as the crisis of unionism she here records (152) is one of theoretical understanding, worker consciousness and appropriate strategy, I will concentrate on her second half.

Chapter 7 is concerned to distinguish, both conceptually and empirically, between unions as institutions and as movements. This follows her initial opposition between the rank-and-file and union leaderships, between the 'intrinsic status of the institution' and the fact that 'most examples of explosive growth and organisation take place *outside* the existing union organisation' (150; original italics). Cohen's discussion of various theories of union leadership and bureaucracy surpasses the binary oppositions suggested above by reference to her favoured agents of militancy, 'workplace representatives' (163). It is these who, in her view, do, or have to, preserve the difficult balance between direct shop-floor democracy on the one hand and a broader and more effective (industrial and national) perspective and organisation on the other. Cohen also tries to overcome conventional Leftist political and economic contradictions by insisting once again on shop-floor militancy. This is conceived as containing an essential, if implicit, class consciousness and transformatory potential.

Chapter 8 seems to reject the opposition of 'false' and 'true' consciousness, yet reformulates it by an opposition between what the working class does '*objectively*' and how it thinks '*subjectively*' (175; original italics). In an attempt to surpass 'false consciousness' Cohen talks of reformism as a 'default' consciousness, of a 'dialectical *balancing*, within one consciousness, of two "conceptions of the world", one subordinate, one transformative' (187. original italics).

Chapter 9 presents the conclusions. Whilst insisting on her own optimism, on the potential resting on the shop floor, and even on the 'inspiring vision of social movement unionism' (220), Cohen feels obliged to admit that, 40 years ago, workers in her two countries were much closer to worker's power (if not social revolution or transformation) than they are today[9].

Now, as someone who has, like Sheila Cohen, spent a lifetime working in or on the labour movement, who puts considerable energy into both critiquing (mostly international) union leadership, and seeking conceptual and strategic solutions to the dilemmas she identifies, I can sympathise with her effort. I also appreciate the fact that

---

- were doing better. A quick search on relevant keywords suggests that these may be even more trapped within the institutional parameters of their organisations or parties, even more bereft of new ideas, than their UK counterparts. Consider the EuroLeft union network: http://www.european-left.org/positions/work groups/trade.

9   Contrast here the contributions of Berlinguer, Ince and myself to *Networked Politics* (2007).

this book is accessible in style, and that Cohen's argument has been made available online, at least in part.[10] However, I think that whilst her emphasis on the shop floor, on the shop-floor activists, and even on their alliances (cross-class and international) provides a necessary part of any labour movement alternative, it is far from being sufficient.

The problem is not only that she is looking back to the future, but that her language and attitudes are imprisoned within the period she celebrates. Moreover, that period could be considered as representing the peak of national-industrial unionism, and therefore of 'national internationalism'. Even, further, when making gestures in the direction of 'international social movement unionism', she is both short and dismissive (as she is of almost all other left theory or strategy over the last 40 years). Cohen is associated with one of the more open and effective Trotskyist tendencies in the USA, Solidarity, itself behind the union monthly *Labour Notes*, and the socialist magazine *Against the Current*. She also seems to have an independent position within (against?) this current – and to preserve a critical distance from the Trotskyist tradition. I say this to establish that she is her own woman (even making, in her self-review[11], a criticism of her failure to deal adequately in her book with ethnicity, gender and other forms of identity).

What Cohen does, however, preserve from the Marxist tradition is the prioritisation of 'class' as *explanandum*; of the working class as a privileged agent of emancipation; of the union as a universal/eternal organisational form; and of the workplace as the primary site of human social emancipation. Today these are all matters requiring discussion, at very least. What she puts together out of her experience, reading and reinterpretation is a world view which has to be called either 'rank-and-fileist' or, more simply, 'workerist'. Thus, even when Cohen is referring to major multi-class, popular or radical-democratic protests, such as the Battle of Seattle, or the 'petty-bourgeois' protest against petrol tax in the UK in 2000, she cannot but insist on what she calls, in the second case, its 'working-class trajectory' (133). She holds, in other words, to a Marxist eschatology (though in the Marxist case, of course, the Chosen are not simply the Saved but also the Saviours).

Whilst, I think, 'rank-and-fileism' or 'workerism', are quite understandable amongst rebellious workers – and for that matter amongst revolutionary thinkers and activists during earlier phases of capitalist development – they are hardly adequate for those concerned with social emancipation today. Marxist traditionalists like Sheila Cohen sit on the horns of a dilemma that they have themselves created: that proletarianisation is the most extreme form of human alienation, yet (or therefore) the proletariat is the privileged agent of human emancipation. In the face of repeatedly contradictory evidence, Marxist traditionalists fall back on rationalisations such as 'the labour aristocracy', 'bureaucratisation', 'incorporation', or, here, 'default ideology'. But the Marxist paradox is today sharpened rather than blunted, given first, the simultaneous de-construction and reconstruction of the working classes (and the multiplicity of those whose dream is primarily of decent work within them[12]; second, the dispersal of

---

10   See www.plutobooks.com/cgi-local/readingroom.pl and her own self-critical review, http://uin.org. uk/content/view/170/71/)

11   http://www.solidarity-us.org/atc.

12   'Decent Work' is *the* slogan and campaign that presently joins, in subordinate partnership, the international unions to capital and state in the International Labour Organisation.

working-class communities; third, the crisis of the union form (developed against but also within earlier capitalist development models); fourth, the rise of more significant order-threatening social movements worldwide – whether of the left or the right; and finally, the growing recognition that working-class people exist also outside the union-ised/-able workplace (Trott 2005), that they have other interests (as consumers, as women, as 'precariat', as the citizens they were not in Marx' time, as species-beings confronted by ecological meltdown), and many other identities, whether sexual, religious or cultural. The notion that all such identities are subordinate to, or have to be subordinated to, a working-class consciousness, pre-defined by one or other socialist intellectual, is a seriously counter-productive class reductionism.

As already noted, Sheila Cohen criticises her own failure to deal with gender and race as well as class. These are, indeed, damaging absences, insofar as their recognition can qualify workerism, and suggest other sites of struggle, or negotiation, than the workplace alone, including the neighbourhood, the media, the household and the bed. In other words, such recognitions can broaden one's world view. As serious, however, is the virtual absence, within her account, of an international perspective, and the *almost* total absence of what I call a globalised, informatised, service and financial capitalism. Her passing references to international solidarity are not always balanced, as when she repeats a crude Trotskyist condemnation of the Liverpool dockers for preferring international 'globaloney' (122) to local solidarity. (It was actually because of the *limitations* of the latter that they opted for the former – in innovatory if ultimately unsuccessful ways[13]). Her meagre attention to the international can be attributed both to her disinterest in globalisation/globaloney (101-2) and to a fixation on the shop floor …despite the movement of so many of these shops to floors in China.

It is a pity, perhaps, that Cohen fails to give serious attention to 'social movement unionism', a concept developed and popularised, in overlapping if distinct ways, both by myself (Waterman 2004b) and by Kim Moody (1997) – who, I am enchanted to discover (viii), is her husband. This concept hovers around her argument but is never explained, far less either integrated into it, or, for that matter, surpassed. It is quite possible that this notion is either undeveloped or simply omitted in error. But, confronted by the global crisis of the trade union movement, discussion of such new ideas is more likely to get us off the horns of the Marxist dilemma than endless repetition of 'shop floor' or 'rank-and-file'.

Labour's (Limited) place in the new global contestation

Globalisation and Contestation is a book that places internationalised labour and labour internationalism within the new world and discourse of global social protest. Ronaldo Munck has long given labour a special place (most recently, Munck 2002; 2003) amongst a wide range of interests, including nationalism, Latin American politics, development studies, social exclusion, and more. This book shows him, again, as a superb synthesiser of relevant theory and as someone who uses appropriate case

---

13   For a more complex view of the matter, see Castree (2000) and Castree et. al. (2004). Noel Castree and his colleagues have, indeed, written a pioneering work on labour and labour solidarity, which considers workers as not only existing in particular social spaces and at particular scales, but also as productive of such spaces. Such a view leads them to consider, in technical terms, previously unexplored aspects of labour internationalism. Given that this is, again, a British work, it should have been included in this review. By way of compensation, see the review by Salman (2006).

studies to illustrate and communicate his argument and ends up with a well-structured and highly-readable whole. The work, it seems to me, is likely to become a standard textbook on the topic. It is also likely to impact on activists in the global justice movement. I especially appreciated his chapter on the new and (literally) reactionary global movements; it is easy to forget that in the brave new world of social movements it is these that have the widest spread and greatest impact.

What we must focus on here, however, is the place that labour occupies within this work and how this is understood. In fact, labour and socialist internationalism appear only in a couple of sub-sections in a chapter on transnational social movements, and unions in one part of a chapter on 'local transnationalisms'. The section on labour and socialist internationalism both recognises and relativises this tradition and the chapter as a whole presents a concise and thought-provoking background to thye movement that many contemporary activists assumed had begun in either 1999 (Seattle) or, at best, 1994 (Chiapas). But his conception of contemporary labour internationalism as a 'local transnationalism' is somewhat contentious. This may make sense if 'local' also means 'particular'. But the concept of a 'working class' has customarily referred to at least the state-national, or colonial, parameter. And since Marx, if not Flora Tristán[14], both social scientists and socialists have recognised or argued that there are senses in which working classes have been, could or should be more than this.

Munck's understanding is influenced, if not determined, by his preference for the 20th century Karl Polanyi over the 19th century Karl Marx. But if we can reduce Marxism to the notion of an international working-class-led socialist revolution against capitalism, we can also reduce Polanyism to the notion of a 'double-movement' within capitalism, in which the attempt to subordinate the social to the economic is confronted with social struggle to reimpose social control over the economic. Whilst I can appreciate that, in the continuing absence of an international proletarian revolution, it is tempting to either abandon or surpass Marx (preferably the latter), I would have thought that the exhaustion of the social evolution (the national Keynesianism that Polanyi prefigured) requires that one should surpass Polanyi also. So I clearly have problems with Munck's Polanyian turn, as also with the role of the working class in Munck's double movement on a world scale.

Munck's reasoning for following Polanyi is presented in these words:
'Writing just when the long post-[second world] war boom was looming on the horizon, Karl Polanyi foretold a great expansion of the free market but also a great social counter-movement that he saw as "the one comprehensive feature in the history of the age"...For Polanyi, capitalism was moving towards 'an attempt to set up one big self-regulating market'..., nothing less than a global economy where the market ruled supreme. However, there was a counter-movement from within society to protect itself from the anarchy of the market. Powerful social movements and institutions would emerge in a veritable 'double movement' to check the actions of the market and reinstate

---

14   Flora Tristán (1803-1844), a French-Peruvian woman, was the author of *The Workers Union* (1843), considered by many as a precursor to the *Communist Manifesto* of 1848 (Lorwin 1929:23. She clearly considered the working class as a national entity. And - as a socialist and feminist cosmopolitan - of its interests nationally as embracing or expandable to workers everywhere.

human interests over those of a utopian market economy. My basic thesis
is that we are not now witnessing a 'clash of civilizations' (Huntington) at a
global level but, rather a clash between the free market and society.' (ix)

Munck is not an uncritical Polanyian, however, since he declares further that:

'we cannot simply assume Polanyi's rather functional analysis of its response to the
market mechanisms. Polanyi does tell us that: "The 'challenge' is to society as
a whole; the 'response' comes through groups, sections and classes"…but that
is still quite under-specified in terms of a political sociology, for a globalised
complex era.' (xiii)

The problem for me, however, is that Polanyi's double movement ends not with a surpassing of capitalism through either revolution or evolution, but a reinsertion of the economy into society and under social control. This was surely the vision and practice of Labour Prime Minister Attlee (a former social worker) and Foreign Minister Bevin (a former union boss) in 1945. Munck, it is true, does bring in numerous other concepts and theories to enable him to make an enthusiastic case for the democratic global movements of the present day. However, he seems to at least allow for the Polanyian vision of a civilised capitalism and thus, implicitly, of a global neo-Keynesianism. I would consider the latter as a possible successor regime to global neo-liberalism. And a tendency within the global justice and solidarity movements would also consider this desirable. However, what I (and other tendencies in the movement, including new labour movements) are interested in is a surpassing not only of neo-liberalism but also of capitalism. And one thing we have surely learned from the past of national Keynesianism is that, whilst it might imply a gentler, kinder capitalism, it in no way guarantees us against another movement in which the economy again escapes from society and destroys not only the contending classes but everyone and everything. Surely we now need to seek for or create new guides for the 21st century to social emancipation – as well as to labour's role within such a process[15].

In Munck's analysis of labour's local and limited role in the global counter- movement there are here, for me, several problems. One is the limitation of any discussion of labour in this work to five or ten out of 161 pages. Another is Munck's use of the descriptive term 'transnationalism' in place of the analytical/theoretical/ethical one of 'internationalism'. A third is in Munck's consideration of contemporary labour internationalism.

This third aspect is illustrated by three cases. These are: first, his model of a local transnationalism, a 1998 strike by a small number of workers in Flint, Michigan, that snowballed internationally and was effective against the globalised General Motors corporation; second, the Liverpool dock strike that began in 1997 and revived a flagging dockworker internationalism; and third, the creation of a union network within the Mercosur free-trade zone in the south of Latin America. These cases are all problematic. The first certainly demonstrates workers' struggle against transnationalisation/ globalisation but reveals no expansion of a global solidarity awareness or ethic. The second struggle was not supported, as Munck suggests (96), by the international union structures: The International Transportworkers Federation was trapped in both state and

---

15   A starting point here might be Sousa Santos (2006), a substantial compilation on labour and social emancipation, which considers contemporary non-capitalist forms of production and land-based movements, as well as new forms of labour internationalism.

union legalities and felt threatened by a locally-initiated dockworker internationalism (of a kind previously denounced by one of its leaders as 'strike tourism'). And, finally, Munck produces no evidence to show that the Mercosur union structure has increased workers' solidarity across the zone, rather than riding, like its European counterpart and model, on the coat-tails of a regional capitalist and state initiative (as strongly suggested by an Argentinean supporter, Julio Godio (2004)). Munck fails to deal with cases in which workers' – if not necessarily union – protest has linked up in one way or another with the new social movement internationalisms. I find this absence odd insofar as such cases – like those involving such 'atypical workers' as street-traders – would have strengthened his general case for a 21st century re-invention of a 19th-20th century internationalism[16]. Munck nonetheless has a dialectical view of the relationship between the local and the global:

'To move beyond the global/local optic we need to foreground the complex interplay of social scales in the construction of globalization. We cannot operate with the tacit rather simple divide between the global as smooth and the local as the place where difference is generated. Nor is it simply the case that the economy is always global and culture is situated at the local level. The cultural political economy of globalisation needs to constantly bear in mind both inextricably linked elements. We also need to foreground all the scales including the regional, the still extremely relevant and the supranational that is not yet global. In terms of political practice, the same way that global managers may 'download' problems to the national level, so the agents of contestation may take local issues 'upwards' in an imaginative 'jumping of scales' as it were. (108)

This is, in sum a book about globalisation and the movement response to it that provokes as much as it rewards.

The internationalism of Labour's 'others'

There has, in the previously-reviewed books, been little questioning of the trade union form, a model developed against but also within the period of what I call 'national, industrial, (anti-)colonial' capitalism. And, insofar as there has been any mention of 'networking', this has been mostly in terms of relations between unions or extensions beyond them. The term 'networking' here leaves unchallenged the traditional national-industrial, pyramidal form, with its extensions upward to Brussels, Geneva or other global centres. Along with this form has gone the ideal of collective bargaining and social (i.e. capitalist) partnership, again extended either upwards to the international union or downwards from the 'tripartite' International Labour Organisation (ILO)[17].

---

16   Evidence for these criticisms can hopefully be found in those of my works already cited. For a provocative case study written in the same spirit, consider Dinerstein (2003). Interestingly, this is about an innovatory workers' movement in Argentina, and Dinerstein is another UK-based Argentinian. The struggle may have been short-lived and its international impact more notional than demonstrable, but of its radically innovatory nature there can be little doubt. Another Argentinean phenomenon that demands attention, particularly for its particular international relations, would be the relatively young and innovative CTA (Central de los Trabajadores Argentinos), the website of which is itself a source for consideration of its internationalism http://www.cta.org.ar/base/principal.php3.

17   For some (very rare) criticism of this quite central yet profoundly ambiguous international labour

Yet many of the reviewed authors would agree that neo-liberal globalisation has profoundly – if not fundamentally - transformed this old world of labour and, just as profoundly, undermined the union form, its traditional parameters of action and its equally traditional hopes or assumptions. Yet, reflecting on the massive influx of immigrant workers into the USA, Immanuel Ness (2005:187-8) argues that

'We often think of unions as militant or even radical organisations, but in fact most are conservative institutions wedded to preserving the past. By their very nature, unions will oppose any change in a labour market that may weaken the bargaining power of their members. Unions are relatively inflexible institutions that have difficulty reacting to changes in capital formation that alter the predictable composition of work and thereby threaten standards established in the past.'

So the question arises of whether another model of worker self-articulation (organisation plus expression) is not necessary, either for the new work and workers, or for the international labour movement as a whole.

Threads of Labour: Garment Industry Supply Chains from the Workers' Perspective, by Angela Hale and Jane Wills, reveals such a necessity - at least for new forms of work and workers, both nationally and internationally. Insofar, indeed, as the book was produced by academics and organisers within an international labour network, Women Working Worldwide (WWW), it exemplifies such a new kind of international labour solidarity project. Taking the estimated 40 million, mostly women, workers in the global garment industry, it considers the global garment industry chain. It reports cases from both Western and Eastern Europe and from South, South-East and East Asia, as well as from Mexico. With the exception of the last, the cases are all drawn from a research project organised by the WWW network itself. The fundamental issues raised by the study are many: whether to understand the industry in 'supply-chain' or 'network' terms; the relevance of union and workplace-based organising to such a fractured industry and vulnerable workforce; the relevance of a collective bargaining model of labour relations; the hypothetical value of 'Corporate Social Responsibility' projects to such workers; the problems of diverse national and international alliances between the worker-support campaigns, community-based organising, traditional unions and consumer-based organisations; and the nature of the action-research project itself:

'The book seeks to contribute to debates about the globalisation of the economy, the operation of international commodity chains and new developments in labour organising from the perspective of the workers involved. Drawing on internationally coordinated but locally developed action research has allowed us to highlight local experiences alongside global trends. We have sought to embody supply chain analysis, and bring it to life by looking at the experiences and situation of some of the workers involved in the contemporary garment industry. The action research data has already been used by local organisations that support women garment workers, informing educational programmes, political action and organising work.' (15)

It is concluded that

---

hegemon, see Germanotta 2007a, b.

'The work of WWW can be seen as part of a new form of industrial action which involves political alliances between workers, trade unions, local and regional activists and consumer-based organisations in the key markets and central locations of major buyers. The significance of these alliances...is demonstrated by the evidence we have provided of cases in which there have been notable improvements in working conditions...and...examples of how internationally co-ordinated campaigns have successfully contributed to the establishment of trade union rights in a number of different locations... And, significantly in the case of workers in Bombay/Mumbai, how their support for workers in the USA helped those Northern workers win a trade union recognition dispute... Although Threads of Labour is focused solely on the garment industry, the research and action reported...can also be seen as relevant to those tackling the economic and social injustices in other economic sectors, as well as...the wider global justice movement.' (237-8)*

Hale and Wills do not claim to have discovered the secret of fire, but the book does have an original vision and it does open new doors. It is also a professional piece of work, with numerous diagrams and boxes to explain the immensely complex structure of the industry (varied according to place, level, process or product) and to illustrate its arguments. It has a chapter on the WWW network itself, as well as a theoretically-informed and self-reflective chapter on the action-research process.[18]

One of the most important characteristics of this book is, for me, the bridge it provides between the shop-floor internationalism of the 1980s and the global justice movement of the present day. WWW was founded in Britain in the early 1980s, has survived and, apparently, thrived. Several of the authors are names I recall from that earlier period, Angela Hale (who regrettably died just before the book was launched), Lynda Yanz, from Canada and Rohini Hensman from Mumbai. The book does not trumpet its feminist credentials. Yet I wonder whether we do not have to put its survival through hard times down to the socialist- or labour-feminist tradition which nurtured these women. But maybe it is simply a matter of their individual or collective staying power. For this reason I would like to know more about WWW. We can never simply rely on activists' accounts of the projects to which they may have devoted their lives for 10 or 20 years. One question that remains in my mind is the nature of international solidarity when this is primarily on the North-South axis and running in a North-to-South direction. Another is the relationship of WWW and its members to the profoundly-ambiguous CSR industry. A third would be the always-problematic relationship with the funders. The fact that the book provokes such questions is suggestive of its value to those it is about.[19]

Threads of Labour does not necessarily provide answers to the questions I originally posed. The labour network is not presented as *the* answer to the organisation question. Nor is international solidarity networking presented as *the* alternative to institutionalised union internationalism. And neither does it take definite positions on the various old and new forums for negotiating or establishing improved wages or extended rights. The

---

18   This book invites comparison with the pioneering one on 'fashion, free trade and the rights of garment workers' (Ross 1997). Ross, British born but US based, pioneers in drawing the connections between production, workers, labour organising, consumption and commodity culture internationally.

19   For extensive further discussion and comparison, see the excellent review article by Ferus-Comelo (2006)

impression it gives is, rather, of a pluralistic orientation. In other words, it relativises the previously universal forms and processes of labour self-activity. And it reveals some of the possible activity and organisation forms taken by some of labour's 'others'. It thus provides a rich source of material for further discussion on such matters.

The Vital Force of Working Class Cultures Across Time and Space

With *Live Working or Die Fighting: How the Working Class Went Global*, Paul Mason has invented a new genre - one which reaches places not commonly touched in either recent academic labour history or accounts of contemporary labour struggles. It should communicate that history and those struggles, and the relationship between them, to new generations of workers as well as to those in the global justice and solidarity movement unaware of them.

As someone who grew up with British and European labour history, who has long studied and written about historical and contemporary labour struggles, national and international, I felt enlightened and inspired by this book. Much of this has to do with the genre, a quasi-cinematic one, consisting of flash-backs (or forwards) or montages, that create above all an image of the working class as a continuing, if irregular, presence, existing on a worldwide stage. What Paul Mason is both recording and urging upon us, it seems to me, is recognition of the moments and places in which there have existed working-class cultures of protest that had or have messages for humanity more generally:

'[This] history needs to be rediscovered because two sets of people stand in dire need
of knowing more about it: first, the activists who have flooded the streets
in Seattle, Genoa and beyond to protest against globalisation; second, the
workers in the new factories, mines and waterfronts created by globalisation
in the developing world, whose attempts to build a labour movement are at
an early stage. They need to know...that what they are doing has been done
before...Above all they need to know that the movement was once a vital
force: a counterculture in which people lived their lives and the the main
source of eduction for men and women condemned to live short, bleak lives
and dream of impossible futures.' (x)

Quite how Mason manages the leaps in his narrative between mutilated workers in Shenzhen in China, today and the Battle of Peterloo in Manchester, in 1819 is something of an artistic mystery. I can only say that it works, without parallels being forced or fingers being wagged. Other chapters compare: silkworkers in Varanasi (Benares), India now and in the Lyons, France, revolt of 1831; the casual labourers of a Lagos slum in 2005 and the Paris Commune of 1871; oilworkers in Basra, Iraq in 2006 and the invention of Mayday in Philadelphia in 1886; and immigrant office cleaners in London's East End in 2004, and the Great Dock Strike of unskilled workers in London's East End in 1889. If we eventually reach the globalisation of unskilled workers' unionism in 1889-1912, we are later confronted by 'wars between brothers' amongst miners in Huanuni, Bolivia, today and German workers' failures to condemn the war of 1914-18 and to bring about a revolution at its end. Most exotic of all is Mason's 25-page account of the Bund, the socialist union of Jewish workers in interwar Poland. This is preceded by a sketch of the struggle in El Alto, a giant squatter city (on a plateau 500m above the city and the high-rises of a literally downtown La Paz). There are several more such stories in this panoramic work, often expressed in the words of the men and women activists involved. Coincidentally, I have been, as an international labour researcher, in several of the countries or towns visited by Paul Mason as a journalist. Yet my feeling in reading his accounts is less that of recognition than of admiration for his capacity to evoke them, and to do so with sympathy but without sentimentality or paternalism.

But what on earth is it that holds this patchwork narrative together? I think it is Mason's insistence on a counter-culture of resistance, of rebellion and of creativity from the class's own resources, and of aspirations that go beyond the social and human relations of capitalism. He himself argues that

'If there is a recurrent theme amid all this, it is control. Politically, the labour movement has debated strategy in terms of reform versus revolution. Practically, to the frustration of advocates of both approaches, workers have been prepared to go beyond reform but settle for less than revolution.' (xiii)

In his concluding chapter, Mason does go into interpretation, offering an explanation for the Post-World War Two loss of working-class independence, and incorporation into two ruling-class projects, one in the West, the other in the East. However:

'It is very different now. Today the transnational corporation is the primary form of economic life. In addition, global consumer culture is breaking down all that was local, insular and closed in working-class communities. There is, for the first time, a truly global working class. But it has not yet had its 1889 moment,' (280)

Mason sees the leadership once offered by philanthropists, social democrats, anarchists or communists now resting with the 'new social reformism' of the anti-globalisation movement. For myself, as someone equally concerned with labour internationalism and the global justice movement, this is a dying fall. Perhaps the author, at the end of his marathon, ran out of puff. It is not simply that we get a gesture where we need at least a picture. It is because the gesture is to the ameliorative tendency within a movement that also has a powerful emancipatory wing and because Mason appears unaware of the extent to which the labour movement is (an admittedly contradictory) part of this movement.

Paul Mason's comparative lack of attention to the labour, socialist and anarchist parties and ideologies that have played such a dominant role in the history of labour, and labour history (for better or worse) is due to his stress on the socio-cultural rather than the party-political. I find this focus (on a rank-and-file of flesh and blood, not one seen through ideological spectacles) refreshing. If the old labour and the new social movements are to be fruitfully articulated, Paul Mason's pathbreaking book will have made a not insignificant contribution. It should be read, taught and discussed. And translated, as a start, into Spanish, Hindi and Chinese.

Mason's is a romance of labour but one without sentimentality. Although neither a theoretical nor a policy-oriented work, it is certainly informed by both sympathy and understanding of the uneven (if rarely combined) struggles of labouring people. Many of the major movements he presents have actually fused, in varied measure, labour and nationalism, labour and ethnicity, labour and democracy. These movements, and their leaders and activists both known and forgotten, are, it is shown, never archetypal proletarians, nor paragons of left or socialist virtue. They were and are, however, our forebears and our *compañer@s*[20] - people with whom we can in our turn empathise, learn from and with.

In concluding, I have to return to where I began, with this book as a new genre. The book has its own website, which is both elegant and transparent.[21] Here it is possible to find photographs, a 60-second video clip of the author promoting his book in a Nairobi slum, resource lists, and reviews. The photographs and other graphics could be taken as illustrations for a book that regrettably has none. The site as a whole reinforces my feeling that this work is cinematic.

From the Page to the Screen

The cinematic qualities of Mason's book, and the audio-visual and computer skills demonstrated in its promotion, presage a welcome and overdue shift of international(ist) labour communication from the page to the screen. The activist tendency within international labour studies has long been connected with labour education and occasionally with the audio-visual (cinema, sound, video)[22]. Yet a marriage between international labour studies and international labour media has yet to be consummated. Today this seems less something to be desired than something which is an essential prerequisite for a new global working-class culture. Two projects, one based in Britain, the other largely involving expatriate Britons and Antipodeans, suggest some ways that research and reflection and communication and organisation may be moving together.

Whilst there has clearly been an explosion in international union uses of computers over the last 10-20 years, there seems to have set in, at this level, some kind of web-disillusionment or web-fatigue. The prime exemplar here has to be the site of the new International Trade Union Confederation (ITUC) founded in 2006. Here, a previously adequate, if conventional, site has been converted into something which combines quite soulless design with information both limited in extent and late in delivery[23]. The various Global Unions sites also seem to be marking time[24]. We might conclude that unions get the websites they deserve. If so, the booby-prize goes to the former Communist World Federation of Trade Unions[25]. Unsuccessful attempts to go beyond its index page suggest not so much WFTU fatigue at the pace demanded by a computerised globalisation as a failure even to enter this new reality and master the relevant technology. If the Web had existed in the 1960s, when I worked for the WFTU, this is what its site might have looked like.[26] Finally, and significantly, none of

---

20   This is a Spanish figure which has the advantages of surpassing the much-abused 'comrade' and of combining the male and female form.
21   http://www.liveworkingordiefighting.co.uk/
22   A pioneer here, and a survivor where others have faded or died, is Steve Zeltzer's San Francisco-based LaborTech, http://www.labortech.net/. A visit to this site and its links reveals the extent to which this project combines researchers, media-makers, computer specialists and internationalists. For a recent labour-relevant video see *The Big Sell-Out*.
23   http://www.ituc-csi.org/spip.php?rubrique1&lang=en
24   http://www.global-unions.org/. When last visited it was still carrying an item dated January 26, 2005.
25   http://www.wftucentral.org/
26   The WFTU also got the history it deserved (Ganguli 2000). Rambling in style, restricted to conferences and declarations, sycophantic in tone, it has a back-cover Congress photo, showing an ageing, portly and exclusively male leadership paying respects not to some working-class or popular hero but the President of

these sites has a feedback feature, far less a space for discussion, or significant access to independent research.

In strong contrast to these are two highly useful and innovative sites: *New Unionism* and *Union Ideas Network*.[27] *New Unionism* appears to be based fairly closely – in more senses than one - to the Geneva headquarters not only of various international unions but also of the International Labour Organisation (ILO). It is, however, institutionally independent. Moreover, it is a quite brilliant new website that seems to me a possible winner of the competition organised annually by *LabourStart*.[28] It is, however, not only its aesthetics that are innovative. So too are its thematic foci, which break radically with those both customary and predictable from, for example, the ITUC site. Whilst the ITUC menu directs readers to: 'About Us', 'Press Room', 'Campaigns', 'Equality', 'Human and Trade Union Rights', 'Economic and Social Policy', 'Members Section', 'Global Unions', *New Unionism* offers: 'Forums', 'Younionize', 'Inspirations', 'Free Resources', 'Success Stories', 'Lessons Learnt', 'Online Library', 'Cast a Vote', 'Union Work', 'Contact Us' and 'Join'.

Whilst this may seem to exemplify the difference between an institutional union website and a labour network one, *New Unionism* also innovates in relation to other new labour sites. It might, again, be suggested that the *New Unionism* concept and aesthetic is more likely to appeal to call-centre operators than to sub-contracted auto industry workers. But, then, it is the first rather than the second who are likely to have computer access, and we have no evidence to suggest that the latter, or their organisers, *prefer* sites designed by, or for, Brother Apparatchik the Union Officer. *New Unionism* declares boldly that it is

'a network, not an organisation. We do not have formal meetings, special task-forces, triennial congresses, steering committees, or annual conferences. We do not decide on collective policies, nor do we elect network officials. We do not run collective lobbies, nor across-the-board campaigns. This is what trade unions are for! And that is why we strongly believe you should join them. They, in turn, are often part of global federations and organisations which promote workers' interests at global level. We do not for a moment pretend to be offering an alternative to this. On the contrary, we want to help in the building these organisations.

'This involves building input from the ground up. If you want to network with other working people, industrial relations commentators, experienced union reps, labour communicators, and/or social movement activists at an international level, and to work with them in developing a community of support which reaches across borders, then here's the place to start.'

My questions about, or challenges to *New Unionism(NU)* start with its self-confinement within the existing parameters of the international and national union institutions.

an increasingly neo-liberal and globalised India.

27   http://www.newunionism.net/, http://uin.org.uk/.

28   http://www.labourstart.org/lwsoty/2007/results.shtml. *LabourStart* was the pioneer international union website, with increasingly worldwide news coverage and regular solidarity campaigns. It also has lots of bells and whistles (labour radio, labour videos), and discussion of the latest technologies. What it does not have, at time of writing, is regular open discussion on the crucial international labour issues.

My doubts continue with its self-definition, which seems to be a combination of 'organising strategy' (assertive union-building rather than servicing existing members) and 'partnership' (the extension of 'economic democracy' within and under capitalism). I am not sure whether the combination of a possibly recent US strategy with a certainly old European one amounts to a strategy that is relevant for labour worldwide in the era of globalisation. But, in any case, each of the conditions assumes the institutions, procedures and norms of Northern tradition, with questionable relevance to a globalised and neo-liberalised world of labour.[29] NU adds 'internationalism' to the formula, but hardly questions traditional understandings or practices here either. However, I am more concerned that this innovative and original site demands of would-be affiliates that they buy the package. And that contributions will be removed if someone (the owners?) consider their contributions inappropriate. Both conditions seem to me in contradiction with those of networking as increasingly understood, and of the kind of dialogue increasingly practised within the global justice and solidarity movements.[30] Given, however, the energy and originality of the site, it is likely to be one worth watching ... and learning from.

Paradoxically, it is the more union-dependent of these sites, *New Union Ideas*, that seems the more open of the two. This is an initiative, apparently, of the British Trades Union Congress – not a body known historically for its interest in new union ideas. It is a much more modest innovation, in terms of both appearance and themes. Yet, whilst clearly also oriented towards the traditional institutionalised union movement, it seems so far to be open ideologically, and to be attracting a rather wide range of (younger?) union organisers, activists and academics. Its major themes are traditional: 'Conferences; Economic/ Social Policy; Education and Skills; Employment Law; Employment Relations; Equality and Diversity; Europe/International; Health and Safety; Union Modernisation Fund; Union Organising; Unions and Politics'. But its current forums include 'Union Futures', and 'Union Engagement with Academia'. And its contributors include, for example, Sheila Cohen (see above) and Andreas Bieler, currently coordinating the international Global Working-Class Project at the University of Nottingham[31].

Conclusion: From Creep to Leap?

What would be required for me to add a third cheer to the two originally expressed? Well, I would clearly like to see a leap where so far there has been mostly creep. Those of us raised within the Marxist tradition are always awaiting the turning of water into steam, of quantity into quality, of ideology into science, for the transformation of the working class 'in itself' to one 'for itself', from reform to revolution; we are always searching for the weak link in the capitalist chain (or at least for uneven development that is also combined) and, of course, for the final solution to the capitalism question.

It seems to me, however, that neither in international labour studies nor in labour

---

29   For a summary statement of the Organising Strategy + Partnership strategy, see Cradden & Hall-Jones 2005. For a critique of the West European tradition of social partnership, see Wahl (2004).
30   Consider here the earlier-mentioned *Networked Politics*. This is a Wiki site, designed for collective thought. As a project, however, *Networked Politics* also has some print publications and is taking an interest in international labour networking. In both content and procedure it suggests a more radically-democratic model than does *NU*.
31   http://www.nottingham.ac.uk/politics/gwcproject/. This project, which was present and active at the World Social Forum, Nairobi, 2007, is currently producing a book.

internationalism are we likely to witness any such apocalyptic transformation. Even less than at state-national level is a transformation within traditional emancipatory paradigms or long-existing social movements/institutions likely to take such dramatic form. Two passages from Raymond Williams, reflecting on Gramsci and Marx (cited by Stillo, 1998-9), seem apposite here :

'A lived hegemony is always a process. It is not, except analytically, a system or a structure. It is a realised complex of experiences, relationships and activities, with specific and changing pressures and limits. In practice, that is, hegemony can never be singular. Its internal structures are highly complex, as can readily be seen in any concrete analysis. Moreover (and this is crucial, reminding us of the necessary thrust of the concept), it does not just passively exist as a form of dominance. It has continually to be renewed, recreated, defended, and modified. It is also continually resisted, limited, altered, challenged by pressures not at all its own. (Williams 1977:108)

'The key to 'revolutionary' social change in modern societies does not therefore depend, as Marx had predicted, on the spontaneous awakening of critical class consciousness but upon the prior formation of a new alliances of interests, an alternative hegemony or 'historical bloc', which has already developed a cohesive world view of its own.' (Williams 1992:27).

The first of these passages surely also relates to what is hegemonic within the international labour movement. The second is suggestive of the task before the global justice and solidarity movement.

It seems to me, in any case, that what is crucially required for an emancipatory movement within international labour studies and labour internationalism (whether in the UK or globally) is the creation of autonomous spaces and places where these can be developed. In the 1980s, at a time of the growing crisis and exhaustion of the previous such wave, I argued, unsuccessfully, that there was such a necessity amongst those writing about or practising 'shopfloor internationalism'. Given the development of the global justice movement, of the World Social Forums, and of cyberspace today, the possibility of such (relatively) autonomous agoras or foci is today even greater (Caruso, 2007). Demonstration of such autonomous initiatives can be found not only at global level but also within Europe and the UK itself[32].

Let us finally reconsider universalism and internationalism. Whilst it is easy to deconstruct or dismiss the naïve Communism of Mariátegui, the desire he expressed predated that movement and survives its demise. So here is a post-Communist formulation, from a new forum of emancipatory ideas, that makes at least a provocative contribution toward the renovation of those intertwined concepts:

'We need to think in terms of the circulation of commons, of the interconnection and reinforcements between them. The ecological commons maintains the finite conditions necessary for both social and networked commons. A social commons, with a tendency towards a equitable distribution of wealth, preserves the ecological commons, both by eliminating the extremes of environmental destructiveness linked to extremes of wealth (SUVs,

---

32   For the WSF, Nairobi, 2007, see Waterman 2007.

incessant air travel) and poverty (charcoal burning, deforestation for land) and by reducing dependence on 'trickle down' from unconstrained economic growth. Social commons also create the conditions for the network commons, by providing the context of basic health, security and education within which people can access new and old media. A network commons in turn circulates information about the condition of both ecological and social commons (monitoring global environmental conditions, tracking epidemics, enabling exchanges between health workers, labour activists or disaster relief teams). Networks also provide the channels for planning ecological and social commons – organising them, resolving problems, considering alternative proposals. They act as the fabric of the association that is the sine qua non of any of the other commons.' (Dyer-Witheford, 2007:25)

When the best that the hegemonic tendency within the international labour movement can come up with by way of inspiration is 'decent work', this kind of notion would seem to combine the necessary subversion of the ruling common sense with the equally necessary leap of the imagination.

© *Peter Waterman, 2008*

REFERENCES AND RESOURCES

Agustín, L. (2007) *Sex at the Margins: Migration, Labour Markets and the Rescue Industry*, London: Zed Asia Monitor Resource CentreAccessed on July 1, 2007 from http://www.amrc.org.hk/about.htm

Caruso, G. (2007) 'Open Spaces and Hegemonic Practices in Global Civil Society: The World Social Forum 2004'. Draft PhD Thesis. Department of Development Studies, School of Oriental and African Studies, University of London

Cradden, C & P. Hall-Jones. (2005) 'Trade Union Reform - Change is the only Constant'Accessed on July 1, 2007 from http: http//www.world-psi.org/TemplateEn.cfm?Section=Focus _magazine&CONTENTID=7253&TEMPLATE=/ContentManagement/ContentDisplay.cfm.

Dinerstein, A. (2003) 'A Silent Revolution: The Unemployed Workers Movement in Argentina', *Labour Capital & Society/Travail,Capital & Societe*, Vol. 34, No. 2:166-183

Dwyer-Witheford, N. (2007) 'Commonism', *Turbulence: Ideas for Movement*, No. 1Accessed on July 1, 2007 from http:http//turbulence.org.uk/turb_june2007.html

Ferus-Comelo, A. (2006) 'Garment Industry Supply Chains from the Workers' Perspective. Book Review: Research in Action for Workers' Rights: Threads of Labour', *European Journal of Women's Studies*, Vol. 13:381-4. Accessed July 1, 2007 from http://www.ejw.sagepub.com/cgi/reprint/13/4/381.pdf

Germanotta, P. (2007a) 'On ILO Principles and Social Justice', *International Union Rights*, Vol. 14, No. 1:12-12

Germanotta, P. (2007b) 'ILO "Principles" on Freedom of Association: Prospects for Proletarian Power Beyond the State', *WorkingUSA*, Vol. 10, June:163-74

Global Labor Strategies. Accessed on July 1, 2007 from http://www.laborstrategies.blogs.com/

Godio, J. (2004) *El MERCOSUR, los trabajadores y el ALCA* (MERCOSUR, the Workers and ALCA). Buenos Aires: Biblos

Gobin, C. (1997) 'Taming the Unions: The Mirage of a Social Europe', *Le Monde Diplomatique*, Accessed on July 1, 2007 from http://mondediplo.com/1997/11/europe

Gobin, C. (Pending) 'La Confederation Europeenne Des Syndicats (CES) et le developpement du marché interieur. Vers une reconnaissance de l'euro-syndicalisme en trompe-l'œil et une devalorisation de la norme sociale?'. GRAID, Institut de Sociologie, FNRS and Université libre de Bruxelles

Gobin, C & D. Mezzi. (2007) 'La CES, un œil sur l'Europe' (The ETUC, An Eye on Europe), Accessed on July 1, 2007 from http://www.europe-solidaire.org/spip.php?article 6289#top

Huws, U. (2003) *The Making of a Cybertariat: Virtual Work in a Real World*, New York: Monthly Review and London: Merlin

International Association of Labour History Institutions (2007) Conference on Transnational Networks of Labour Accessed on July 1, 2007 from http://www.ith.or.at/konf_e/zeitpl_2007 _e. htm

International Union Rights/International Centre for Union Rights. Accessed on July 1, 2007 from http://www.ictur.org

International Union Rights (2005) 'Sex Workers Organising', *International Union Rights*, (Special Issue), Vol. 12, No. 4:2-13

International Union of Sexworkers. Accessed on July 1, 2007 from http://www.iusw.org/ start/ index.html

Kester, G. (2007) *Trade Unions and Workplace Democracy in Africa*, Aldershot: Ashgate

Kloosterboer, D. (2007) *Innovative trade union strategies: Successful examples of how trade unions meet the challenges of the 21st century*, Amsterdam: Federatie Nederlandse Vakbonden:128 Accessed on July 1, 2007 from http://www.fnv.nl/helpjezelf/lokaal/achtergrond/publicaties/ vakbondsvernieuwing_rapport.asp.

Lorwin, L. (1929) *Labor and Internationalism*, London: Allen and Unwin

Mariátegui, J. (1986/1923-4) 'Internationalism and Nationalism', *Newsletter of International Labour Studies* (The Hague), Nos. 30-31:3-8

Mather, C. (2004) *Garment Industry Supply Chains: A Resource for Worker Education and Solidarity.* Manchester: Women Working Worldwide:80 Accessed on July 1, 2007 from http://www.poptel.org. uk/women-ww/pdfs/www_education_pack.pdf.

Moody, K. (1997) 'Towards an International Social-Movement Unionism', *New Left Review.* No. 225:52–72

Munck, R. (2002) *Labour and Globalisation: A New Great Transformation?*, London: Zed Books

Munck, R. (2003) *Labour and Globalisation: Results and Prospects*, Liverpool: Liverpool University Press

Networked Politics. Accessed on July 1, 2007 from http://www.networked-politics.info/index. php/Main_Page

Networked Politics. (2007) *Networked Politics: Basic Reader. Rethinking Political Organisation in an Age of Movements and Networks*, Berlin Accessed on July 1, 2007 from http://networked-politics. info/index.php/Main_Page:26

Ness, I. (2005) *Immigrants, Unions, and the New US Labor Market.* Philadelphia: Temple University Press

New Labor Forum. Accessed on July 1, 2007 from http://www.newlaborforum.org

No Border Network. Accessed on July 1, 2007 from http://www.noborder.org/news_index.php

Prol-Position. Accessed on July 1, 2007 from http://www.prol-position.net/

Ross, A (ed). (1997) *No Sweat: Fashion, Free Trade and the Rights of Garment Workers*, London and New York: Verso

Salman, T. (2006) 'Book Review: Spaces of Work: Global Capitalism and Geographies of Labour', *Anthropological Theory*, Vol. 6, No. 2:259-261

Santos, B. (2006) 'De lo posmoderno a lo poscolonial y más allá de ambos' (From the Postmodern to the Postcolonial and Beyond Both), in *Conocer desde el Sur: Para una cultura política emancipatoria*, Lima: Universidad Nacional Mayor de San Marcos

Stillo, M. (1998-9) *Antonio Gramsci*, Accessed on July 1, 2007 from http://www.theory.org.uk/ctr-gram.htm

Streetnet International. Accessed on July 1, 2007 from http://www.streetnet.org.za/english/page10.htm.

The Big Sell-Out. Accessed on July 1, 2007 from http://www.thebigsellout.org/bongani.html

Trott, B. (2005) 'Gleneagles, Activism and Ordinary Rebelliousness', in David Harvie et.al. *Shut Them Down! The G8, Gleneagles 2005, and the Movement of Movements.* Also: Accessed on July 1, 2007 from http://www.shutthemdown.org/

Wahl, A. (2004) 'European Labour: the Ideological Legacy of the Social Pact', *Monthly Review,* Vol. 55, No. 8. Accessed on July 1, 2007 from http://www.monthlyreview.org /0104wahl.htm

Waterman, P. (1989) '"New Realism" at ILR?', *International Labour Reports*, No. 31:26-27

Waterman, P. (1998) 'The Second Coming of Proletarian Internationalism? A Review of Recent Resources', *European Journal of Industrial Relations*, Vol.4, No.3:349-77

Printed in the United Kingdom
by Lightning Source UK Ltd.
128740UK00002B/1-69/P

05378003